Masculinities in Text and Teaching

Also by Ben Knights

ACTIVE READING: Transformative Writing into Literary Studies (2006, *with Chris Thurgar-Dawson*)

FROM READER TO READER: Theory, Text and Practice in the Study Group (1992)

THE IDEA OF THE CLERISY IN THE NINETEENTH CENTURY (1978)

THE LISTENING READER: Fiction and Poetry for Counsellors and Psychotherapists (1995)

WRITING MASCULINITIES: Male Narratives in Twentieth-Century Fiction (1999)

Masculinities in Text and Teaching

Edited by

Ben Knights

palgrave
macmillan

First published 2008 by
PALGRAVE MACMILLAN
Houndmills, Basingstoke, Hampshire RG21 6XS and
175 Fifth Avenue, New York, N.Y. 10010
Companies and representatives throughout the world

PALGRAVE MACMILLAN is the global academic imprint of the Palgrave
Macmillan division of St. Martin's Press, LLC and of Palgrave Macmillan Ltd.
Macmillan® is a registered trademark in the United States, United Kingdom
and other countries. Palgrave is a registered trademark in the European
Union and other countries.

ISBN-13: 978-0-230-00341-5 hardback
ISBN-10: 0-230-00341-9   hardback

This book is printed on paper suitable for recycling and made from fully
managed and sustained forest sources. Logging, pulping and manufacturing
processes are expected to conform to the environmental regulations of the
country of origin.

A catalogue record for this book is available from the British Library.

A catalog record for this book is available from the Library of Congress.

10   9   8   7   6   5   4   3   2   1
17   16   15   14   13   12   11   10   09   08

Printed and bound in Great Britain by
CPI Antony Rowe, Chippenham and Eastbourne

Contents

Preface

The performance of masculinity in English does not concern men alone. The dual subject of this book is the experience of men in English Studies, and – simultaneously – the significance of masculinities for *all* those who practice in this family of subjects. *Masculinities in Text and Teaching*, as its title suggests, seeks to weave together the critical study of text with reflection upon the experience of teaching. The textual disciplines, we suggest, have always provided a scene for the more or less tacit articulation of male subjectivity and roles. This book invites readers to consider the implications for teaching and curriculum of rendering masculinity visible. Skills developed for the interpretation of texts may, the authors believe, also enable teachers – and students – to unpick the meanings of the groups in which they participate. The informed creation of pedagogic narratives allows teachers to become in a sense ethnographers of their own experience. This means that in terms of its evidential base – and to use a metaphor to which we shall have to return – the book is rooted in 'soft' processes. We are aware that to some other disciplinary traditions such ways of making knowledge might appear merely impressionistic or anecdotal. The editor is therefore particularly grateful to all those whose faith in the project sustained him through a very long-drawn-out process. That gratitude extends to the chapter authors themselves (including those who for one reason and another had to withdraw along the way).

Acknowledgements

Many people have sustained the intellectual and human environment from which this book emerges. I would especially like to give warm thanks to Paula Kennedy and the team at Palgrave Macmillan; to Michael Kimmel for support and ideas, and the anonymous publisher's reviewer for their challenging but sympathetic response to the proposal and the draft; to Pamela Knights for going on believing that the work was interesting, and thus helping in no small measure to make it so; to the staff of the Higher Education Academy English Subject Centre for being such wonderful colleagues; the English Subject Group at the University of Teesside who were so receptive to the original idea; Ina Schabert and the organisers of the 2003 University of Munich 'Gendered Academia' Conference at Kloster Seeon; and to John Brannigan and his colleagues at University College Dublin who invited me to give an early version of the introductory chapter as a paper to their departmental research seminar. Rebecca Price gave invaluable help in the final stages of formatting and organising the text. The voices of many scholars of masculinities in relation to English will be heard throughout the book, and are – I hope – duly acknowledged in the introductory chapter.

Notes on Contributors

Dennis W. Allen is Professor of English at West Virginia University. He is the author of *Sexuality in Victorian Fiction* and has published articles on topics ranging from queer pedagogy to aesthetic activism in journals such as *Narrative, Genders* and *Modern Fiction Studies*. He is currently working on a book on the impact of post-industrial capitalism on contemporary gay male culture.

John Beynon is Head of Communication, Cultural and Media Studies in the Cardiff School of Creative Industries, University of Glamorgan. An ethnographer, he has been teaching and writing about masculinities in one form or another for over 20 years – from *Initial Encounters in a Secondary School* (1985), through to *Masculinities and Culture* (2002). He is now completing a study of 'prison masculinities', based on inmate mitigation narratives.

Robert Burden is Reader in English Studies in the School of Arts and Media at the University of Teesside where he teaches modern literature and culture. He is the author of *Radicalising Lawrence* (2000), and co-editor of *Landscape and Englishness* (2006). He is currently writing a book on travel writing and modernism.

Rachel Carroll is Principal Lecturer and Subject Group Leader in English Studies at the University of Teesside. Her research interests are in feminist theory, queer theory, critical heterosexuality studies and twentieth century and contemporary literature and culture.

Ranita Chatterjee is Assistant Professor of English at California State University, Northridge where she teaches British Romanticism and critical theory. She has published articles on Mary Shelley, Gothic fiction and Irigaray. She is working on a book on the libidinal politics of the Godwin–Shelley circle.

Mark Dooley is Senior Lecturer in English at the University of Teesside and previously taught at Manchester Metropolitan University. He has published work on gender, sexuality, food, medicine and the body in

Renaissance culture. The main focus of his research is on the dramatic works of the Elizabethan playwright John Lyly. He has previously been Programme Leader for Cultural Studies and retains an interest in gender and contemporary popular culture.

Alice Ferrebe is Lecturer in English at Liverpool John Moores University. Her book *Masculinity in Male-Authored Fiction, 1950–2000* was published by Palgrave Macmillan in 2005.

Ruth Helyer is a Senior Lecturer at the University of Teesside; her research interests are contemporary fiction and film (particularly American), visual culture and gender studies (particularly masculinity). Her publications include a chapter in the forthcoming *Cambridge Companion to Don DeLillo*.

Ben Knights is Director of the English Subject Centre of the UK Higher Education Academy. He has a long standing interest in the interplay of subject and pedagogic research, and in the study of masculinities in fiction and in education.

Wayne Martino has recently moved to the University of Western Ontario. His research focuses on gender and education with a specific focus on boys, masculinities and schooling. He has also conducted research into the sex- and gender-based dimensions of bullying in schools which has explored the implications for educational policy and practice. His books include: *So What's a Boy? Addressing Issues of Masculinity and Schooling* published in 2003 and *Being Normal is the Only Way to be: Adolescent Perspectives on Gender and School* published in 2005. His latest book is entitled *Gendered Outcasts Sexual Outlaws*.

Ruth Page is interested in the many different ways in which gender might influence narrative strategies. Her published work includes both sociolinguistic and literary studies in this area, including her recent *Literary and Linguistic Approaches to Feminist Narratology* (Palgrave, 2006). Her current research also explores developments in new media from a feminist perspective. She is a senior lecturer at the University of Central England in Birmingham.

Having lectured in the Czech Republic, **Chris Thurgar-Dawson** is currently Programme Leader for English Studies at the University of Teesside. He has research interests in the long poem, cultural geography and critical-creative writing. With Ben Knights he is co-author of *Active Reading: Transformative Writing in Literary Studies* (2006), and from 2008 he will be leading the Teesside MA in Creative Writing.

Cris Yelland is Principal Lecture in English Studies at the University of Teesside, UK. His research interests include Thomas Hardy, the use of critical linguistics with student groups, and the oral/written interface in nineteenth-century radical journalism. He has just completed a book on Jane Austen's languages.

1
Masculinities in Text and Teaching

Ben Knights

> As a woman, I am a consumer of masculinities, but I am not more so than men are; and, like men, I as a woman am also a producer of masculinities and a performer of them.
>
> – Eve Kosofsky Sedgwick, 'Gosh, Boy George, You Must be Awfully Secure in Your Masculinity' in Berger *et al.* (1995)

> Reading and the associated behaviours of sitting quietly with a book can... be understood as gender marked behaviours.
>
> – Millard 1997: 20–21

Masculinity, it is now widely accepted, can no longer be treated as an unmarked or tacit norm. As the reflexive or estranged study of masculinities takes root, one side effect in the English disciplines is that we are likely to become increasingly aware of the ubiquity of literary discussions of manliness and masculinity. Examples start to leap off the page. Take a moment in a superficially unremarkable nineteenth-century realist novel. 'Why is it that we hate a suicide?', rhetorically asks the eponymous vicar of Trollope's *The Vicar of Bullingham* (1870) of his despairing friend. Then answers himself:

> 'Because he is a coward and runs away from the burden that he ought to bear gallantly. He throws his load down on the roadside, and does not care who may bear it, or who may suffer because he us too poor a creature to struggle on! Have you no feeling that, though it may be hard with you here,' – and the Vicar, as he spoke, struck his breast, – 'you should so carry your outer self, that the eyes of those around you should see nothing of the sorrow within? That is my idea of manliness...' (Chapter 68)

1

There is a paradox here. This recipe for 'manliness' as defined by a necessary, ethical disjunction between subjectivity and outward conduct occurs in a male-authored text ostensibly dedicated to bringing to light the inner – even unconscious – springs of behaviour. This paradox focuses the problem of masculinity in textual studies. The association between affect, disclosure and subjectivity has over the years created a predicament for those men who engage in literary studies, one which becomes most acute as we contemplate what sort of conversations can be sustained through and around texts.

This book attempts a case study in the politics at once of inter-pretation and of pedagogy: its focus is the simultaneous production of masculinities within text and their performance upon the stage of teaching. Through the interweaving of the chapters that follow, we seek to articulate an ethical and political response to the discourses and narratives of masculinity as they are lived out in textual studies. This, we believe, is the minimum contribution that our topic can make to a much greater and more urgent political – even in the largest sense environ-mental – imperative. For across multiple cultures, religious and political traditions, men's pursuit of atavistic or resurgent patriarchal agendas, and their fear of declining relative material and symbolic power, appears to be among the most threatening forces at loose on earth today. This may appear a dramatic, overblown claim. But consider the import-ance of the nexus between patriarchy and textuality. Monotheistic neo-fundamentalisms have in common an uncompromising effort to restore society to the patriarchal law of the father. Where fidelity to the father's word is a matter of life or death, the immersion of masculinity in text is hardly a sideshow: education has responsibilities that are far from trivial. But textual education, we shall insist, must be understood as comprising far more than exegesis.

While over the past 25 years there has been in Britain, Australia and North America an explosion of critical interest in the study of masculin-ities, it is on the face of things surprising that the growing study of literary and textual masculinities has so far had little to say about the pedagogic implications. Thus, for example, the special issue on 'literary masculinities' of the journal *Men and Masculinities* (Vol. 4, No. 4, 2002) only obliquely touched on pedagogic issues. It does not seem to be easy for English and Cultural Studies (at least in Higher Education) to rise to the challenge posed by Michael Kimmel of 'Integrating Men into the Curriculum'.[1] As has so often been the case with the development of 'theory' in the cultural studies, it seems that 'business as usual' models of teaching have largely been assumed. In contrast, the premise of this book is that it is increasingly necessary to take the debate beyond textual analysis as such, and enquire into how the gender politics of textuality are played out in the classroom. Not least because English as a university subject is predominantly studied by women – indeed in Britain the most recent figures suggest that after several years when relative male participation in the subject was slowly increasing (partly because of the rise of A-level English Language which attracts a higher proportion of male students), full-time intake is not far off 75 per cent female.[2] Young males who choose to study English are generally assuming a position in many ways counter-cultural, not the least of whose attractions may be an extended struggle for superiority with female teachers of reading (e.g. Millard 1997: 81–82). As a minority, men in English groups are apt to form homosocial bonds against other students. And yet this is a field one of whose pre-occupations over the past 30 years has been the critique and subversion of traditional assumptions about gender. Fundamental to the present book is a belief that 'English', as a critical study of discourses, can potentially provide a terrain on which gendered identities and narratives may be reflexively questioned and even rewritten.[3] The book comprises a number of short case studies at once textual and pedagogic with the intention of creating a mosaic of insights into the mutual influence of processes at once cultural and pedagogic.

There are three related and confluent sources for this book. It derives from an ongoing enquiry into the representation, performance and reproduction of masculinities, through narrative and pedagogy (Beynon 2002; Connell 1995, 2000; Knights 1999). This, in turn, finds its context in an enquiry into the overlaps and synergies between subject scholarship and the intellectual practices of the discipline as they are embodied in teaching occasions. The embodied nature of learning is in fact an implicit if elusive theme throughout. And a key feature of this orientation towards pedagogy must be attention to the discursive formation of student identities within disciplines, specifically here within a broadly defined 'English and Cultural Studies'. Those identities, we suggest, are formed in the daily process of educational socialisation and derive as much from student constructions of what is expected of them as from the stated intentions of academics.

Throughout, this book will build upon the vigorous debates on gender within the subject domain, the formative influence of both gender and queer studies, the profound transformation feminism has wrought in both subject matter and (to a lesser extent) in how the subject is practised. Yet we see it as imperative that the weight of debates over gender should not simply fall (as in the curriculum it so often does) upon women's or gay studies. The formation of male subjectivity needs itself to be made visible.[4] At the moment, debates on gender in tertiary education are (mostly) carried on at the level of textual – or linguistic, or cultural historical – analysis. Here we intend to take a leaf from the study of secondary education and explore them as well at the level of the classroom, actual or virtual. As will be evident, this book invites and practices the critical discussion of text. Thus, for example, in their respective chapters, Robert Burden discusses D.H. Lawrence, Ranita Chatterjee Charlotte Dacre, Ruth Helyer Don De Lillo and Chris Thurgar-Dawson the long twentieth-century poem. But the book further seeks to fold the study of text back into a speculative, though experientially informed, account of the gendering of *oral critical practice*, and the making of symbolic power in and around the classroom. In different but complementary ways, the authors are concerned with how masculinities may be reproduced, affirmed, policed or subverted in educational practice, and, quite specifically, in a subject domain where biological males – at least at A-level and undergraduate level – are and have been for many years in a minority. Between us, we are thus concerned with the (largely tacit and unacknowledged) processes through which footing, influence, symbolic power and access to privileged meanings are acquired and maintained through the discussion of text. The invitation to readers is to join in a reflexive enquiry into the co-production of gendered meanings within that simultaneously social, intellectual and affective space where text and the group meet. We need to ask questions such as by what rhetorical moves is the authoritative 'voice' achieved? Where is the disposing, adjudicating gaze located? Does the tactical disruption of the flow of reading itself propagate intellectual superiority? Who achieves access to 'high' meanings? (Those adjudicating propositions that 'place' in a hierarchy of significance the other observations made within a seminar or within a critical text.) Do transactions surrounding text legitimate or question gendered forms of power?

Located in a particular group of disciplines, this whole book is simultaneously offered as a contribution to the scholarship of learning and teaching. This itself requires a *caveat*. Our approach is embedded in what Martha Nussbaum refers to as 'narrative imagination' (Nussbaum 1997). In appealing to teachers to become reflexively aware of the processes and rituals in which they are likely to find themselves unwittingly caught up, we are closer to literary ideals of defamiliarisation or estrangement than to 'evidence-based' educational research. We nevertheless suggest that future qualitative research of an empirical or phenomenographic kind could productively complement the kind of discussion around the text carried on here.[5]

As will be explained at greater length below, this whole book builds on the working hypothesis that there is a symbiosis between intellectual and pedagogic habits. Subjects are themselves *produced* in the arguments and dialogues of the corridor and classroom, in the encounters between initiates and experts, on feedback forms and in the margins of student essays, as much as in the monograph or learned journal (Knights 1992). In the case of this particular group of subjects we make and shall revisit later in this chapter, the historical assumption that the covert gender struggle within English Studies in its formative years still in certain ways influences the reproduction of the subject today. Or to put it another way, that to uncover some of the predicaments faced by the pioneers of the discipline can throw light not only on our own contemporary efforts to induct our students into our modes of discourse and study, but also on the roles – compliant or adversarial – that students find themselves playing. This is a discipline which – and despite the rhetorical, outward turn we associate with the era of 'theory' – has treasured affect, interiority and the 'soft' discourses of interpersonal relations.[6] In doing so, it found the need to manage the very forces it had itself let loose, a compulsion to legislate for what *ought* to matter within the interior of the self. And constructionists and essentialists alike might agree that interiority and the private domain have historically had to some extent different meanings for – typical – females and males and at different points along the gay/straight spectrum.

In this introductory chapter, then, we shall next offer a working theory of masculinities as a rationale for the book, before going on to locate its argument in pedagogy and specifically the pedagogy of higher education. That will then lead in a final section to a speculative account of masculinity in relation to the history of English Studies.

Thinking about masculinities

Since the 1970s, cultural studies have campaigned vigorously against all forms of essentialism, not least those attached to sexual dimorphism. Contemporary literary and cultural studies almost invariably assume a cultural or social constructionist view of gender. Such an orientation was fundamental to the rise through the 1980s of masculinity studies in sociology and social psychology.[7] The primacy of social learning in the formation of identity as a sexed being and in the construction of experience has become a category of thought for professionals in social, language and cultural studies. From this perspective, masculinities (the term is rhetorically contrasted with the connotations attached to simply being male) are seen (in Michael Kimmel's summary) as a

> constantly changing collection of meanings that are constructed through relationships with themselves, with other men, and with the world. A social constructionist perspective understands gender definitions as neither static nor timeless, but historically articulated within and through people's interactions with their worlds.
>
> http://www.law.duke.edu/journals/djglp/articles/gen4p181.htm

As articulated above, the meanings of masculinity vary across cultures, through history, among men within any one culture, and over the course of a man's life. Thus, one cannot speak of masculinity as though it were a constant, singular, universal essence, but rather one must approach masculinity as an ever-changing fluid assemblage of meanings and behaviours. Vulnerable as such propositions would seem from the standpoint of evolutionary biology or cognitive neuroscience, they have come to seem well-nigh unassailable from the point of view of literary and cultural theory. While this chapter is not the place to review the current research literature on masculinities, a book devoted to masculinities in textual study owes it to its subject and its readers to articulate its key term.[8] The best thing under the circumstances seems to be to state a series of working hypotheses as an allusion to longer and more complex arguments. Our first hypothesis is both the most difficult and – in our field – the most controversial. But since we aim not simply to appropriate arguments about masculinity from other disciplines, but rather to argue for textual studies as themselves an arena for the development of masculinity studies, we have to get it over with first.

'Theory' as it is embedded in English Studies has usually been characterised by cultural relativism in pursuit of a vigorous politics of anti-essentialism. In short a preference on the part of this particular academic tribe for thinking in terms of gender rather than sexual dimorphism. Yet it is possible that the case for the social and linguistic construction of gender espoused by literary theory (one which reached its acme in the reception accorded to the performative arguments of Judith Butler, in *Gender Trouble* and *Bodies that Matter*) has actually passed its high-water mark. Even if we disagree with them, those of us in English and Cultural Studies cannot simply dismiss arguments about maleness and femaleness emerging from a variety of sources: from the new cognitive sciences and from Simon Baron-Cohen's work on autism as an extreme version of 'the male brain' (see below), as much as from evolutionary biology. In any case, a *purely* performative account of gender risks pulling the rug from underneath a necessary critique of real inequalities and injustice. Recent theory has sometimes made it seem as though identification with victims of historical oppression was simply a matter of consumer choice. A similar argument concerns the effect on any concept of human rights of the trick taught in any first year theory module of disposing of 'human nature'. All this said, we can and in our view should continue to acknowledge that gender power (while resting on biological foundations) is articulated and reinforced through the medium of language and culture. To borrow the term Benedict Anderson put into currency about nationality, we might say that to be a man is to belong to a highly culturally variable 'imagined community' – a community with its paradigmatic narratives for 'self-fashioning', its folklore and dramatis personae.

This book seeks to avoid being trapped in the extremes either of essentialism or of a constructivist/performative account of gender and masculinity. We see both as dead ends, and as derived from the sort of primitive dualism and disembodiment of mind taken to task by Antonio Damasio (*Descartes' Error* 1994 and *The Feeling of What Happens* 1999). In general, the new neuroscience provides a constant reminder of the inter-penetration of the biological and the cultural.[9] Dualisms tend to favour one of their binary terms, and the dualist tradition in western thought has tended to privilege the bearers of intellect (cf. Lloyd 1993). (We might, in passing, hazard the suggestion that reverence for 'monuments of unageing intellect' is itself derived from a long patriarchal tradition of associating the male with spirit and the female with the somatic.[10]) Doreen Kimura (who has invited and taken her share of criticism for insisting on the biological origin of cognitive difference between the sexes) is quite clear:

> It is by now a truism that behaviour is determined by both physiological and environmental factors, acting interdependently.
>
> (Kimura 2004 and see Kimura 1999)

Biological and evolutionary pre-dispositions of personality and behaviour (themselves layered and various) are lived out and mutually influenced through culture and language. And there seems little doubt that many of the effects of genetic and evolutionary endowment can be muted or enhanced by environmental factors. In what follows, then, we are talking about the production of the masculine subject on the basis of an already diverse (though indisputably real) biological infrastructure. 'Masculinity', we propose, is an aspirational identity rather than descriptive fact. Forms for exhibiting it in the classroom (or anywhere else) do not simply exist: they are perpetually in formation, and hence at least potentially changeable. As Dennis Allen documents (below), the meanings of masculinity, of manliness, of the behaviours and dispositions proper to being a man are perpetually under negotiation – a fact which has immediate relevance to those places where languages, codes and genres come under reflective scrutiny. That said, the performance of identities is not simply a matter of unconstrained individual choice. We suggest that narratives of male identity hold an attraction endowed by the memory (albeit often a false memory) of an entitlement to power.

Men of all sorts and orientations have been attracted to an epic narrative of male supremacy not because they were hard-wired to do so (the jury is out), nor because historically they all shared equally in the benefits of hegemony (they didn't). To take an analogy: many years ago, in her classic study of the US South, *Killers of the Dream* (1949), Lillian Smith demonstrated how many of those who in any objective terms were themselves victims of an economic and social regime could be persuaded to identify with the wealthy and powerful and act as though they 'really' belonged to a master race. Material differences could be brushed aside in bonding together to defend a supremacy which was in many ways imaginary. It might help to think of the 'imagined community' of hegemonic masculinity working in rather the same way. As a working generalisation, men have characteristically sought to assert an identity based upon an acquired memory of the historical experience of dominion – an experience that was only ever attainable by some and only locally attainable by others. On that proposition rest the propositions that follow. We are not here attempting a general theory of masculinity: simply to articulate some hypotheses which we believe to be of particular relevance to the immersion of self-identified males in textual experience.

1. Hegemonic masculinity seeks to impose unity upon plurality. A vast deal of historical and cultural evidence exists that – at all events in western cultures – *typically* (we will have to insist on the qualifier throughout), being male has been associated with a drive to exorcise anxiety by rituals of bonding, by contempt directed against those perceived to undermine manliness and by demonstrative acts

of heroism. These tend to involve taking risks (with one's own body and the bodies of others), in courting danger beyond what would in any practical sense be required by actual circumstances. Exaggerated performance seems to derive from the male subject's obsessive need for reassurance about his own continuity, physical integrity and even existence. Narratives of heroism provide the medium of symbolic bonding into what can be understood as an 'imagined community'. For it is a mistake to assume that the dominant masculine modality is simply one of physical assertion. Even violence operates in the symbolic domain as much as in the realm of deeds. As the present editor became conscious many years ago when teaching in a men's high-security prison, violent narratives (whether of triumph or of failure) are not simply a celebration of individual or group experience. Addressed to an audience, they constitute a distinct kind of speech act: menace. Such speech acts present interlocutors with an acute situational choice: follower or victim? On a more highly wrought level, epic endeavour has always been about giving enduring form to social memory. The originals of Achilles, Aeneas or Beowulf would have faded from the world pretty fast were it not for the cultural forms which celebrated and perpetuated deeds. So the Carlylean longing to award ontological superiority to the (male) act is a non-starter. And in any case if violent self assertion were *simply* instinctual, what function would be served by celebrating it in word or image?[11] The standpoint of this book is that atavistic, competitive heroism is no longer sustainable. Humankind, says the military historian John Keegan (hardly a soft touch himself), 'needs not new hardware but a change of heart. It needs an end to the ethic of heroism in its leadership for good and all'.[12] This may be akin to what Headlam Wells – who speaks of the 'will to myth'– is driving at when he says of Coriolanus that in the assumed nobility of his tragedy, Martius' 'greatest conquest is not of Corioli, but the hearts of theatre audiences and critics alike' (Wells 2000: 83 and 146).

2. A number of simultaneously textual and social phenomena follow. One concerns the strengthening and purifying of boundaries.[13] Baron-Cohen's key characteristic of what he calls 'the male brain' is the propensity to 'systemise' (as opposed to the empathising 'female brain').[14] The pragmatics of system building, we might add, involve a compulsion to police a dominant definition of manliness or male attributes. One of the boundaries that appears to have given most trouble is that marking off the subjective or inner domain. *Typically*

(again), men have tended to treat their own interiority or inner world as a strange (and even threatening) land.[15]

3. Historically the suspicion attaching to interiority has also applied to its correlative, empathy (dangerous proximity to the innerness of others). Recalling Ian Suttie's formulation 'the taboo on tenderness' (Suttie 1963), we suggest that one (typical) phenomenon of male-affiliation is unease about affect, about the demands of intimacy and the resulting compulsion to manage the boundaries of the securely contained self.[16] Once again, this suggestion impinges upon the domain of literary culture and its reproduction through criticism and educational institutions. In particular, the forms of subjectivity and interiority associated with the rise of the novel and with Romantic and post-Romantic poetry[17] – and anticipated in the development of the soliloquy in the early modern period – required male authors and those who identified with them to negotiate a danger zone of affect and blurred edges conventionally associated with the feminine. Over the ensuing vertigo loomed a Carlylean spectre that introspection would sap the ability to act. In Kristevan terms, this fear of abjection, of disintegrating under your own gaze and under the gaze of significant others follows on the dissolution of strong boundaries. Conversely, many literary representations of masculinity have been drawn precisely to the narrative dynamics of failure. Thus one consequence (going back at least as far as Dostoyevsky) has been a thread of enquiry into the male abject as anti-hero: 'I really was a coward and slave', asserts the protagonist of Dostoyevsky's *Notes from Underground*.[18] Reciprocally, literary fictions from Defoe's *Moll Flanders* to Allan Warner's *Sopranos* have provided a pretext and instrument for male authors and commentators to divert attention from their own vulnerability by probing the interior of female experience. But this itself is not a risk-free procedure: the problem of identification with the object of the gaze has been felt acutely in relation to male creativity, as also in relation to the male gaze implicated in critical reading ('Portrait of the Artist as a Man' in Knights 1999). In male-authored fictions, one way of managing the risk of engulfment by feminised subject matter has been to project the sense of threat upon female protagonists who subsequently – like Desdemona, Cordelia, Anna Karenin, Emma Bovary, Effie Briest or Tess Darbeyfield – come to grisly ends as sacrificial victims. Later in the chapter we shall extend this argument about narrative predicaments: English Studies being organised to ward off or engage in ritual expulsion of the feminine and the domestic.[19]

Let us conclude these propositions by saying that in this book we are going to take a pragmatic – even phenomenological – approach to the question of masculinities. While believing that it is meaningful to talk about a spectrum of publicly produced manhood, we see no reason to collapse the discussion back into essentialism or any unmediated form of quasi-biological determinism. At the same time, we can see no way of theorising masculinities within a cultural – constructivist perspective that is not itself susceptible to deconstruction (MacInnes 1998). Pragmatically, though, there is a job for educationists to do: it would be intellectually and politically retrograde to revert either to 'blank slate' (in any of its many variables), or, on the other hand to deny that gender modalities – however sustained – exist and have 'real world' effects. Let us grant that the masculine identities and performances towards which men are tempted almost certainly have roots in evolutionary biology, and in foetal responses to intra-uterine androgens. Outside the womb, these dispositions are in due course overdetermined by the fraught relationship to embodiment that arises from the drive to dissociate from the mother. But the identities which result from these overlapping bio-cultural processes are themselves experienced and performed in symbolic, cultural (and *to some degree* therefore mutable) forms: the experience of embodiment is itself mediated through interaction with other embodied subjectivities.

Among those forms are the very narratives which literature, film and drama make available to enquiry as public and sharable dramas of self-fashioning. Almost needless to say, such texts are not simply available to the always already gendered reader as items for solitary consumption. Among the places where they take on meaning and perlocutionary force is the scene of teaching within institutions dedicated to study. This book adopts the working hypothesis that printed cultural forms – analogous in a sense to the world wide web – constitute a form of virtual, collective intelligence. This is what we might refer to as 'peri-text': the buzz of conversation which surrounds the text as an enactment of social meanings. In this view, poetry, drama or the novel constitute a form of software for social intelligence. To take our immediate topic: narratives of manliness do not have to be explained as simply epiphenomenal upon a somatic or psychic base. Ruth Page's empirical research (see chapter below) constitutes a salutary warning against stereotypical ideas of masculine or feminine narrative procedures. Nevertheless, social participation in fictive narrative constitutes a theatre where the meanings of masculinity may (among infinite other topics) be explored. Fictive texts – as the chapters by Ruth Helyer, Ranita Chatterjee and Robert

Burden demonstrate – can themselves be read as commentary upon the pedagogic formation of masculinities. (Even, as in Helyer's discussion of De Lillo's *White Noise*, the parodic formation of academic man himself.) In turn, John Beynon shows us how self-conscious understanding of narrative can help make sense of the crafting of memory outside fiction. Without going down an essentialist road, we shall therefore frame the chapters that follow in terms of a history of the management of gendered subjectivity. But in doing so we must at the same time insist upon heteroglossia: the idea that discourses are almost inevitably fraught, self-divided and internally inconsistent. As textual critics we are in many ways trying to read texts and textual occasions 'against themselves', with the prompts they themselves provide.

This book, we have said, is intended to be more than a collection of critical studies as such. In a proceeding akin to David Bleich's 'double perspective' (Bleich 1988), the chapters which follow work through an underlying supposition that while scholarly and critical knowledge inform the processes of teaching and learning, the latter simultaneously inform the creation and re-making of knowledge. We need next to turn to the context within institutional pedagogic regimes.

Pedagogic orientation

While this book concentrates on the production of masculinities within textual studies in Higher Education, we must make clear that there is a substantial research literature on masculinity in initial education, (and even to some degree specifically on masculinity in English).[20] Higher Education is in fact coming late to an already developed debate. One way of explaining the ambition of the present book would be to say that it represents a tentative application to higher education of research which has been carried on for many years on schooling and with young persons of school age. As long ago as 1994 student cultures of masculinity and the idea of schools as a masculinising agency were the subject of Mairtin Mac An Ghaill's *The Making of Men: Masculinities, Sexualities and Schooling* (1994). Mac An Ghaill's work (see also Mac An Ghaill 1996) draws upon and returns to a tradition of research and critique strongly represented in the pages of the journal *Gender and Education* (e.g. the 1997 'Masculinities in Education' special issue 9.1). If we turn specifically to the domain of English and reading, we must note that such research studies have taken place in a context of widespread and volatile public debates concerning boys and reading.[21] There is and has been for 10 years or more a lively public and media debate in the United

Kingdom, in North America and in Australia around ideas about why boys are failing (or why the education system is failing boys – a media trope repeatedly and cogently critiqued by Lynne Segal[22]), above all in the skills of literacy. Many of the implications were drawn out by Elaine Millard in her *Differently Literate: Boys, Girls and the Schooling of Literacy* (Millard 1997), a study from which – although its research effectively antedates the impact of the Internet – those who teach in Higher Education could learn much. For comparatively little has been written on masculinity in Higher Education (Michael Kimmel's 'Integrating Men into the Curriculum' is a significant exception) and of what there is, little of it directly concerns men in English subjects. (An important, if now rather dated, exception is Kim Thomas 1990; see also a handful of articles in *Studies in HE*, and in *Gender and Education*, a few pages in Evans 1993 and Knights 1999.) This book proposes itself as a contribution to filling that gap.

The implications of much of what follows are explored further in Wayne Martino's chapter (below). Where he will concentrate on the experience of men who have elected to become English teachers, it seems important here to suggest some further cross-sector threads. Especially now that universities are no longer an experience of an elite only, there is, we shall assume, an even greater need to explore and understand the 'gender regime' (Connell 2000) of English in universities. What Mac An Ghaill says of school as a masculinising agency has relevance across the sectors, as will be apparent in the chapters by Allen and Dooley (below).

> A main argument of this book is that we need to consider not only gender *differences* but also *relations between* young men and women and *within* young men's peer groups. It is important to see masculinity not simply as complementary to femininity. . . . Masculinities are also developed in specific institutional contexts in relation to and against each other.
>
> (Mac An Ghaill 1994: 61)

While historically men have dominated university teaching (a situation however which in the Humanities has changed dramatically over the past 15 years), teaching has paradoxically been by tradition been a lower status and a women's profession. At the same time, children (as much as students) have to be seen as active agents in producing gendered positions and resisting or creolising the educational languages with which their teachers attempt to endow them. While they are unlikely to use the term, students whether at school, college or university are quite as sensitive to the implicit messages of 'the hidden curriculum' as are its left wing critics. That English as a subject had colluded in producing the subjectivities required by the state became in the 1980s a commonplace of one strand of critique (e.g. Hunter, *Culture and Government* 1988). From observation and the research literature, we might derive the related suggestion that dominant boys have tended to identify English and English teachers as having designs upon them. For as Mark Dooley has pointed out:

> English is a subject more profoundly engaged with the processes of identity formation than any other. Every engagement with every text involves, at some level, the negotiation of our sense of self with the external world. When that engagement takes place in a public space, with a group of people, there is no telling how many personal stories could be circulating, how many narratives are being written and rewritten, challenged and affirmed.
>
> (p. 73)

Inasmuch as teacherly ideologies are perceived as threatening cherished masculinities, resistance takes shape against teachers as well as their subject matter and 'soft' empathetic approaches. Martino's article 'The Tyranny of Surveillance: Male Teachers and the Policing of Masculinities. . . .' (*Gender and Education* 2006) vividly portrays the attempts of male teachers to operate under the 'normalizing [and frequently homophobic] gaze' of male pupils. One frequent result is the display of forms of humour and toughness by which to curry favour with dominant boys. Simultaneously, Millard's summary of research will come as no surprise.

> Boys learn at an early age to control both the girls in their class and the women who teach them by adopting a 'male' discourse which emphasizes negative aspects of female sexuality, and embodies 'direct sexual insult' . . . Boys act as if the very fact of working with girls will demean them.
>
> (Millard 1997: 9)

In higher education too, fear of feminisation can be countered by taking control of the symbolic space. A quotation from Kim Thomas's interviews is likely to ring bells:

> With my current tutor, I tend to be rather argumentative because she's a talker, she would talk if you let her – so I cut across her

sometimes, which might mean she thinks I'm aggressive, but...she probably respects me in that respect.

(Male student interviewee quoted in Thomas 1990: 150)

The ambiguities of a situation in which a woman tutor is identified with masculine subject matter are highlighted in Alice Ferrebe's chapter (below). But while those influenced by Pierre Bourdieu would reach for the term 'symbolic violence' to characterise the power relation between teacher and taught, we would prefer here to draw attention to the problematics of nurture.[23] How, in the pedagogic environment, do nutrients circulate, and who controls their flow? In particular, we are dealing with a discipline that foregrounds the role of nurture and attentive sympathy, yet at the same time is embarrassed by what to do with it. In any case, how does an educational subject *do* nurturing? How does it practise in that fuzzy, ordinary, in all senses *virus-ridden* domain where subjectivities meet and may be exposed to shame or humiliation? How does it call out and then in turn protect the vulnerability of teachers? (The question will emerge again in the context of Mark Dooley's and Dennis Allen's chapters below.) Disciplines that pride themselves on their rigorous intellectual challenge may by the same token give scant attention to the emotional or social needs of either their practitioners and students. Self-evidently, this is a problem that extends far beyond the family of English subjects or even the Humanities. But we suggest that it has taken on a peculiar force in a discipline whose very subject matter foregrounds the giving and receiving of nourishment (metaphorical and literal) and relationships of care and attentiveness to others. The intellectual and affective vulnerability of the teacher in this discipline constitutes a model for the student. How teachers manage and students internalise or reject their vulnerability constitutes a central element of the classroom production of the subject. As Higher Education (in the United Kingdom at all events) moves steadily towards a nurturing paradigm – though admittedly in a highly routinised, even managerial, sense – such issues (with their implications for managing the boundaries of embodiment) become even more acute. They have, we suggest, implications for all levels of practice in our subject group, from the lone reader, to the classroom and the dialogue within virtual learning environment (VLE) and chat room, from the social and institutional organisation of academic departments, to the practice of scholarship in the subject. We shall explore below the protocols of male teachers in a subject widely perceived as feminising. Here, let us note that one resolution of this gender conundrum is the projection of the male English teacher as charismatic hero, a role crystallised in Peter Weir's 1989 film *Dead Poets' Society* (starring Robin Williams). Yet, charisma, too, with its resonances of heroism and masculine leadership has to be understood as operating within regimes that are simultaneously textual and social. Fictional studies of the English – and more recently the Creative Writing – lecturer also enlarge on the possibility that the elaborate, erotic discourse of the subject may itself become a medium of seduction (e.g. J.M. Coetzee's *Disgrace* [1999]). In a contrasting mode, we can often observe the perpetation of symbolic violence as a bonding force in male reading. The male Cultural Studies students I remember testing their squeamish male tutor (and female peers) by insisting on talking and writing assignments about *American Psycho, Fight Club* or *Omen* were anticipated in the late 1970s 'sub-cultures' period of the Birmingham Centre for Contemporary Cultural Studies.[24]

The present book builds on ideas developed over many years by the Development of University English Teaching Project about the isomorphic relations between text and pedagogic practice (Evans 1995; Knights 1992). These ideas are grounded in a psychodynamic tradition. Applied to educational groups, they concern how groups negotiate authority, police relevance, deal with material felt to be dangerous; how they manage internal relations, and strive for coherence. With its vocabulary of splitting, projection and of inter-group fantasy, the discipline of group relations provides lucid insight into the fantasies and patterns of expectation which govern gendered behaviours. Yet the Tavistock tradition in group relations is itself vulnerable to critique on grounds of its tacit gendering. The present study is simultaneously influenced by the constructivist tradition in educational thought. And while Foucault and 'technologies of the self' are another strong influence, the book is committed simultaneously to ideas about heteroglossia and dialogism, to a belief that educational institutions can provide sites in which to explore difference, change, possibility. Contrary to the critique launched in the 1980s by the anti-humanist left, we take a liberatory view of the potential of textual study for cultural learning and renewal. Reading and the collaborative discussion of books can be, as Rachel Carroll suggests below, one road to alternative realities. Cris Yelland's chapter proposes a line between the study of transitivity and a revived sense of human agency. But for such – admittedly utopian – routes to be unobstructed, teachers and students have to become consciously aware of Kimmel's 'hidden gender meanings' within the dialogue between students, teachers and texts. The underlying argument is that (while aiming to avoid reductive treatment of texts and discourses) gender power and performance can be raised to the level of awareness through dialogue over and through texts.

Earlier on, we suggested that literature (in a broad sense) might plausibly be seen as analogous to a form of software for social intelligence. Underlying this point was the idea that text understood in this way exists not solely in its one-to-one relation with individual readers, but as mediated, argued-over, interpreted in social groupings which include those which are our subject here: those at work in the socio-intellectual space of academic institutions. Thus, in terms of the topic in hand, interaction with narratives (literary and otherwise) is one of the ways in which masculinity is produced. But the arena of higher education study could simultaneously be one where that very process could be held up to the light.

In what follows, then, we shall be talking not about text as such, but about the *study* of text as a social practice: the protocols of argumentation, the disciplinary rhetorics, the conventions of evidence and styles of thinking that from a scholarly point of view constitute the subject but which, simultaneously, from a pedagogic point of view, are enacted within the classroom or other encounters between professional initiates and learners. I will argue as I have elsewhere that it is necessary for those of us who study disciplinary 'tribes' to consider what I have – on the analogy of the 'implied reader' – called the 'implied student' of the discipline (Becher and Trowler 2001; Knights 2005). Disciplines – like novels – can be studied in terms of their addressivity. The practice of the subject invites the formation of a paradigmatic identity. This is of course an invitation which students do not have to accept – like readers, they too may comprehend their subject 'against the grain', or be selective about which attributes they internalise. But even where their students will not follow them into their profession, we have to see academics as in some sense gatekeepers. This gatekeeping function operates within the border rituals of the classroom (e.g. how it establishes relevance or irrelevance in discussion) as well as its policing of its own scholarly discourse. To examine a discipline is thus also to ask about its addressees, those whom its discourse attempts to enlist in its intellectual style.

In the identification of the 'implied student', questions of gender are unavoidable. Above all, in English and Literary studies, pedagogy and the construction of masculine roles have to be understood as taking place within a subject widely experienced as implicitly feminising. T.S. Eliot's much-quoted dictum about poetry being an escape from personality continued to be lived out in the conflicted homage paid by English Studies to impersonality (Ellmann 1987). We are talking about a subject constellation which over the past century has formed defences against its own tendency to blur cognitive borderlines. The practice of the subject at once renders the subjective impersonal and disciplined and then re-immerses apparently unambiguous knowledge in interpretation. This dialectic, its proponents are likely to agree, is a fundamental element in its pedagogic and developmental strength. Yet the affective snags of this dialectical process are little understood. In the history of the subject itself what started out as hard, objective knowledge (about literary history, or philology or linguistic structures, about contexts or about authorial biography) has tended to dissolve under scrutiny into the reflexive, the ambivalent, the tentative, the inexorable slither of signified into signifier.[25] In this context, Ranita Chatterjee's chapter (below) might well suggest to us that what the pedagogic situation and the Gothic have in common is a susceptibility to the uncanny. From Freud's reading of Jensen's *Gradiva* (1904) to Derek Attridge's *The Singularity of Literature*, hospitality towards the haunting unspoken requires of both critic and student a receptive mindset far removed from that traditionally associated with hegemonic masculinity.

Masculinity and English Studies

This brief contribution to a speculative history of the subject is different (and in intention less dismissive) to that developed during the New Left challenge of the 1980s.[26] A critique of the dynamics by which gender superiority is pursued provides no grounds for a reprise of the 1980s assault on the discipline, if only because such an assault would unerringly reproduce earlier male attempts to take back ownership of the subject. Literature as an institutionalised study has many and various virtues, and we have no intention of denying these in suggesting that it has also frequently formed a terrain for a covert struggle over the gendering of symbolic power. Let us return to a fundamental (and, we would argue, gendered) metaphor.[27] Drawing on the earlier work of Anthony Biglan, Becher and Trowler have demonstrated that the soft/hard metaphorical set is endemic in the constitution of educational disciplines (2001: 34–36). The English group have from the beginning felt compelled to explain that what appeared to be a 'soft' subject matter was actually hard if you looked rigorously enough. Between 1919 and 1921 the authors of the Newbolt Report, *The Teaching of English in England* were exercised by a charge that has been repeatedly heard since. Having reviewed the sources of difficulty, the Report concluded that

It is suggested that [English] is a 'soft option'. This is an accusation which affects the whole of our inquiry. If it were made good, it would go a long way towards providing a justification for denying English the place in our education system which we demand for it. Above all it would be fatal to the claims of English at the University stage.... Our answer to it is that the charge is untrue and the danger imaginary.... [It] is a pure delusion to suppose that the fact that a boy or man knows enough English to talk to his brother, or take a railway ticket, or even conduct a business, leaves him nothing hard or difficult to learn when he comes to study English Literature.

In short, the

man who enters an English 'School' hoping for an idle or easy time should at once find he has deceived himself.

(§ 194)

But the celebration of Englishness and English culture into which Newbolt and his colleagues hoped to engage the nation turned out not to be the dominant gene within the new subject.

Literary studies soon turned out to represent a form of liminal activity. Not only were they perched uneasily on the boundaries of everyday and esoteric discourse, but, like psychoanalysis, alongside which they grew up, they proposed to bring to the surface and articulate disturbing unconscious material.[28] Rapid and frequently disconcerting code-switching has been and remains central to their performance. To the extent these subjects' boundaries leak, they are, in Mary Douglas's terms, dangerous.[29] Critical activity – whether working with everyday or with literary texts – is precarious, and in many senses counter-intuitive. To re-immerse the written or spoken world in its moment of production, to engage in elaborate interpretation, is to undermine everyday assumptions about making secure sense. Cris Yelland's chapter (below), which explores transitivity in war narratives, is simultaneously an object lesson in the estrangement of apparently common-sense discourse, a necessary but disturbing activity. The pedagogic value of unpacking transitivity rests, indeed, upon its unsettlingness. Critical studies have characteristically privileged hidden meaning, indeterminacy, unconscious shadowing – all the ambivalences, concealments and contradictions inherent in language.

Yet, paradoxically, 'English' as a self-avowedly transgressive subject has raised its own transgressions to a form of superior orthodoxy. The site of teaching is therefore one which breeds anxieties all the more urgent for the sense that only to the initiated can access the secret. To borrow and adapt Basil Bernstein's terms, the subject appears to invite 'horizontal' (everyday) discourse, then reveals that the high status language was 'vertical' (esoteric) all the time (Bernstein 1996). Crucially for our purposes here, this propensity of the subject to re-immerse the achieved word and well-wrought artefact back into indeterminacy has particular resonances in terms of the history of gender. The emergence of a community of professional textual interpreters may derive from the same sources that have historically, in so many cultures, fuelled a perceived need for a male caste of exegetes: those entrusted with the sacred task of an engagement with the word seen as too dangerous for the laity.

Quite specifically, the years when English Studies was being formed were years of considerable gender turbulence and an agitated debate over the nature of male subjectivity. I have written about this elsewhere, and shall merely summarise here (Knights 2005). One way of getting hold of this would be by allusion to the recent explosion of fictional interest in Henry James.[30] These doublings and re-doublings of James, with their prurient attention to his sexuality and troubled subjectivity provide us with a way of orienting a discussion of an educational subject that emerged out of a moment when male aestheticism and the range of male cultural expression had been so forcibly restrained. In distinctly Jamesian circumstances, Nick, the young protagonist of Alan Hollinghurst's *The Line of Beauty* (2004), tries to explain his PhD thesis to Lord Kessler.

> 'And what is your chosen field?'
> 'Mm. I want to have a look at *style*,' Nick said. This flashing emphasis on something surely ubiquitous had impressed the admissions board, though Lord Kessler appeared uncertain. A man who owned Mme de Pompadour's escritoire could hardly be indifferent to style, Nick felt; but his reply seemed to have in mind some old wisdom about style and substance.
> 'Style *tout court*?'
> 'Well, style at the turn of the century – Conrad, and Meredith, and Henry James of course.' It all sounded perfectly pointless, or at least a way of wasting two years, and Nick blushed because he really was interested in it and didn't yet know – not having done the research – what he was going to prove.
> 'Ah,' said Lord Kessler intelligently: 'style as an obstacle.'

Nick smiled. 'Exactly... Or perhaps style that hides things and reveals things at the same time.' For some reason this seemed rather near the knuckle, as though he were suggesting Lord Kessler had a secret. 'James is a great interest of mine, I must say.'
'Yes, you're a James man, I see it now.'

(2004: 54–55)

In the 1890s and early 1900s, expressions of male melancholy became endemic alongside wholesale propaganda for a new, toughened imperial masculinity. Those poets of male doubling, Wilde, James, Stevenson or George du Maurier, were surrounded by a frenzy of disambiguation: notable instances include the discourses of nationalism; race, and – here most pertinently – male bodies. From the mid-1890s on, social attempts to regulate the male ran the gamut from military-style drill, to imprisonment, and on to surgical mutilation (Budd 1997; Darby 2005; Knights 2004). While Queer Studies have been inclined to read late nineteenth-century heterosexual melancholy in the light of the repression of the homosexual other (e.g. Butler 1993; Sedgwick 1991), we make a complementary suggestion.[31] That is that the haunted masculinities of the proto-modernist moment may also represent an act of mourning for an earlier conception of male childhood. Much recent research has explored the emergence of the new, toughened masculinities of the late nineteenth century out of the more heterogeneous, even androgynous version of manliness current in the mid-nineteenth century (Robson 2001; Steedman 1995; Tosh 1999). Thus Catherine Robson concludes that in the 1890s 'the boy returned from his long obscurity to be childhood's supreme representative for the twentieth century' (2001: 193). In a complementary argument, Claudia Nelson argues that it was a mix of Darwinism and homophobia that generated the strengthening distinctions which destroyed the old androgynous ideal (Nelson 1991).

Obviously there are differences of emphasis and approach here. But between them they nevertheless lend substance to the suggestion that by the early years of the twentieth century a re-alignment of the relationship between adult and child male self was for many generating a sense of disorientation and loss. A gothic pathos associated with the death of the small boy famously attracted Henry James as much as, later, it did Benjamin Britten (cf. Bradley 2000; Ohi 2005). In an era when childhood was increasingly the subject of educational and social regulation, we might speculate that James's *Kindertotenlieder* 'The Pupil' or *The Turn of the Screw* prefigure an anxiety that pedagogy might smother its objects.

The trope of the 'lost domain' or *Temps Perdu* of boyhood came to be extensively mined in Modernism – by Proust as by Alain-Fournier.[32] As James put it in his late memoir *A Small Boy and Others* (1913):

> To look back at all is to meet the apparitional and to find on its ghastly face the silent stare of an appeal. When I fix it, the hovering shade, whether of person or place, it fixes me back and seems the less lost.

At the same moment in the history of masculine subjectivity, J.M. Barrie re-wrote his hugely successful play *Peter Pan* as a novel. In the narrator's identification with the figure of Peter, Barrie, like James, located the male onlooker in a lost and excluded subjectivity. As he did so, he established for the new century the paradigm of the little boy as exile (cf. Rose 1984).[33]

> However, as we are here we may as well stay and look on. That is all we are really, lookers-on. Nobody really wants us.
>
> (*Peter and Wendy* 5th edition 1911: 236)

Cultural repetition (acts of writing, reading or performance) could be both the nostalgic performance of the moment of loss and a symbolic rescue of the boy self. One might suggest that the pervasive literature of male doubles – to which one hundred years later David Lodge, Colm Tóibín and Alan Hollinghurst have now, as though under the sway of some overpowering transference, returned – derives from the power of the written word to hold in suspension multiple latent identities. But also – and more to the point here – that the uncanniness and leaky borders of so much turn of the century male writing rang warning bells for those who sought to develop an educational practice based on literature.

In short, we seem to have in the turbulence of masculine identities a common genesis both for the gothic hauntings of *fin de siècle* fiction, *and* a matrix for the new English Studies. This was perhaps another aspect of that 'paranoid articulation of charisma among middle-class professional men at the turn of the century' of which David Trotter speaks (Trotter 2001: 152). Here was a domain which had roots in activities and orientations widely perceived as feminine – or at least opposed to those coercive versions of masculinity fashioned in the controversy over aestheticism which surrounded the trials of Oscar Wilde. Simultaneously, as the study of vernacular literature spread through the university extension movement, it became apparent that most of the students were actually women. As the authors of the Newbolt Report commented,

> literature courses found their audiences chiefly among women of the middle class. But this fact by no means prevented them from being valuable.... It was an invaluable opportunity to thousands of women in London and still more in large provincial towns or country districts to have lectures of high quality brought within their reach.... Many of the women who now have the right to vote at elections... have learned in University Extension classes to understand and appreciate more fully those national traditions which find in our literature their highest expression.
>
> (1921 §245)

In these circumstances, there was a social as well as an intellectual sense of the threat to a male monopoly over the 'monuments of unageing intellect'. This, I suggest, is one context for what Robert Scholes was to say of the men of 1914: 'by their disparagement of the sentimental, as opposed to the ironic or the paradoxical, they had made the typical modernist move of assigning feeling to the female and thought to the male....' Scholes (*Crafty Reader* 2001: 34). 'Men's modernist culture', argues Peter Middleton, 'is one means of sustaining modern masculinities' (1992: 44).

The fear of a potential feminising influence within the new subject reflected also an orientation derived from a longer history of anxiety about the rise of a mass reading public. In the nineteenth century and on into the twentieth, mass literacy was associated with novel reading and a feminised readership (Brantlinger 1998; Leavis 1932; Pykett 1995). The masculine style and manliness in writing were a recurrent trope of the period.

> Manliness in art, what can it be, as distinct from that which in opposition to it must be called feminine quality there, – what but a full consciousness of what one does, of art itself in the work of art, tenacity of intuition and of consequent purpose, the spirit of construction as opposed to what is literally incoherent or ready to fall to pieces, and in opposition to what is hysteric or works at random, the maintenance of a standard.
>
> (Walter Pater, *Plato and Platonism: A Series of Lectures* [1893] New York, 1969: 280)

Intellectually as well as socially, the new English Studies represented a gender border zone, and many practitioners went to considerable lengths to regulate the perils of their new domain. As Colin Evans has shown, in taking poetry and fictions as its objects of study the subject had to guard against both the accusation of 'softness' and of 'play', thus warding off the potential childfulness and femininity of the subject (Evans 1993). In the work of the pioneers of the subject, there was a covert gender struggle over the mastery of creative language. Those early struggles have left their traces in continuing practice. The (mostly) male pioneers of 'ambiguity' had to make sure there was no room for error over the attribution of their key concept. Inasmuch as the subject embraced polysemy as a literary and ethical value it had simultaneously to disambiguate its own practices. The subject both invited and as a consequence felt compelled to regulate interiority and intimacy. There were, potentially, several ways of re-assuring oneself and other stake-holders that the new subject possessed 'hard' subject attributes.

This dynamic may be seen as a kind of disciplinary deep structure or sequence of transferences of which – even through subsequent fission and metamorphoses – the subject still exhibits the archaeological traces. Over the years, bulwarks against its own dangerous, boundary nature have included, variously:

1. asserting the scholarly credentials of the subject by doing difficult textual or historical work, or working on texts that required the mastery of Old English or Old Norse (an approach rejected by the Cambridge and US New Critical schools);
2. demonstrating that the new subject had 'edge' and bite: that while it might take poetry and novels as its subject matter, its approach was rigorous, and uncompromising in making discriminations. Real critics might discuss emotions, but they would do so with detachment and a dry lack of sentimentality; they would be very strict about 'self-indulgence', aiming to promote forms of maturity where affect was subordinated to intellect and judgment;
3. forming some version of a 'high' language: a language which, precisely because it shared its syntax and a good deal of its lexis with the vernacular, required study and prolonged immersion in order to be initiated. (Thus parallel in many ways with Classics or academic Latin). English Studies analogues included the difficult and deeply ambiguous discourses of modernist poetry (and to some degree the modernist novel); more recently, the proliferating languages of various kinds of 'theory'.

Founded as it was on the domain of verbal play (and thus open to accusations of infantilism as well as effeminacy), the new subject felt obliged to mark out clear boundaries in arguing its case for its own essential seriousness. In the classroom as much as in its published writings it had to simultaneously *invite* and then in turn *manage* 'play'. How otherwise were its students to cope with the lack of set rules and clear-cut answers? The theatre of the subject generated forms of competition and hierarchy that relied on the internalisation of tacit rather than explicit rules of discourse. Hegemony within class as within the profession was generated through verbal facility, irony, the art of the put-down, ritualised aggression: drawing on those adversarial, agonistic traditions which Walter Ong has identified as characterising the institutions of male knowledge (Ong 1981). This polemical assertion of the validity of the subject converged with argumentative or cognitive styles which advantage those who have invested most in those attributes traditionally understood as 'masculine'. Some (male) colleagues can still be heard to distinguish between the kind of 'brilliance' tacitly associated with the 'male mind' and an idea of 'good' but plodding compliance associated with the 'female'.

As I have tried to show in an earlier article, the educational practice of literary modernism was characterised by contempt for the feminine lowbrow – the assumption being that reading, and the reading of fiction in particular had become feminised, aligned with consumption, passivity, 'substitute living'; all the phenomena of standardisation that in 1930, in a polemical pamphlet that was in many ways a programme for *Scrutiny*, F.R. Leavis (building on Queenie Leavis' work) identified with 'mass' civilisation ('Mass Civilisation and Minority Culture' 1932).[34]

A central task of the new subject 'English', then, was to save heroic readers from the fate of Emma Bovary: to ward off that regression into a life of wish-fulfilment and social mimesis understood to be fostered by the addictive habit of reading commercial best-sellers (Huyssen 'Mass Culture as Woman' in Modleski 1991; Trotter 2001 especially Chapter 9). Practical criticism was in effect a homeopathic ritual designed to defend mind and strenuous reading from feminisation. In a subject which constructed maps of interiority through evoking the unconscious and the emotions, there was a perceived need to draw clear boundaries and impose rigorous structures. A 'habit of fantasying' as Queenie Leavis sternly remarked 'will lead to maladjustment in actual life' (*Fiction and the Reading Public* 1932: 54). Such fears carried a particular force for the reconstruction of masculinity in the wake of the spectacular trauma of the First World War.

As David Gilmore has argued, rituals of masculinity are designed to ward off regressive wishes and fantasies: 'a defense against the eternal child within' (1990: 29). The reverse of the coin for a discipline that took as its subject matter linguistic and emotional play was an implicit equation between the female and the infantile.[35] In the 1920s and 1930s, the Peter Pan-like implications of deriving sustenance from poetry were peculiarly threatening. The new subject's prickly fear of feminisation fed into a practice designed to demonstrate the mature, masculine rigour of its cultural enterprise. 'Sentimentality' became an implicitly gendered code word for all that the student should eschew. With their cult of impersonality and the 'objective correlative', those who aspired to form a new professional caste sought to demonstrate the 'hard' nature of their subject, leaving behind them a legacy in a discipline which offered normative models for subjectivity. Writing about Hemingway, Peter Schwenger once referred to an attempt to become an object in order to evade your nature as a subject (*Phallic Critiques* 1984: 54). In its horror of the domestic, the interior, the local – the conventionally feminine – modernist literature (and the discipline erected upon it) tended to treat attention to the inner, intimate world as warranted only if projected – like the comings and goings of Leopold Bloom upon *The Odyssey* – onto a larger, even mythic canvas. We might here appropriate Trotter's insight that 'masculinity was for some Modernist writers not so much a posture or a doctrine as a form of symbolic capital' (2001: 252). The corresponding institutionalised procedure was built on the foundation of a modernist canon (a particular reading of Metaphysical Poetry and of Hopkins; early Eliot, Pound, and in due course Yeats, Lawrence and Joyce) in which crises in masculine subjectivity were raised to the level of 'universal human' dramas – dramas on which literature with its own 'anxiety of influence' could be read as a privileged commentary. This propensity to universalise the masculine subject of literature has occluded both male bodies and male sexuality, and – in relation to our argument here – obscured the power relationships set up in the pedagogic field that surrounds the text. Despite the anti-essentialism of Theory, such pedagogic heroics were in many ways re-affirmed in both English and Cultural Studies during the early years of the 'theory wars',[36] the heroic avatar now the fearless controversialist who could tear apart the veils of mystification. Arguably, indeed, 'theory' (not least in its Freudian variants) gave a whole new lease of life to the father-fixated Oedipus narrative.

Time and again what has been offered by 'canonical' literature (and the pedagogic style it entailed) has been the opportunity of occupying the gaze of the male viewer. For pedagogy is a kind of deixis – nudging, shaping, directing attention. Consciousness, readers of Vygotsky or Bakhtin will not be surprised to hear, is being increasingly regarded as social. The evolutionary anthropologist Michael Tomasello speaks of the profound significance within the speculative origins of culture of 'joint attentional activities' (1999: 6). Or again, Nicholas Humphrey, writing from the standpoint of evolutionary psychology seems to return to a Vygotskian insight that 'empathy is mediated by imitating bodily action' (*Seeing Red* 2006: 104). The affinities between the jointly attentional gesture of pedagogy and the nurturing role discussed above militate against any obtuse lumping into separate boxes of the cognitive, the affective and the bodily. The gestural and physically grounded practice of pedagogy constructs the objects of attention in the same way as the text creates its imaginary scenes, characters and incidents.

Literature (text and peri-text) may be seen as a performative anthropology: one of the sites where humans can practise what it means and might mean to be human. While this book has no intention of suggesting that other interpretative ventures are invalid, it does propose to estrange the study of masculinity and manliness as a cultural aspiration. The subject of culture, we have suggested, has frequently been implicitly asked to develop a theory not so much of mind as of their own or others' *male* mind. Between them, the chapters that follow concern ways of *authoring and authorising* masculinity within the domain of social consciousness, but in ways that do not take masculinity as a default or normative property. We propose to question or disrupt the situation described by Bronwyn Davies.

> While those inhabiting an ascendant category have difficulty recognising their dependence upon the subordinate term for their own meaning, the imagination of the person who is not in the ascendant category is trained in an education system which takes those in the ascendant... to be the major source of meaning making.... In a fundamental sense, those who inhabit subordinate categories are bi-cognitive, or bi-modal.... 'Constructing and Deconstructing Masculinities through Critical Literacy'.
>
> *Gender and Education* 9.1 (1997: 27)

Like her, we have no intention of replacing one dominant discourse with another. But we would argue that the cultural performance of masculinity should acknowledge and celebrate its own bi- or multi-modality. While few English lecturers in the United Kingdom would be likely to be comfortable with the degree of disclosure recommended by David Bleich,[37] they might reflect that in the history of the discipline both sensibility and Althusserian approaches to 'the subject' (in the other sense) have provided a field for the regulation and subordination of suspect elements.

This book invites engagement in a reflexive poetics of pedagogy. We make the hypothesis that the predicaments embedded in the history of the subject go on being lived out in the transferential relations between mentors and learners and between learners themselves. Pedagogic androgyny may yet be a long way off, and living in the unequal sort of society we do, might in any case be for the moment a disingenuous aim. Nevertheless, as part of our professional reflection, we who teach should become self-aware about our own propensity – however inadvertent – to reproduce or to collude in the gender dynamics of the subject. We do not in this book seek to make a simplistic case about the roles of actual women and men in the classroom or in the staff group. But we should all acknowledge that a discipline that calls forth the intricacies and indeterminacy of meaning also generates its own forms of analytical heroism and professional quest – forms which all too readily dignify the more sordid everyday dramas through which gender and gender identity is established and symbolic power assigned. In her chapter, Rachel Carroll urges us to recognise that 'a refusal of empowered forms of masculinity is not necessarily reducible to a state of powerlessness' (pp. 151–2). The historically grounded dynamics, which we have sketched in this chapter, hold out to male participants the lure of asserting symbolic mastery over proceedings. It is an invitation which men must find the courage to refuse.

Notes

1. The same criticism can also broadly be made of the otherwise excellent essays collected in (eds) Still and Worton (1993).
2. In 2004–2005, of the UK students listed by the Higher Education Statistics Agency in English Studies, 36,810 (73.1 per cent) were women and 13,515 (26.9 per cent) men. (These figures include postgraduates, but not students on combined or joint honours programmes.) The comparable figures for 2003–2004 were 36,885 (73.6 per cent) women and 13,230 (26.4 per cent) men, and for 2002–2003, 33,470 (71.3 per cent) women and 12,405 (28.7 per cent) men. For comparison, in 2004–2005, 54.6 per cent of UK History students were women and 53.25 per cent of Media Studies students. In the same year 85.5

per cent of Engineering students were men. (My percentages, based on HESA tables: http://www.hesa.ac.uk/holisdocs/pubinfo/student/subject0405.htm.) English Language attracts a slightly higher proportion of males at A-level. See Adrian Barlow's appendix to the English Subject Centre Report *Four Perspectives on Transition*, 2005.

3. The academic study of masculinities as it emerged in the late 1970s and 1980s has been predominantly associated with the social sciences and psychology, yet it has also in various ways entered into and influenced the study of text. While this book does not seek to provide a history of the impact of research on masculinity upon literary and critical studies, it must acknowledge the productiveness of such approaches to texts across a wide historical span. Such work goes back of course to Kate Millett's *Sexual Politics* (1971) and takes in pioneering studies by Peter Schwenger (1984), and Robert Scholes' 'Reading Like a Man'. Its sweep includes distinguished work on the Early Modern (Mark Breitenberg, Juliana Schiesari, Coppelia Kahn, Janet Adelman, Bruce Smith, Gary Taylor, Robin Headlam Wells), to the eighteenth century (Raymond Stephanson), through Romanticism (Tim Fulford), the Gothic and Fin de Siècle (Joe Bristow, Scott McCracken, Andrew Michael Roberts) to work on contemporary and near-contemporary novelists (e.g. Berthold Schoene, Susan Brooks, Alice Ferrebe) and poetry (Peter Middleton, Steve Clark).

4. This is in essence a 'men in feminism' perspective: we also note the need for male students and teachers to 'do their own work' on their relations to subject matter, authority, colleagues/fellow students and each other (cf. Jardine and Smith 1987). We further need to acknowledge, however briefly or inadequately, that this field of masculinity studies is deeply fraught and not a little contradictory. It is not the least of its problems that a field of research and practice that arose in dialogue with and as a complement to feminism can have the paradoxical effect both of surreptitiously re-asserting the centrality of the male and of colluding with (or appearing to collude with) a highly suspect narrative of the male as victim (e.g. Faludi, MacInnes).

5. An initial report on a fascinating example is to be found in Ken Jones, Monica McLean, David Amigoni and Margaret Kinsman. 'Investigating the Production of University English in Mass Higher Education: Towards an Alternative Methodology'. *Arts and Humanities in Higher Education*. 4. 2005: 247–264.

6. 'To be "literate"', says David Bleich, 'means to be a social being. One is committed to "read" the inner life of other, and to "write" one's own life on the blank space of one's pre-given relatedness to others. In these terms, any literate act is a development of one's implication in the lives of others'. And, he continues, to 'cultivate literacy is to refine and enhance our mutual implication in one another's lives and to discover and exercise our mutual responsibilities' (1988: 67).

7. There is a helpful discussion of the idea of social construction by the classicist and philosopher Martha Nussbaum in her *Cultivating Humanity*. 1997: 226–232. This is not the place to illustrate the variety of masculinity studies. But in relation to this book, we should mention Lynne Segal's formative *Slow Motion* (1990), R.W. Connell's *Masculinities* (1995) and *The Men and the Boys* (2000).

8. A number of relevant anthologies have been published during the last 10–15 years. Examples include (eds) Stephen M. Whitehead and Frank J. Barrett,

The Masculinities Reader (Polity 2001); (eds) Rachel Adams and David Savran, *The Masculinity Studies Reader* (Blackwell 2002); (ed.) Judith Kegan Gardiner, *Masculinity Studies and Feminist Theory* (Columbia 2002); Máirtín Mac An Ghaill, *Understanding Masculinities* (Open University 1996); (eds) Harry Brod and Michael Kaufman, *Theorizing Masculinities* (Sage 1994).

9. There is a rich source on the website *Literature, Cognition and the Brain* – http://www2.bc.edu/~richarad/lcb/.

10. And see Peter Middleton's commentary on Yeats's 'Sailing to Byzantium' 1992: 63–65.

11. Barbara Ehrenreich's point seems capable of analogous extension: 'War... is too complex and collective an activity to be accounted for by a single warlike instinct working within the individual psyche. Instinct may or may not inspire a man to bayonet the first enemy he encounters in battle. But instinct does not mobilise supply lines, manufacture rifles, issue uniforms, or move an army of thousands from point A on the map to B'. (*Blood Rites: Origins and History of the Passions of War*. London: Virago. 1997: 9).

12. *Mask of Command* 350. Robin Headlam Wells (2000) draws attention to this passage.

13. Carole Gilligan teasingly suggests that a male identity is forged in relation to the world rather than in relation to another person (Gilligan 1993). Gilligan's book (especially Chapter 7) has been an influence on this section.

14. Simon Baron-Cohen is himself careful to stress that he sees these as tendencies on a spectrum and sees the distribution of 'male' and 'female' brains as statistical averages only. See his popularising work *The Essential Difference* (2004), and a number of articles on the website of the Cambridge Autism Research Centre <http://www. autismresearchcentre.com/research/cogneurogen.asp>.

15. Though our subject here is only indirectly creativity, there are suggestive implications for the Orpheus syndrome, that recurrent question of through what faculty men create. Is it the case, as versions of the Eurydice story from the 6th century BCE through Rilke's *Sonnets to Orpheus* to Coupland's *Girlfriend in a Coma* suggest, that male creativity may often derive its energy from its position 'over her dead body' (Bronfen 1992)? As Raymond Stephanson has demonstrated, a debate about the internal space in which men created was already being vigorously carried on in the early eighteenth century (Stephanson 2004) The 'traffic in male creativity caused a disjunction between... the inner site and public status of creativity' (p. 95). This led to 'self-alienating consequences for male authors as their sexually embodied creativity became a rhetorical commodity....' (p. 157).

16. Simon Baron-Cohen's definition of empathising is suggestive: 'Empathising is defined as the drive to identify emotion and thoughts in others and to respond to these appropriately... It is not simply about inferring what someone else is thinking or feeling, though this is an important part of empathising. Rather, it includes an appropriate spontaneous emotional reaction'. John Lawson, Simon Baron-Cohen and Sally Wheelwright. 'Empathising and Systemising in Adults with and without Asperger Syndrome'. *Journal of Autism and Developmental Disorders*. 34.3. 2004: 302.

17. See for example Nancy Armstrong, *Desire and Domestic Fiction*; Juliana Schiesari, *The Gendering of Melancholy*, Francis Barker, *The Tremulous Private Body*.

18. Trans. Jessie Coulson, Penguin Classics. p. 48. The story is discussed in relation to narratives of abject masculinity in Knights 1999: 121–125. We speculate that the fascination held by Samuel Becket for so many males in the critical profession may have to do with the way he raises male abjection to the level of intellectual heroism.

19. See Valerie Walkerdine's *The Mastery of Reason* (1988) on the power of decontextualised knowledge, depersonalisation and the illusion of mastery.

20. See Millard, Martino, Connell, Mac An Ghaill and Paechter. An early and still important study of gender in education is (ed.) Henriques, Walkerdine, 1984.

21. In the United Kingdom, what has now become a media commonplace – that boys are failing in the education system (or alternatively that the education system is failing boys) – might be seen to have received its first official acknowledgment in the 1993 OFSTED report *Boys and English*. See Millard pp. 2–3. Compare Janet White, 'On Literacy and Gender' in (ed.) Carter 1990.

22. For example in http://www.guardian.co.uk/Archive/Article/0,4273,4117316,00.html.

23. Nurturing, like the giving of gifts, can of course itself be an ambivalent, even dominating behaviour.

24. The gendering of such work is explored by Susan Brook in her *Literary and Cultural Criticism: The Feeling Male Body*. 2007: 136ff.

25. Witness the disorientation and puzzlement of first year students over their teachers' aggressive insistence on 'the death of the author' or the arbitrary nature of the signifier.

26. Cf. the critique of the now conventional history in Atherton, *Defining Literary Criticism*. 2006.

27. Many relevant connotations hover around the systemic hard/soft metaphorical set. While there are clearly pitfalls for the layperson, it appears that recent research in the cognitive sciences enables a more grounded account of the systematicity of metaphor as developed earlier by Lakoff and Johnson, *Metaphors We Live By* (1980), Turner, *The Origins of Thought and Language* (1996), Lakoff, *Embodied Mind* (1999), *Women, Fire and Dangerous Things* (1987). A number of studies lend weight to the intuitive recognition that the 'soft'/'hard' binary is gendered, and gendered in ways that are of direct importance for the history of disciplines and educational processes. See the summary by Melnick who demonstrates the alignment of this binary metaphorical set with (largely) unconscious beliefs about the nature of fe/maleness. http://www.clas.ufl.edu/ipsa/journal/1999_melnick01.shtml.

28. Among the influences on this section are Peter Middleton's *The Inward Gaze* (1992, especially Chapter 3), Gilbert and Gubar (1988) and David Trotter's *Paranoid Modernism* (2001).

29. '...all margins are dangerous. If they are pulled this way or that the shape of fundamental experience is altered. Any structure of ideas is vulnerable at its margins'. Mary Douglas, *Purity and Danger*. 121.

30. In particular, David Lodge's *Author, Author*, and Colm Tóibín's *The Master* (both 2004).

31. Christopher Lane has cautioned us both against the assumption when dealing with texts like these that all opacities stem from a closeted sub-text, and against the reductivism present in resolving textual ambiguity by providing the missing 'answer' (1999: 235–236).
32. It is also, though with yet another valency, the dominant trope of Thomas Mann's *Death in Venice* (1912). I have explored masculinities in *Le Grand Meaulnes* (1913) in Knights 1999: 28–34.
33. Cf. Kenneth Kidd's account of Pan as liminal, even feral figure... 'Men Who Run with Wolves' http://muse.jhu.edu/journals/lion_and_the_unicorn/v020/20.1kidd.html.
34. See Kauko, Mieszkowski *et al.* (eds) *Gendered Academia*, especially chapters by Elfie Bettinger, Ina Schabert and Ben Knights.
35. Or even explicit. 'Mrs. Woolf as we all know, is a Poet in Prose; or rather she has... a range of sensuous impressions which would have stood a poet in good stead. But sensuous impressions... are not an end in themselves; if they were, most normally sensitive children would be great poets. Of course Mrs. Woolf is an "intelligent woman" but, as a reviewer in the *Calendar* pointed out... her intellectual capacity is oddly disproportionate to, and immature compared with, her sensitiveness, and, if she ventures outside the narrow range imposed on her by her sensuousness, she becomes a child...'. Wilfred Mellers (*Scrutiny* VI 1937: 71–75).
36. Evans has explored the 'contribution Theory has made to the masculinization of English...' (1993: 129), and see Chapter 6.
37. See for example his nuanced argument in 'Collaboration and the Pedagogy of Disclosure.' *College English*. 57.1. (1995).

Works cited

Adams, Rachel and David Savran. *The Masculinity Studies Reader*. Oxford: Blackwell. 2002.

Alloway, Nola, with Pam Gilbert, Rob Gilbert and Robyn Henderson. 'Boys Performing English'. *Gender and Education*. 15.4. 2003: 351–364.

Anderson, Benedict. *Imagined Communities: Reflections on the Origin and Spread of Nationalism*. London: Verso. 1991.

Armstrong, Nancy. *Desire and Domestic Fiction: A Political History of the Novel*. Oxford: Oxford University Press. 1987.

Atherton, Carol. *Defining Literary Criticism: Scholarship, Authority and the Possession of Literary Knowledge 1880–2002*. Basingstoke: Palgrave. 2005.

Barker, Francis. *The Tremulous Private Body: Essays on Subjection*. Ann Arbor: Michigan University Press. 1995.

Baron-Cohen, Simon. *The Essential Difference*. London: Allen Lane. 2004.

Becher, Tony and Paul Trowler. *Academic Tribes and Territories: Intellectual Enquiry and the Cultures of Disciplines*. Buckingham: Open University Press. 2001.

Berger, Maurice with Brian Wallis and Simon Watson (eds) *Constructing Masculinity*. New York: Routledge. 1995.

Bernstein, Basil. *Pedagogy, Symbolic Control and Identity: Theory, Research, Critique*. London: Routledge. 1996.

Beynon, John. *Masculinities and Culture*. Buckingham: Open University Press. 2002.

Bleich, David. *The Double Perspective: Language, Literacy, and Social Relations*. New York: Oxford University Press. 1988.

Bradley, John R. *Henry James's Permanent Adolescence*. Basingstoke: Palgrave. 2000.

Brantlinger, Patrick. *The Reading Lesson: The Threat of Mass Literacy in Nineteenth-Century British Fiction*. Bloomington, IL: University of Illinois Press. 1998.

Bristow, Joseph. *Effeminate England: Homoerotic Writing After 1885*. Buckingham: Open University Press. 1995.

Brod, Harry and Michael Kaufman (eds). *Theorizing Masculinities*. Thousand Oaks, CA: Sage. 1994.

Bronfen, Elisabeth. *Over Her Dead Body: Death, Femininity, and the Aesthetic*. Manchester: Manchester University Press. 1992.

Brook, Susan. *Literature and Cultural Criticism in the 1950s: The Feeling Male Body*. Basingstoke: Palgrave. 2007.

Budd, Michael Anton. *The Sculpture Machine: Physical Culture and Body Politics in the Age of Empire*. Basingstoke: Macmillan. 1997.

Butler, Judith. *Gender Trouble: Feminism and the Subversion of Identity*. New York: Routledge. 1990.

——. *Bodies That Matter: On the Discursive Limits of 'Sex'*. New York: Routledge. 1993.

Carter, Ronald. (ed.) *Knowledge About Language and the Curriculum: The LINC Reader*. London: Hodder and Stoughton. 1990.

Coetzee, J.M. *Disgrace*. London: Secker and Warburg. 1999.

Connell, Robert W. *Masculinities*. Cambridge: Polity Press. 1995.

——. *The Men and the Boys*. Cambridge: Polity Press. 2000.

Damasio, Antonio. *The Feeling of What Happens: Body, Emotion and the Making of Consciousness*. London: Vintage. 2000.

——. *Descartes' Error: Emotion, Reason, and the Human Brain*. Reprinted. London: Vintage. 2006.

Darby, Robert. *A Surgical Temptation: The Demonization of the Foreskin and the Rise of Circumcision in Britain*. Chicago: University of Chicago. 2005.

Davies, Bronwyn. 'Constructing and Deconstructing Masculinities Through Critical Literacy'. *Gender and Education*. 9.1. 1997: 9–30.

Douglas, Mary. *Purity and Danger: An Analysis of Concepts of Pollution and Taboo*. London: Routledge. 1966.

Ellmann, Maud. *The Poetics of Impersonality*. Brighton: Harvester. 1987.

Evans, Colin. *English People: The Experience of Teaching and Learning English in British Universities*. Buckingham: Open University Press. 1993.

——. (ed.) *Developing University English Teaching: An Interdisciplinary Approach to Humanities Teaching at University Level*. Lampeter: Edwin Mellen. 1995.

Faludi, Susan. *Stiffed: The Betrayal of the Modern Man*. London: Chatto and Windus. 1999.

Gender and education

Gilbert, Sandra M. and Susan Gubar. *No Man's Land: The Place of the Woman Writer in the Twentieth Century*. Vols. 1 and 2. New Haven: Yale University Press. 1988, 1989.

Gilligan, Carole. (Revised edition) *In a Different Voice: Psychological Theory and Women's Development*. Cambridge, MA: Harvard University Press. 1993.

Gilmore, David. *Manhood in the Making: Cultural Concepts of Masculinity.* New Haven: Yale University Press. 1990.

Graff, Gerald. 'The Problem and other Oddities of Academic Discourse'. *Arts and Humanities in Higher Education.* 1.1: 27–42. 2002.

Henriques, Julian *et al. Changing the Subject: Psychology, Social Regulation and Subjectivity.* London: Methuen. 1984.

Hollinghurst, Alan. *The Line of Beauty.* London: Picador. 2004.

Humphrey, Nicholas. *Seeing Red: A Study in Consciousness.* Cambridge, MA: Harvard University Press. 2006.

Hunter, Ian. *Culture and Government: The Emergence of Literary Education.* London: Macmillan. 1988.

Huyssen, Andreas. *After the Great Divide: Modernism, Mass Culture, Postmodernism.* Basingstoke: Macmillan. 1986.

Jardine, Alice and Paul Smith (eds). *Men in Feminism.* New York: Methuen. 1987.

Kauko, Miriam, with Sylvia Mieszkowski and Alexandra Tischel (eds). *Gendered Academia: Wissenschaft und Geschlechterdifferenz 1890–1945.* Göttingen: Wallstein. 2005.

Kimmel, Michael. 'Masculinity as Homophobia: Fear, Shame, and Silence in the Construction of Gender Identity'. In (eds) Stephen M. Whitehead and Frank J. Barrett. *The Masculinities Reader.* Cambridge: Polity. 2001.

——. *The History of Men: Essays in the History of American and British Masculinities.* Albany, NY: State University of New York Press. 2005.

Kimura, Doreen. *Sex and Cognition.* Cambridge, MA: MIT Press. 1999.

——. 'Human Sex Differences in Cognition: Fact, not Predicament.' *Sexualities, Evolution and Gender.* 6. 2004: 45–53.

Knights, Ben. *From Reader to Reader: Theory, Text and Practice in the Study Group.* Hemel Hempstead: Harvester Wheatsheaf. 1992.

——. *Writing Masculinities: Male Narratives in Twentieth-Century Fiction.* Basingstoke: Macmillan. 1999.

——. 'Men from the Boys: Writing on the Male Body'. *Literature and History.* 13.1. 2004: 25–42.

——. 'Reading as a Man: Women and the Rise of English Studies in England'. In (eds) Kauko and Mieszkowski. *Gendered Academia: Wissenschaft und Geschlechterdifferenz 1890–1945.* Göttingen: Wallstein. 2005.

Kriesteva, Julia. (Trans. Leon S. Roudiez) *Powers of Horror: An Essay in Abjection.* New York: Columbia University Press. 1982.

Lakoff, George and Mark Johnson *Metaphors We Live By.* Chicago: Chicago University Press. 1980.

Lakoff, George. *Women, Fire and Dangerous Things: What Categories Reveal About the Mind.* Chicago: University of Chicago Press. 1987.

Lakoff, George. *Philosophy in the Flesh: The Embodied Mind and Its Challenge to Western Thought.* New York: Basic Books. 1999.

Lane, Christopher. *The Burdens of Intimacy: Psychoanalysis and Victorian Masculinity.* Chicago: Chicago University Press. 1999.

Leavis, F.R. *Mass Civilisation and Minority Culture.* Cambridge: The Minority Press. 1930.

Leavis, Q.D. *Fiction and The Reading Public.* London: Chatto and Windus. 1932.

Lloyd, Genevieve. *The Man of Reason: 'Male' and 'Female' in Western Philosophy.* London: Routledge. 2nd Edition. 1993.

Mac An Ghaill, Mairtin. *The Making of Men: Masculinities, Sexualities and Schooling.* Buckingham: Open University. 1994.

——. (ed.) *Understanding Masculinities: Social Relations and Cultural Arenas.* Buckingham: Open University Press. 1996.

MacInnes, John. *The End of Masculinity.* Buckingham: Open University Press. 1998.

Martino, Wayne and Frank Blye. 'The Tyranny of Surveillance: Male Teachers and the Policing of Masculinities in a Single Sex School'. *Gender and Education.* 18.1. 2006: 17–33.

Men and masculinities

Middleton, Peter. *The Inward Gaze: Masculinity and Subjectivity in Modern Culture.* London: Routledge. 1992.

Millard, Elaine. *Differently Literate: Boys, Girls and the Schooling of Literacy.* London: Routledge. 1997.

Millett, Kate. *Sexual Politics.* Reprinted 1993. London: Virago. 1971.

Modleski, Tania. *Feminism Without Women: Culture and Criticism in a 'Postfeminist' Age.* London: Routledge. 1991.

Nelson, Claudia. *Boys Will Be Girls: The Feminine Ethic and British Children's Fiction, 1857–1917.* New Brunswick: Rutgers University Press. 1991.

Nussbaum, Martha C. *Cultivating Humanity: A Classical Defense of Reform in Liberal Education.* Cambridge, MA: Harvard University Press. 1997.

Ohi, Kevin. *Innocence and Rapture: The Erotic Child in Pater, Wilde, James, and Nabokov.* Basingstoke: Palgrave. 2005.

Ong, Walter J. *Fighting for Life: Context, Sexuality, and Consciousness.* Ithaca: Cornell University Press. 1981.

Paechter, Carrie. *Educating the Other: Gender, Power and Schooling.* London: Falmer. 1998.

Pykett, Lyn. *Engendering Fictions: The English Novel in the Early Twentieth Century.* London: Edward Arnold. 1995.

Redman, Peter. 'Who Cares About the Psycho-Social? Masculinities, Schooling, and the Unconscious'. *Gender and Education.* 17.5. 2005: 531–538.

Robson, Catherine. *Men in Wonderland: The Lost Girlhood of the Victorian Gentleman.* Princeton: Princeton University Press. 2001.

Robson, Jocelyn, Becky Francis and Barbara Read. 'Gender, Student Confidence and Communicative Styles at University'. *Studies in Higher Education.* 29.1. 2004: 7–23.

Rose, Jacqueline. *The Case of Peter Pan, or, The Impossibility of Children's Fiction.* London: Macmillan. 1984.

Schiesari, Julia. *The Gendering of Melancholy: Feminism, Psychoanalysis, and the Symbolics of Loss in Renaissance Literature.* Ithaca: Cornell University Press. 1992.

Scholes, Robert. 'Reading Like a Man'. In (eds) Jardine and Smith. *Men in Feminism.* New York: Methuen. 1987.

——. *The Crafty Reader.* New Haven: Yale University Press. 2001.

Schwenger, Peter. *Phallic Critiques: Masculinity and Twentieth-Century Literature.* London: Routledge. 1984.

Sedgwick, Eve Kosofsky. *Between Men: English Literature and Male Homosocial Desire.* New York: Columbia University Press. 1985.

——. *Epistemology of the Closet.* Hemel Hempstead: Harvester. 1991.

———. *Tendencies*. London: Routledge. 1994.

Segal, Lynne. *Slow Motion: Changing Masculinities, Changing Men*. London: Virago. 1990.

Smith, Lillian. *Killers of the Dream*. New York: W.W. Norton. 1949.

Steedman, Carolyn. *Strange Dislocations: Childhood and the Idea of Human Interiority 1780–1930*. London: Virago. 1995.

Stephanson, Robert. *The Yard of Wit: Male Creativity and Sexuality 1650–1750*. Philadelphia: University of Pennsylvania Press. 2004.

Still, Judith and Michael Worton (eds). *Textuality and Sexuality*. Manchester: Manchester University Press. 1993.

Suttie, Ian. *The Origins of Love and Hate*. Harmondsworth: Penguin. 1963.

Taylor, Gary. *Castration: An Abbreviated History of Western Manhood*. New York: Routledge. 2000.

The Teaching of English in England. Being the Report of the Departmental Committee Appointed . . . to Inquire into the Position of English in the Educational System of England. London: His Majesty's Stationery Office. 1921. [The Newbolt Report]

Thomas, Kim. *Gender and Subject in Higher Education*. Buckingham: Open University Press. 1990.

Thurgar-Dawson, Chris and Ben Knights. *Active Reading: Transformative Writing in Literary Studies*. London: Continuum. 2006.

Tomasello, Michael. *The Cultural Origins of Human Cognition*. Cambridge, MA: Harvard University Press. 1999.

Tosh, John. *A Man's Place: Masculinity and the Middle-Class Home in Victorian England*. New Haven: Yale University Press. 1999.

Trotter, David. *Paranoid Modernism: Literary Experiment, Psychosis, and the Professionalization of English Society*. Oxford: Oxford University Press. 2001.

Turner, Mark. *The Literary Mind: The Origins of Thought and Language*. New York: Oxford University Press. 1996.

Walkerdine, Valerie. *The Mastery of Reason: Cognitive Development and the Prodcution of Rationality*. London: Routledge. 1988.

Wells, Robin Headlam. *Shakespeare on Masculinity*. Cambridge: Cambridge University Press. 2000.

Whitehead, Stephen M. and Frank J. Barrett. *The Masculinities Reader*. Cambridge: Polity. 2001.

2
Training to be an English Teacher: Negotiating Gendered Subjectivities and the Gendered Curriculum as Inter-linked Cultural Processes

Wayne Martino

Introduction

This chapter draws on research into the influence of masculinities on male students who are training to be English teachers. I am interested in examining how issues of masculinity impact on their developing identities and pedagogical practices as English teachers, given the perception of English as a specific gendered curriculum domain and, hence, feminized learning area (see Martino 1994; Millard 1997; Thomas 1990). This forms the basis for exploring the extent to which English functions as a specific gendered site for amplifying male teachers' tensions or anxieties about masculinities and what the implications of this might be for their pedagogical practices and relations with students in the high school classroom (Martino and Frank 2006; Roulsten and Mills 2000). Thus, by raising important questions about the perception of English as a feminized domain, a space is created for investigating the extent to which such signifying practices mediate relations of masculinity for prospective male English teachers. For example, being associated with *the feminine* can often activate defensive practices of masculinity which lead male teachers feeling compelled to reassert or rather project hegemonic heterosexual masculinity as a protective strategy in order to deflect any suspicion or attribution of imputed homosexuality (see Francis and Skelton 2001; Skelton 2001). This may result in anxiety-ridden practices of intensified self-surveillance and regulation motivated by homophobia and regimes of compulsory heterosexuality (see Martino and Frank 2006). It may also translate into practices of masculinizing or defeminizing the curriculum in schools in terms of text selection to ensure that male interests and values are taken into consideration (see Greig 2003; Martino and Meynn 2002; Martino *et al.* 2004; Rowan *et al.* 2002 for a critique of such boy-friendly approaches). Such pedagogic strategies are tied directly to the negotiation and reproduction of gendered subjectivity in male teachers' lives. These inter-linked processes involving the performative dimensions of masculinity and pedagogical practices serve as a basis for understanding the negotiation of gendered subjectivities in male educators' lives and how these are enacted within the pedagogic space of the gendered curriculum.

While research has been conducted into the lives of male student/primary teachers and their perceptions of doing women's work (Carrington 2002; Johnston *et al.* 1999; King 1998; Skelton 2002, 2003; Smedley 2006; Smedley and Pepperell 2000; Thornton 1999), scant attention has been directed to investigating how masculinities impact on secondary male teachers' professional identities and pedagogical practices, particularly within the context of the gendered curriculum (see Martino and Frank 2006; Roulsten and Mills 2000 as exceptions). Foster and Newman (2005), for example, focus on the stories of male primary teachers in the United Kingdom to highlight the complexities of men's experiences within the context of how they 'made sense of other people's gendered perceptions of their professional identity' (p. 346). In fact, they claim that the 'range of competing masculinities that is representative of the complexities of men's experiences in the world outside remains scarcely acknowledged inside the primary school, either by men themselves or by their female colleagues' (p. 342). This is particularly significant in relation to investigating male high school teachers' experiences and practices of masculinities in schools. As Francis and Skelton (2001) argue, what is needed is a focus on the various ways in which discourses of gender and sexuality are employed by men in their professional lives as teachers and how these are manifested in terms of both their pedagogical practices and relations with students.

This chapter is thus motivated by such concerns in its focus on male students studying to be English teachers. In following Smedley (2006), it aims to look closely at individual men's negotiation of their professional identity and pedagogical practices within the context of a domain often perceived to be associated with the feminine: 'Looking closely at individual men's ideas and perspectives has shed light on assumptions about masculinity and men as teachers, highlighting a sense of not fitting in disjunctions, and feelings of unease and conflict'

(p. 128). It is at this nexus of negotiating gendered subjectivities and the gendering of the curriculum as interlinked cultural processes that this chapter makes a particular contribution to the field in addressing the following question: How do gender regimes impact on male pre-service English teachers, both in terms of their own professional identities and also their pedagogical practices in the classroom? This is important given the moral concern motivating recruitment drives for more male teachers in the United Kingdom, North America and Australia, where the call for more male role models and, hence, a more gender-balanced workforce eschews any discussion of the gender politics implicated in doing women's work and its status vis-à-vis regimes of hegemonic masculinity (see Carrington 2002; Elementary Teachers' Federation of Ontario 2003; Foster and Newman 2005; House of Representatives Standing Committee On Education and Training 2002; Martino and Kehler 2006; Williams 1993).

About the study

This chapter is based on research undertaken in 2000–2001. Sixteen pre-service male students completing their Bachelor of Education program at an Australian university (three of whom were studying to become high school English teachers) and five students enrolled in a similar program in a Canadian university (two of whom were studying to become high school English teachers) were interviewed.[1] The focus of this research was to investigate how these men's experiences of masculinity impacted on their self-perceptions and identities as student teachers.[2] In drawing on both Foucault (1977, 1982) and Butler (1993) I was interested to investigate how these men come to understand themselves as gendered subjects within the context of a dominant culture in which normalization and gender hierarchies are endorsed. In short, to what extent did these men demonstrate an awareness of their embodied practices of masculinity? To what extent did their own insights into 'doing masculinity' (Coleman 1990) inform their understanding about their developing skills and pedagogical capacities as prospective English teachers? To what extent did the signifying potential of English as a feminized learning area impact on the self-fashioning and performative practices of masculinity in terms of how these men talked about their own experiences of schooling and initial teaching? In short, to what extent did these men's self-perceptions as gendered subjects and, hence, their experiences of doing or embodying masculinity mediate their pedagogical relations and practices in the English classroom? In addressing these sort of questions, I draw on interviews with two men studying to be English teachers – Matthew, aged 23 (Australian) and Jackson, aged 22 (Canadian) – who raise important issues about the performative dimensions of masculinity and the pedagogical significance of this in terms of their developing understanding about the limits imposed by the 'regulatory apparatus of heterosexuality' and, hence, a gender system built on the repudiation of the 'feminine'[3] (Butler 1993: 12).

The gendered dimensions of English as a pedagogical and learning domain

In the interview with Mathew the gendered dimensions of English, as both a pedagogical and learning domain, are examined. Reflections on his experiences of being an adolescent boy studying English play an important part in his developing understanding about the gendered significance of pedagogical practices and relations in a domain that is often associated with the feminine. For instance, Matthew had a passion for English teaching which he attributed to his own experiences of English in high school and to one particular male English teacher. He grew up in a small rural community and talked about the significance of the relationship/friendship he developed with this teacher. Within this small community sport and farming were central and, as Mathew suggests, almost antithetical to what English, as a subject and his English teacher, more specifically, offered – an appreciation of life and the space for deep reflection and meaningful learning connected to personal experience. For example, Mathew claims:

> My English teacher was the one who really got me to want to do something with academics rather than sport and other sort of work that I was used to, farm work...I really enjoyed English and writing and reading and stuff, and I thought maybe I could transfer that in a way of my experience into a teaching situation. I just felt that was the closest I had come to feeling good about, confident about some sort of work other than being on a farm chasing horses and stuff.

In the interview he talks at length about the influence of his English teacher:

> He just got me interested in the stuff that I was studying at school. It became like a transferral from the sport and we'd go on bush walks and long bike rides and lots of chats about sorting out the universe

and sorting out where you're at when you're a 14 year old boy. He was able to say, 'Well look at this poetry by John Keats and see how he was going through similar emotional stages and he's dealing with loves, losses', all these sort of things that I actually could see in the text. And then we started studying Malouf and the questions about dying, all these things just became interesting to me. From that point on I also started to write poetry about the bike rides, the beauty of a morning bike ride, stuff like that which in my way was my sort of outlet. Sort of I suppose making a bit of sense of it really, just creative sense and I thought it was good.

So for Mathew, it is something about the quality of the relationship fostered by this teacher which mediated his engagement with literature in the classroom. He seems to be highlighting the significance of this relationship as a powerful influence in being able to connect literary texts to his everyday experiences in the world. Thus for Mathew, the quality of the pedagogical relationship that he valued with this teacher was supported by approaches to teaching English which endorsed both the personal growth of the student and the philosophical significance or relevance of reading literary texts. This highlights the experience of English for Mathew as facilitating a distinctive set of learning experiences and pedagogical relations which did not appear to be as readily available in other subject areas. As Ian Hunter (1988) points out, the reading practices fostered by this teacher and endorsed within English are governed by norms for undertaking a particular work on the self through engaging in certain acts of moral self-problematization and reflection. However, for Mathew the reading practices fostered by such pedagogical relations are consistent with those fostered by the English teacher with his students outside of the classroom.

The gendered significance of this learning experience and pedagogical relationship as curriculum specific is highlighted by Max in his interview. He differentiates learning English or being an English student from studying maths and science. For instance, he mentions that he introduced his 'best mate' to this teacher, who tended to be more of 'a Mathematics/Science based academic learner' and indicates how they developed a great friendship which 'really improved his attitude towards learning and especially English'. Thus for Mathew English as a learning domain is governed by norms that require different modes of relating and responding and he frames such practices in antithetical and oppositional terms to those fostered by teachers of other subjects such as maths and science. The gendered significance of such a curriculum divide or split, as dictated by the regulatory 'apparatus of heterosexuality', are made much more explicit later in his interview, where he talks about the compulsion he felt as a male school student to be enjoying those subjects considered to be more sex-appropriate:

> I think one of the main gender issues for me, as far as going to be a teacher, would be to encourage the sort of diversity of mix between subject areas. That comes again from me enjoying English, whereas I should have been enjoying maths, science, blah, blah, which I was hopeless at of course. But because I enjoyed English I was put into a category, I was labelled gay, homosexual, for enjoying English. I mean this is in a country school, mind you, where people are much more blinkered ... But that sort of attitude ... how girls are encouraged with the humanities and English and things like this and boys are steamrolled into the maths and sciences ... you've got an amazing, like a skewedness about where the girls go and where the boys go. It's all boys in the maths and science, just about all boys. So I think that gender issue really needs to be addressed in our schools and we need to get rid of the stigma.

However, while Mathew's aim is to engage boys in the humanities, and more specifically in English, he does not appear to be committed to masculinizing the curriculum to accommodate boys' expressions of hegemonic heterosexual masculinity. He wants to foster particular pedagogical relationships and responses to texts that do not resort to supporting the perpetuation of sexism, misogyny and homophobia as means by which to establish his 'masculine credentials' (see Francis and Skelton 2001: 15). In short, his experiences of marginalization do not lead him to assert hegemonic masculinity – the attribution of the feminine is not experienced as a threat, but rather as something to be embraced. Mathew is only too aware of the limits imposed by a gender system that enforces polarization grounded in the differentiated sexed body (Harding 1998). This is most clearly manifested when he talks about the stigma that is attached to English due to its perceived focus on expressing emotion and studying poetry:

> Everyone seems to have this stupid notion that poetry is effeminate, where it comes from who ever knows. Secondly to talk about things such as love, relationships, even death that kids are scared of. When you're 15, 16 year olds dealing with issues and the mere fact that

they're coming out in the open just embarrasses so many people and also the showing of emotions.

This leads him to talk about a particular incident involving a unit on studying poetry in English class which involved a task where students were required to choose a poem and to read it out to the class. He was 16 years old and the incident stands out as very significant for him in that it brought with it a particular knowledge about being placed under the homophobic surveillance of other school boys as a consequence of choosing to engage in what was considered to be a transgression of normative masculinity. For example, he chose to stage a performance of part of Coleridge's, *The Ancient Mariner*, which he had learnt by heart, as opposed to just reading it out to the class. He talks about having long hair at the time down to his shoulders, which he had wet and ruffled in order to personify the mariner. His performance involved a dramatic reconstruction of the mariner, 'almost dead' and with this 'very raspy look'. When he finished his presentation he indicates that 'a couple of the guys just pissed themselves laughing' and he explains their reaction in these terms:

> I could hear them at the start sort of going phphph, and it was because I'd shown some sort of putting your whole person into something and not caring what other people thought. And just guys seem to have a real problem with that. Even though the girls didn't, no one else in the class actually did that and the teacher said to me afterwards – he didn't know I was going to do it – but he said that's great that people can express themselves, he said we need to get more of that.

The attribution of the feminine within the pedagogical space of the English classroom appears to be related to being open and expressing emotion, behaviour which is subjected to the normalizing and homophobic gaze of other boys who police the limits of acceptable heterosexual masculinity (see Alloway *et al.* 2003). Such regimes of normalization, Mathew intimates, impose gender straightjackets for boys, particularly in terms of governing the ways in which they learn to relate as boys and respond in the English classroom (see Martino and Pallotta-Chiarolli 2003). This appears to be intensified in a small rural community dominated by farming and sport as culturally sanctioned 'masculinity confirming practices' (Renold 2003). Thus for Mathew, the teaching of English must necessarily involve a moral imperative to engage boys and to facilitate the development of quite specific capacities

for engaging with literary texts, which appear to be at odds with normative constructions of masculinity: 'But the gender issues for me are to
try and get rid of [this stigma] and ... maybe encourage some of the guys
to not be afraid to want to do English if they do want to, and then I'll
obviously encourage them then as a class, try to get people more open
about their feelings'.

The limits of such a culture, in which the feminine is repudiated,
are further highlighted by Mathew who, as an adolescent boy, worked
actively to challenge the 'regulatory apparatus of heterosexuality' and
the normative embodied practices of masculinity that it supported. His
commitment to challenging such a regime is attributed to his own
experiences of being targeted for engaging in what were considered to
be non-normative practices for an adolescent boy, such as expressing
himself in English and cultivating a close student–teacher relationship.
This stigmatization is further situated within a broader homophobic and
sexist community from which he actively worked to dissociate himself:

> When I went through school I was labelled homosexual and attrib-
> uted all the language that's carried with homosexuality, and all these
> things for three or four years at high school. And me and a couple
> of mates who just happened to enjoy English and my relationship
> with my English teacher was said to be homosexual by lots of people
> in the community, even adults and other teachers. My Year leader,
> she was homosexual and she married another female staff member
> and they had to leave the town. So these sort of issues in schools
> they're just so potent and I don't know what we can do about it but
> it's so prevalent. Homophobia is just everywhere ... The word 'poof'
> is almost an accepted form of slang. So it's a huge problem.

And he relates such homophobia to the stigmatization that is attached
to gender non-conformity, both in terms of performing masculinity and
in terms of attributions of the feminine regarding perceptions of the
curriculum:

> It all comes back to people being put into roles, stigmas being
> attached to gender, the fact that boys do maths. All that sort of thing,
> the fear of expression, the fear of being creative, all these things, I
> think, lead into this, not that homophobia is by any means the only
> sort of outlet and horrible thing that comes out of all these stupid
> stigmas and things that are attached to gender and people. But it's
> definitely probably the most harmful and I think one of the most

negatively geared one that happens in schools. It stops people, especially boys, it really stops boys from following a course that they may
otherwise have followed for fear of having this stigma attached to
them. I mean it's a real thing that kids are afraid of and every 14 year
old boy, whether he is homosexual or not, is dead scared of being
labelled as a homosexual...I think it shapes the whole way people
go in their school lives and their careers.

Mathew's own attempt to challenge the normative gender expectations and homophobia of his school community highlights the signifying potential of the body as performative text. For example, as an
adolescent boy, he and his friend were both conscious of projecting
a different masculine image – they grew their hair long, wore an ear
ring and had a pony tail. In fact, he claims that they were both
'very non-conformist', despite the fact that they embraced learning and
were very successful academically. He recounts an experience which
involved how they had decided to go to school dressed in a sarong
('Fijian style') and leather striped sandals. This performance appeared
to be incited by the already existing homophobia that they had experienced, as a consequence of their refusal to conform to the dominant
norms governing hegemonic masculinity in school and the broader
community. Mathew did not relate to the dominant boys or their sexist
attitudes and his passion for English appeared to be symptomatic of
a deeper sense of rejecting such masculinist values. For instance, he
remembers the homophobic comments that were directed at them as a
result of wearing a sarong, but stresses that 'it was worth doing it':

There wasn't one person in the whole school who didn't look at us
and go, 'Oh my god. There was a whole, I'd say 90 per cent, looked
at us and said, oh my god these guys are gay as it comes...The
feeling that day, so many comments, so many people saying, 'What
are you wearing a dress for? Are you a fairy?' All the bullshit, it
was unbelievable. It was worth doing it just to, I wish I had a tape
recorder that day because if I had brought that tape recorder today
you could write three books on it. The comments that were said
just because we were wearing a sarong, it wasn't a dress, if we came
cross-dressed the attitude would have been the same. The fact was
we were making a concession to something feminine, I mean even
the sandals went down, 'What are these sandals you're wearing?',
because 'blokes' aren't supposed to do this.

Being a 'bloke' – a colloquial and class-inflected term for being a man
in the Australian context – highlights the cultural significance of a particular version of masculinity involving mateship, which Mathew clearly
rejects. This involves men relating in ways that do not compromise their
masculinity through any display of soft, feminine or expressive behaviour. He also mentions in the interview how they walked into town
after school, still wearing their sarongs, only to have 'blokes shouting
abuse from cars and tooting their horns'. Weeks later, they were still
dealing with the towns' people trying to 'pick fights' and threatening
them with violence:

> It was like we were threatening the very existence of this whole town.
> It was like, basically, they were scared of us because we were doing
> this... and I'm sure it just all came back to this fact that we'd made
> a concession, well I wasn't even making concession on my feminine
> side but people said, you're trying to get in touch with it.

Through recounting such an experience, he demonstrates a knowledge
about the 'regulatory apparatus of heterosexuality' and how this is maintained through homophobic policing and surveillance of the gendered
body. He claims that gender transgression for girls also results in similar
questions being raised about the status of their femininity. For example,
he mentions that while girls who excelled at sport were 'sort of given
raps formally', the blokes 'behind their backs' would make derogatory
comments about them such as, 'Oh jeez look how big her shoulders are!',
rather than commending them for their sporting or athletic prowess: 'All
that people could do would be say, she's a bit masculine for my liking'.
In this sense, he highlights the constraints imposed on both boys and
girls for choosing not to conform to traditional gender stereotypes or
normative constructions of femininity and masculinity. However, while
he asserts that it is 'equally harmful both ways... it's worse for boys who
show the effeminate side': 'Like a boy with a high pitched voice, or a
boy with gestures that aren't particularly masculine, it's harder for them
than for girls because girls seem not to pick on them as much'. This sense
of the amplification and intensification of homophobia amongst boys
is significant in terms of Mathew's own lived experiences of gender and
sexuality in school and in the broader community in which he grew up.

The significance of this is that Mathew's own experiences of homophobia as a heterosexual boy led him to develop crucial insights into
the policing of masculinity and its consequences for imposing limits in
the form of a gender straight-jacket. In fact, he is able to distinguish

between sex and gender in his articulation of a disavowal of hegemonic masculinity and attributes this understanding to his own family experiences of growing up with four sisters and a mother who was the primary breadwinner. For example, he reiterates that, while he sees himself as male, he doesn't 'really have a notion of masculinity' or what he terms 'a masculinity ethos'. What he does have an understanding of is how others choose to define masculinity:

> but I do have a notion of what other people have of masculinity which is big, strong, sport playing, perhaps mathematics, sort of money earning, bread winning, all the relevant stigma. That's what I see masculinity as meaning because that's how society places it basically. But I don't really have a concept of masculinity. I think maybe because I have four sisters and I've never really had masculinity in a home situation. My father was never the bread winner, my mother was the bread winner and my dad was the house husband sort of thing. Although he taught, he retired when I think I was 12 and just part time taught, and then worked on the farm, and there was never any sort of he'd make the decisions sort of thing.

Mathew has a particular knowledge about the social construction of masculinity and its embodied significance, which he has lived in terms of being a boy at school who felt marginalized by the values of hegemonic masculinity in a small rural community. The consequence of these values were manifested for him poignantly in terms of his experiences of studying and participating passionately in the English classroom as an adolescent boy, which he frames in gender-specific terms. Such knowledge and understanding informs his commitment to teaching English and to encouraging boys to engage in non-normative practices of masculinity in the English classroom. The link between his lived experiences of masculinity and how this connects to his pedagogical commitment to address the limits imposed on boys by gender regimes in the English classroom are significant. Furthermore, his desire to embrace certain pedagogical practices in the English classroom, which promote particular modes of relating to the self and engaging with texts, is informed by a broader political project of supporting alternative versions of masculinity. Through his own self-fashioning experiences of embodied masculinity, he has experimented with the signifying potential of the body as a site of resistance and transgression. This has translated into a knowledge base that informs his desire to foster certain pedagogical relations and practices within what he understands to be a gendered curriculum domain. I elaborate further on the link between the gendered body and pedagogical relations in the next section, where the focus is on investigating Jackson's commitment to interrupting hegemonic practices of masculinity in the English classroom. Jackson's interview further highlights the significance of the signifying potential of embodied practices of masculinity and their pedagogical potential in the English classroom.

The significance of embodied practices of masculinity and their pedagogical potential or limits

The interview with Jackson also raised important questions about the signifying potential of the male body in terms of the implications of self-fashioning practices of masculinity for engaging in pedagogical relations in the English classroom. He mentions his desire to engage students in the way that his own English teacher in high school did. She is identified as 'a really modern woman' and as a feminist with a 'kind of left wing modern type of influence' who encouraged her students 'to question a lot of things' (see Coulter 2003). This was achieved by relating literature to real-life issues and concerns. She also addressed sexuality and used literature to raise philosophical questions about the meaning of life that he could relate to:

> She got us to think about sexuality and the meaning of it and I guess it's a good time to begin at that age, you're really interested in it then. Sexuality is still pretty new so it's really cool to be able to talk about it in an intelligent and objective way in the high school situation. Because you apply your own life. We talked a lot about death too and existentialism with the book, Albert Camus 'The Outsider' and books like that. I think that's where you know like the big ideas of the world started becoming really interesting to me.

Thus, once again, like Mathew, Jackson presents English as a pedagogical space or site for fostering certain sorts of relationships that are conducive to a particular kind of learning which can be readily applied to 'real life'. Fostering such modes of relating to the self through using literary texts constitutes a particular moral technology that still lies at the heart of producing certain kinds of literate subjects in the English classroom. Jackson, in following in the footsteps of his inspiring English teacher, too wants to embrace such a technology for ethical–moral cultivation and engagement in the English classroom. At the centre of such a pedagogy lies the liberatory potential invested in the teacher's capacity to open up the classroom to an examination of the human condition through the vehicle of using literary texts. This lends itself to creating conditions for learning and relating to the self that become associated quintessentially with the domain of English teaching. However, embracing such pedagogical relations incites certain tensions for Jackson as a male – an attractive male – who is aware of the risks involved:

> So involving them and getting them to talk about their perspectives on their lives, I mean it's a dangerous topic because you don't want to talk too much about their personal experiences for your own protection.

The spectre of being considered sexually suspect hangs over Jackson, particularly, given his desire to raise questions about sexuality in the English classroom by connecting literary texts to the everyday lives of students within the context of cultivating certain personalized relationships. There is a heightened sense of vulnerability as he assesses the risk posed by his embodied heterosexual masculinity and what this might signify for his female students. In this sense, Jackson raises important questions about risky and dangerous pedagogies within the English classroom, given the sort of topics that he wants to address and the relationships with students that he wants to foster (see Martino and Berrill 2004; McWilliam and Jones 2005):

> The things that are the most interesting I think can sometimes be dangerous when you're getting involved with ideas that some of the students aren't going to be comfortable with, or their parents wouldn't be comfortable with. So I mean the things I'm interested in talking about are somewhat precarious in that way ... Like talking about the meaning of the value of sex, or of having sex as a young teenager and what it means and things like that. It's almost like a health class but with the theory and philosophy into it. You get a lot of that when you read books that have that kind of content in it. So it's a dangerous thing but it's something to think about anyway.

Here, Jackson is explicit about deploying literary texts as sites for cultivating pedagogical relations and practices of self-problematization in the English classroom, particularly as they relate to sexual desire and bodies. This becomes accentuated for him while on practicum. He talks about a girl in a Grade 8 class becoming 'really obsessed' with him to the point she would write his name on her pencil case and focus undue attention on him. There was a sense, he claims, that 'she was projecting this identity onto me which as a teacher and as a man and all these things, it just really made me, it really created a distance between us when I was teaching her'. Such experiences provoke a certain degree of anxiety for Jackson and accentuate a particular polemic about heterosexual masculinity and the pedagogical limits imposed by his own embodied self-fashioning practices of masculinity. In short, in order to ward off the signifying potential of his body as inciting sexualized desire, he resorts to dressing differently – wearing more formal clothes such as a suite and tie – as a means by which to downplay his sexuality. This functions as a protective strategy to minimize the risk that such sexualized attention carries in terms of the need to avoid any perception of sexual misconduct within the context of teaching adolescents in schools:

> As a teacher and as a man, it just really created a distance between us when I was teaching her. Because I was protecting myself and trying to reduce the situation and then I started dressing more like an adult. I started wearing a tie and a jacket to school so that I would just kind of reduce my young look... That's one thing about teaching which scares me in a way because you hear a lot about stories of teachers who are accused of things and that's the worst thing... being accused of something that's inappropriate I guess.

In this sense, he believes there are certain limits imposed on male teachers. However, he does talk about negotiating what appears to be a relational pedagogy organized around deploying literary texts as a means by which to raise philosophical, social and challenging issues that are relevant to students' lives, while still protecting himself from being implicated as sexually suspect: 'I mean I'm interested in finding strategies which are positive and helpful but also protecting and I have to think about that'.

Jackson also demonstrates a broader awareness of the sexual and gender politics governing the differential perceptions and expectations that students have of teachers. For example, he talks about how male teachers are treated or perceived differently by students on the basis of their gender. While he claims that male teachers are treated with more respect than their female counterparts, he raises questions about embodied masculinities and about male teachers 'doing women's work', which may also result in questions being raised about their status and legitimacy as men.

> with male students there's almost a higher respect for male teachers than female teachers, and this is a problem because it's shifting the identity, removing the identity from what the actual teacher is doing and placing it onto their body and their image. I think male teachers are, often there's the stereotype of male teachers being gay in primary school, or things like that. And those things I am going to confront them and deal with it. I don't know how they're going to manifest themselves to me but I mean I certainly think it's quite a different thing to be a male teacher than a female teacher.

Here he seems to be suggesting that there may well be parallels between the sort of homophobia and stereotypes that male primary teachers are forced to confront and those that he will have to deal with as a male high school teacher. However, as a result of what he sees as being the limits imposed by hegemonic heterosexual masculinity (Frank 1987), he is committed to developing strategies that are designed to 'break down gender distinctions in the classroom'. A part of this project involves not only deploying literary texts and cultivating particular pedagogical relations, but, more significantly, a conscious attempt to engage in self-fashioning practices of performative and embodied masculinity that, in his eyes, have the signifying potential to interrupt 'gender stereotypes'. He does this by actively fashioning a different kind of masculinity through wearing nail polish – the idea of a man wearing nail polish leads people to raise questions about both the normative status of masculinity and also to a questioning of his sexuality:

> As a man wearing nail polish, it's like people see me and the question of my sexual orientation is immediately prevalent, and that has been really helpful for me. It's been a really good move for me to attach myself to the finger nail polish because that way I found people are less affronted by me as a man. I mean being a man is something that is attached to this higher order of power and your dynamic in culture is somewhat heightened by masculinity. The expectations of being a man is being red blooded and aggressive and all these things which I don't identify with as a man. So wearing nail polish is a way to physically say, 'Hey this is a way that I feel differently from other men', and it's a form of gender bending, it's about erasing the distinctions to create equality and wearing nail polish is kind of a fun

way to get people to question their ideas about me and then in turn their ideas about masculinity.

He sees such self-fashioning practices as potentially destabilizing people's expectations regarding what is considered to be acceptable, normative and embodied masculinity. This is an active intervention, on his part, which appears to be integrated into his own lived experience of gender relations as a concrete commitment to the realization of a transformative gender politics. For example, when I ask him whether he saw himself wearing nail polish as a teacher in the classroom, he responds:

> I can see myself doing that with a class that I'd be able to get to know and get to explain to them what it's about and encourage them to question gender. I think that as a man who has kind of a masculine body I feel like I'm in a privileged position to destabilise gender roles – it's is easier for me. In the classroom I think it's kind of a dangerous thing and this is where I'd be putting myself somewhat at risk of being I guess lumped with homophobic threats and things like that.

He indicates, however, that he has not attempted to wear nail polish during his practicum because he doesn't believe that there is enough time to allow the students to 'get comfortable' with him. Since Jackson already embodies a normative masculinity and, thus, has cultural and social capital in terms of being physically attractive, he acknowledges the privilege that this accrues. For example, he is careful to avoid claiming that he is not effeminate through stating that he has 'a kind of masculine body'. His pedagogical strategy is to get students on side and to create a threshold of acceptance, before launching into any sort of gender-bending practice as a teacher in terms of 'doing masculinity' in the English classroom. This raises crucial questions of the power of homophobic regimes which position effeminate male teachers as the deviant other and, hence, in Jackson's eyes, as significantly de-powered in terms of being able to effectively intervene in a dominant culture that is dominated by the values of the jocks or what he terms 'prom kings'. Part of his rationalization for delaying the application of nail polish relates to the necessity of avoiding the limits imposed pedagogically through any overt invitation for his students to classify him as a 'freak':

> I would like them to get to know me and the nail polish being a part of me but if I'm only there for a short period of time, then it's like

that guy who wears nail polish, he's this freak. And what I don't want is to be cast or exiled as a freak or to be labelled as someone that's different, because I'm very much inside of the culture and I want to show that I'm a part of it and different from the normatives. As soon as you say someone is a freak or an outsider, then it's like, okay then we can just incorporate them into our mind as a freak, or someone that's different. But if you can say oh well that person is normal and they're doing this thing which is different, then it's a much better and more positive way to understand.

This raises important questions about the male body and its signifying potential. Given Jackson's own awareness of such potential, he is conscious of deploying his body strategically and pedagogically to achieve a particular object of interrogating gender regimes and their impact on students' lives and relationships. However, he still fails to realize the significance of the limits imposed by a logic that requires him to establish his normative masculine status as a basis for securing a form of pedagogical legitimacy or authority in his students' eyes. In short, his political agenda of disrupting hegemonic masculinity relies on proving his normality as a man in the students' eyes, which leaves unquestioned the very regimes of homophobia and compulsory heterosexuality upon which the 'regulatory apparatus of heterosexuality' is built. This leaves unquestioned assumptions about status of the effeminate male teacher or more broadly the homophobic system of denigrating the feminine. Inscribing the feminine on the male body as a potentially disruptive strategy for challenging gender binaries can only gain legitimacy, once the male teacher has established the status of his masculinity in the students' eyes (see Martino and Frank 2006). This draws attention to the limits of the signifying potential of the male body that is still caught within a regime of normalization which both dictates the requirement to embody normative heterosexual masculinity and governs the logic driving pedagogical regimes in schools. While Jackson is not committed to consolidating or asserting hegemonic heterosexual masculinity through his pedagogical practices in the English classroom, he is still caught within the limits of a logic which unintentionally authorizes hegemonic male power as a means by which to ward off any attribution of deviancy and, hence, as a basis for realizing a political agenda of gender deconstruction. The polemical significance of such a logic and its implications for those male teachers and students who do not embody normative masculinity are not considered. Does a male teacher's failure to meet students' normative expectations of embodied masculinity detract from his pedagogical potential and status as a transformative intellectual? To what extent does such a strategy leave intact certain regimes of normalization that are sustained by a desire to pander to the homophobia of those hegemonic male students who function as gatekeepers of masculinity for both teachers and their peers (see Martino and Frank 2006)?

This strategic attempt to interrupt hegemonic masculinity though mobilizing the signifying potential of the male body needs to be applauded and is indeed built on a deep knowledge about the cultural politics of gender relations and performativity. For example, Jackson states:

> I don't think masculinity exists. I think masculinity is this facade put on by men who absorb this idea of what it means to be a man and how to culturally behave as a response to what's in between your legs. Masculinity is a creation of body techniques, of walking a certain way, of talking a certain way and thinking a certain way which is completely fabricated by the world. Well I don't know who is to blame but it's all a part of our culture which falsely interpellates all male sex people into this kind of behaviour technique which is disturbing. I mean I've really been frustrated with our culture's insistence on a battle between the sexes and kind of like there's the men's magazines which give you advice about women and then there's the women's advice about how to get your guy to do this. I mean it's all, our culture has dichotomised ideas about men and women. Femininity I think is just as much of a creation as masculinity... I think masculinity is also a masquerade, a kind of performative facade in order to feel comfortable with yourself... Men and women have this set of traits which they choose between but I don't think it's related to your body as much as it's related to the way you've been socialised.

In this sense, Jackson's attempt to pedagogically work at interrogating the limits of gender regimes in the English classroom through mobilizing the signifying potential of the male body as a cultural resource, needs to be situated at the nexus of theory and practice which is always fraught with slippages and indeterminacy in the realization of a transformative gender politics:

> Well I think my objective in school is in terms of deconstructing gender roles and kind of challenging the masculinity is going to be met with resistance by the typical male, people who are insisting

that football is for boys and things like this. I mean I think being a modern man or someone who is trying to figure out a way to be egalitarian and degendering is a real problem. It can be a real problem in the classroom when it comes to people who are going to be immediately dislocated from their previous ideologies. I want to function in the classroom and I want to change the masculine identities or depower them, but working within the system and working within the classroom and culture as a normal person. As a part of it not as an outsider, not as someone who is different but as someone who is the same and who has the same kind of ideas about life that other people who will identify with. I want to be a teacher who, I'm kind of fumbling right now, so it's getting incoherent. The challenges that I'm going to face are going to be in recreating an idea about masculinity which the students will feel comfortable with, and which gets them away from a forced presentation of themselves.

Thus, Jackson is committed to using his privilege and, hence, to working within the limits imposed by the current gender system, while simultaneously creating a pedagogical threshold for using his body to disrupt the notion of a fixed, essentialized masculinity that is grounded in biological sex differences. It is in this sense that Jackson's interview draws attention to the crucial significance of the gendered dimensions of pedagogical relations and textuality in terms of the signifying potential of the male body within the context of the English classroom. Jackson's attempt to disrupt gender binaries and, hence, to interrogate masculinity needs to be understood in relation to understanding the historical significance of the emergence of literature teaching as an apparatus of moral supervision in which a particular teacher–student relation was organized around moral emulation and correction (Hunter 1988). Jackson embraces such a literary pedagogy married with a knowledge about the limits imposed by a gender regime, which leads him to embrace a cultural practice in the service of placing students' own values and experiences of gender under his moral authority and gaze. The analysis undertaken here, however, has been committed to foregrounding the significance of embodied practices of masculinity in mediating such pedagogical relations.

Conclusion

In this chapter I have attempted to highlight the pedagogical implications of masculinities for male university students who are training to be English teachers. The focus has been on an examination of the gendered dimensions of their embodied pedagogical relations in the English classroom. In drawing attention to the significance of authorized pedagogies within the context of English education, which are committing to cultivating a particular student–teacher relation and moral aesthetic involving the imperative to connect the text to real life, my aim has been to raise some critical questions about the significance of hegemonic heterosexual masculinities for male student teachers' developing understanding of their pedagogical practices. It is at this nexus that the interconnected dimensions of negotiating gendered subjectivities and teaching English are foregrounded in an analysis that is committed to exploring the signifying potential and limits of embodied masculinities in terms of their impact on pedagogical relations for male teachers in the English classroom. Such an analysis of masculinities offers a much more nuanced perspective than that represented by recruitment drives to attract more male teachers to the teaching profession and which are grounded in simplistic notions of role models and calls for a more gender balanced workforce (Bernard *et al.* 2004; Elementary Teachers' Federation of Ontario 2003). Such perspectives eschew an analysis of the significance of hegemonic heterosexual masculinities for imposing limits on male teachers 'doing women's work' (Williams 1993) or for those high school teachers responsible for teaching subjects such as English, which are considered to be aligned with developing feminized or *soft* learning capacities and dispositions. In drawing attention to the textuality of the male body, with its signifying capacities for both reinforcing and disrupting representations of hegemonic masculinity, this chapter highlights the need to further investigate the gendered dimensions of pedagogical practices for male teachers and the extent to which their threshold knowledges about gender relations and performativity impact on their teaching of English.

Notes

1. I would like to acknowledge Deborah Berrill, Trent University, for her support in setting up the interviews I conducted with Canadian research subjects. The overall study was funded by Murdoch University, Perth, Western Australia.
2. Male student teachers were asked in the interviews to talk about why they had chosen to become a teacher, whether they thought there were any issues that impacted on them as males training to be teachers and about what they had learnt about being a teacher form their practicum experiences. Towards the end of the interview, they were also asked specifically to reflect on specific issues of masculinity, how they defined it and what they saw its significance to be in their lives as prospective teachers.

3. Only two men are selected for focus in this chapter due to limits imposed by word length and to allow for more in-depth analysis of the individual men's subjective experiences of teaching English.

References

Alloway, N., Gilbert, P., Gilbert, R. and Henderson, R. (2003) Boys performing English, *Gender and Education* 13 (4): 351–364.

Bernard, J., Falter, P., Hill, D. and Wilson, W. (2004) *Narrowing the Gender Gap: Attracting Men to Teaching*, Report commissioned by Conseil scolaire de district du Centre-Sud-Ouest, Laurentian University, Ontario College of Teachers and Trillium Lakeheads District School Board, Canada. http://www.oct.ca/publications/documents.aspx?lang=en-CA.

Butler, J. (1993) *Bodies that Matter: On the Discursive Limits of Sex*. New York and London: Routledge.

Carrington, B. (2002) A quintessentially feminine domain? Student teachers' constructions of primary teaching as a career, *Educational Studies* 28 (3): 287–303.

Coleman, W. (1990) Doing masculinity/Doing theory. In J. Hearn and D. Morgan (eds), *Men, Masculinities and Social Theory*. London: Unwin Hyman.

Coulter, R. (2003) Boys doing good: Young men and gender equity, *Educational Review* 55 (2): 135–145.

Elementary Teachers' Federation of Ontario (2003) EFTO encourages males in elementary, *EFTO Voice* 5 (3): 20.

Foster, T. and Newman, E. (2005) Just a knock back? Identity bruising on the route to becoming a male primary school teacher, *Teachers and Teaching: Theory and Practice* 11 (4): 341–358.

Foucault, M. (1977) *Discipline and Punish*. London: Penguin.

Foucault, M. (1982) The subject and power, afterword. In H. Dreyfus and P. Rabinow (eds), *Michel Foucault: Beyond Structuralism and Hermeneutics*. Sussex: The Harvester Press.

Francis, B. and Skelton, C. (2001) Men teachers and the construction of heterosexual masculinity in the classroom, *Sex Education* 1 (1): 9–21.

Frank, B. (1987) Hegemonic heterosexual masculinity, *Studies in Political Economy* 24, Autumn: 159–170.

Greig, C. (2003) Masculinities, reading and the 'boy problem': A critique of Ontario policies, *Journal of Educational Administration Foundations* 17 (1): 33–56.

Harding, J. (1998) *Sex Acts: Practices of Femininity and Masculinity*. London, Thousand Oaks, New Delhi: Sage.

House of Representatives Standing Committee on Education and Training (2002) *Boys' Education: Getting it Right*. Canberra: Commonwealth Government of Australia.

Hunter, I. (1988) *Culture and Government: The Emergence of Literary Education*. London: Macmillan Press.

Johnston, J., McKeown, E. and McEwen, A. (1999) Choosing primary teaching as a career: The perspectives of males and females in training, *Journal of Education for Teaching* 25 (1): 55–64.

King, J. (1998) *Uncommon Caring: Learning from Men who Teach Young Children*. New York and London: Teachers' College Press.

Martino, W. (1994) Masculinity and learning: Exploring boys' underachievement and under-representation in subject English, *Interpretations* 27 (2): 22–57.

Martino, W. and Berrill, D. (2004) Dangerous pedagogies: Addressing issues of sexuality, masculinity and schooling with male pre-service teacher education students. In Davison, K. and Frank, B. (eds), *Masculinity and Schooling: International Practices and Perspectives*. University of Western Ontario, London: Althouse Press.

Martino, W. and Frank, B. W. (2006) The tyranny of surveillance: Male teachers and the policing of masculinities in a single sex school, *Gender and Education* 18 (1): 17–33.

Martino, W. and Kehler, M. (2006) Male teachers and the 'boy problem': An issue of recuperative masculinity politics, *McGill Journal of Education* 41 (2): 1–19.

Martino, W. and Meynn, B. (2002) War, guns and cool, tough things': Interrogating single-sex classes as a strategy for engaging boys in English, *Cambridge Journal of Education* 32 (3): 303–324.

Martino, W. and Pallotta-Chiarolli, M. (2003) *So What's a Boy? Addressing Issues of Masculinity and Schooling*. Maidenhead: Open University Press.

Martino, W., Mills, M. and Lingard, B. (2004) Issues in boys' education: A question of teacher threshold knowledge, *Gender and Education* 16 (4): 435–454.

McWilliam, E. and Jones, A. (2005) An unprotected species, *British Educational Research Journal* 31 (5): 109–120.

Millard, E. (1997) Differently literate: Gender identity and the construction of the developing reader, *Gender and Education* 9 (1): 31–48.

Renold, E. (2003) 'If you don't kiss me, you're dumped': Boys, boyfriends and heterosexualised masculinities in the primary school, *Educational Review* 55 (2): 179–194.

Roulsten, K. and Mills, M. (2000) 'Male teachers in feminised teaching areas: marching to the beat of the men's movement drums', *Oxford Review of Education*, 26 (2): 221–237.

Roulston, K. and Mills, M. (2001) Male teachers in feminised teaching areas: Marching to the men's movement drums, *Oxford Review of Education*, 26 (1): 221–237.

Rowan, L., Knobel, M., Bigum, C. and Lankshear, C. (2002) *Boys, Literacies and Schooling: The Dangerous Territories of Gender-Based Literacy Reform*. Buckingham: Open University Press.

Skelton, C. (2001) *Schooling the Boys: Masculinities and Primary Education*. Buckingham: Open University Press.

Skelton, C. (2002) The feminisation of schooling or re-masculinising primary education?, *International Studies in Sociology of Education* 12 (1): 77–96.

Skelton, C. (2003) Male primary teachers and perceptions of masculinity, *Education Review* 55 (2): 195–210.

Smedley, S. (2006) Listening to men student primary school teachers: Some thoughts on pedagogy, *Changing English* 13 (1): 125–135.

Smedley, S. and Pepperell, S. (2000) No man's land: Caring and male student primary teachers, *Teachers and Teaching: Theory and Practice* 6 (3): 259–277.

Thomas, K. (1990) *Gender and Subject in Higher Education*. Buckingham: The Society for Research into Higher Education and Open University Press.

Thornton, M. (1999) Reducing wastage among men student teachers in primary courses: A male club approach, *Journal of Education for Teaching* 25 (1): 41–53.

Williams, C. (1993) *Doing 'Women's Work': Men in Nontraditional Occupations*. Newbury Park, London and New Delhi: Sage.

3
Queer Teaching/Teaching Queer: Renaissance Masculinities and the Seminar

Mark Dooley

This chapter takes as its starting point a moment of crisis in my own teaching career that took place several years ago. It was a moment that has stayed with me, scarred me to some extent, and upon which I have reflected many times. Being invited to contribute a chapter on masculinity and pedagogy to this book, then, has given me the opportunity finally to explore that experience more systematically and to unpick some of its more illuminating aspects. In writing about it, I hope not only to lay to rest some of its after effects for myself, but also to turn it into a meaningful experience that may stimulate further thoughts about the complex relationships between gender and sexuality in our teaching spaces and practices.

The highly personal tone of the introductory paragraph will be continued throughout this chapter – I make no apology for it. Indeed, one of the central themes of my contribution here will be to stress the need for teachers of English to reflect more on themselves; to think about the route by which they have entered their profession (or vocation), how their own subjectivity and the ways in which it has been shaped subsequently influence their own pedagogical practice. We are, as a profession, very good at thinking about our students and their experiences and, increasingly, through Personal Development Planning and the like, enabling them to become more and more self-reflexive at a personal, as well as an intellectual, level. But we are not, I would suggest, so accomplished in our own self-reflexive practices and, if we are, we tend to keep the results of our explorations pretty well closeted. I am, of course, generalising here, but my research for this chapter has confirmed in my own mind that even the most sensitive and recent material in this area of study has tended to take as its object the student and pays little real attention to the role of the teacher.

This chapter, then, will be divided into several sections. Firstly, I want to reflect on myself, to examine where I have come from and how this has shaped my own identity, research interests and practices as a teacher. It will then describe and explore the crisis to which I have (albeit obscurely, and perhaps teasingly) referred. It will then proceed to examine the complex relations between gender, sexuality, authority and pedagogy as they are revealed in this episode before moving finally to look outwards and suggest some wider implications for the subject and the profession of such experiences.

English, as an academic discipline, has always provided a particularly important space for the negotiation of identities. As a rather 'bookish' child, growing up on a council estate and attending the local, London Borough comprehensive school, I was made acutely aware of my 'difference' from my male peers. Marked out by my friendships with girls and lack of footballing skills, I was labelled very early on with the usual range of insulting epithets (poof, queer, gayboy, etc.). As the insults began to bite, I retreated further into my books and, it is now interesting to reflect, was also increasingly labelled 'posh'; a term that was intended as an insult, but which also seemed synonymous with 'boffin', another term regularly used to describe me by other pupils. My dubious masculinity and perceived intellectualism, then, were directly related in the minds of my tormentors to sexuality and to class, well before we had a clear sense of what constituted either of these categories. Of course, what made me unpopular with my peers made me popular with my English teachers who clearly saw someone who had a genuine enthusiasm for the subject. As they encouraged me, so I became ever more 'bookish' and so it went on. The standard response of my family as I moved through my teens and they were asked if Mark had a girlfriend yet was to jump in with, 'he's too caught up in his books to have time for girlfriends'. It seems the books gave everyone an excuse!

The English classroom became, for me, a haven into which I could escape from the oppressive models of masculinity operating at home where my father's highly traditional view of masculinity (no doubt reinforced by his job as an heavy goods vehicle driver and shop steward at Ford Motor Company, and his football refereeing at weekends and evenings) and my brother's sporting prowess, became yardsticks against which I was found profoundly lacking. It is impossible to overstate the significance and positive influence of Angela Dale, Jenny Des Fountain and Margaret Berry, my A-level English teachers who, although they never explicitly acknowledged my sexuality (how could they?) made me feel valued and created a space in which it was safe to explore, through texts, issues that were so very pertinent in the lives of all their pupils. They also encouraged me to go to university to read English, and so I became the very first member of my family to go on to higher education.

The move to university was, initially at least, not a happy one. My lecturers in the first year of my undergraduate career in the mid- to late- 1980s were, for the most part, diehard Leavisites and I shall never forget my first essay assignment title: 'Tentative: Is Lawrence that in *The Rainbow?*' The English class went from being a safe and encouraging, imaginative and creative space, enabled by women teachers, to one where father figures seemed once again to dominate and whose expectations I seemed unable to fulfil. These were men in their fifties who were highly authoritative on their subject (the Modernists, of course) and very explicitly heterosexual. I felt alienated from the subject I had loved and threatened by the men who stood at the front effectively telling us it was unlikely that many of us would ever be able to understand the literature we were studying. I saw little in these men that I could, or wanted to, emulate.

Everything changed in the second year. A new lecturer joined the department and threw everything into turmoil. He was, certainly by the standards of the time, a 'theorist', but his use of theory was enabling and, although challenging in many ways, his teaching was exciting and engaging. He was a Renaissance literature specialist and, as he made sure we were aware, gay. He was also, by no means, a father figure. To me, this was a hugely significant moment, both in my intellectual and personal development. To experience a man teaching the literature I had very nearly fallen out of love with and to recognise in that man something of my own emerging identity gave me, at last, a model of masculinity to which I could aspire. There was, after all, a way to be a man, be gay and love literature. From then on, the way forward was, for me, the literature of the Renaissance: that was what he taught and that is what I would study. All this seems very obvious in retrospect, but the effect at the time (and I recognised it as such at the time) was phenomenal. I would not hesitate to say that the influence of that particular man was to shape the rest of my professional life. As George Steiner asserts:

> Every 'break-in' into the other, via persuasion or menace (fear is a great teacher) borders on, releases the erotic. Trust, offer and acceptance, have roots which are also sexual. Teaching and learning are informed by an otherwise inexpressible sexuality of the human soul. This sexuality eroticises understanding and *imitatio*. Add to this

the key point that in the arts and humanities the material being taught, the music being analysed and practised, are *per se* charged with emotions. These emotions will, in considerable part, have affinities, immediate or indirect, with the domain of love.[1]

I have offered this extended and, no doubt, apparently egocentric description of my own journey in order to shed light on the nature of the events to which I alluded at the beginning of this chapter. Those events culminated in my being verbally abused in a threatening manner in my office by two male students late one evening, several hours after a seminar which had not gone at all well from their perspective.

In Early Modern Sex and Sexualities: Lyly to Milton (a final year, double credit module in the BA Hons English Studies programme), students had an opportunity to focus their study of Renaissance literature around the issues of gender and sexuality, while broadening the range of texts with which they engaged. The module also engaged, at a sophisticated level, with feminisms and queer theory and their implications for reading Renaissance texts. It had as a prerequisite a level two module, Renaissance Drama, which introduced students to a range of fairly canonical dramatic texts. In Early Modern Sex and Sexualities, however, they were encouraged to look beyond the canon and actively to seek out texts that would allow them to explore their own areas of interest as they develop. There were no lectures for this module, just a weekly 2-hour seminar. So, the first five sessions of the module were directed, and introduced students to erotic poetry such as Shakespeare's 'Venus and Adonis' and Marlowe's 'Hero and Leander'. Another session explored the importance of Ovid to Renaissance culture. In another session on homoerotics, students studied Marlowe's *Edward II* alongside John Lyly's *Campaspe*; a play from the 1580s about Alexander the Great and his relationships. In another session we studied Lyly's *Gallathea* (a crucially important, though often overlooked, play for those interested in representations of female same-sex desire in the period) and in the final directed session we explored three Jacobean witchcraft plays. After the first five sessions, students on this module submitted a short essay (chosen from a list of titles set by the tutor) based on the texts they had studied so far. This essay counted for 30 per cent of the overall mark for the module.

During the weeks of directed study, students were encouraged simultaneously to begin seeking out new texts, which they could use for their negotiated essay; a longer piece based on their own research interests and which counted for 70 per cent of the overall module mark. The title of the essay had to be negotiated with the tutor and signed off and the students gave a seminar presentation as part of the preparation for this essay. The idea behind the module, then, was that students move from a closely directed mode of study to a much more self-directed approach which allowed them to negotiate their own curriculum and shape their own assessment.

It is particularly significant to me that the challenge from the young men in question came so near the end of their programme but I think their reaction to this particular module can be accounted for if we examine the links between their own sense of their masculine identity and their chosen path through the course up until this point. Both these men were returning to education after some years working locally. As has long been recognised, 'English [as an academic discipline] has battled from the beginning against being classified as a "soft" option'.[2] These students marked themselves off as distinct from the predominantly female student body of their year cohort from the outset and had as little to do with their peers as possible; whether in the seminar room or out of it. They chose their modules carefully, seeking out wherever possible those focused on modern literature and taught by older, established male lecturers that they felt they could look up to. This strategy, I would suggest, enabled them to enact a model of masculinity, which defended their own sense of self and promoted a feeling of community; not with their female classmates, but with their male lecturers. Indeed, they were often referred to by some staff as the brightest and most promising students in their year while some equally bright women were somewhat overlooked. The master/disciple model of pedagogy was one to which these particular students were well suited.

So, having chosen to study English in the first instance, these students found a way to defend their traditional masculine identity through a careful choice of modules and lecturers. As Ben Knights has recently noted:

> The male student of English is going against the social grain...As members of a minority within the student body, males have to negotiate their standing, and fend off the effeminacy that may be attributed to them by other students.[3]

Some male students, it must be noted, would embrace the opportunity to go against the social grain and discover a host of new opportunities for their masculine identity in so doing. The students in question here, though, succeeded in fending off any potential effeminacy by enacting a barely disguised contempt for their female peers and their contributions to seminar discussions. They established their identity almost entirely on gendered lines: they were 'proper' men, working closely with 'real' (male) academics on 'hard' authors and texts whereas the women students, as they later made clear in their own terms, were 'silly housewives' who were playing at being students.

The crisis moment in Early Modern Sex and Sexualities occurred during the session on Homoerotics and Masculinity in Christopher Marlowe's *Edward II* and John Lyly's *Campaspe*. Interestingly, the students under discussion here had little problem with the Marlowe's play. Despite their own reading around our topic, and my reminders that categories of sexuality in the period were far from stable, or even recognisable from a twentieth-century viewpoint, they were reluctant to see Edward II as anything other than 'gay' or 'homosexual'. There is, of course, a real difficulty for students in discussing early modern sexualities in ways that recognise their difference from our own, highly defined notions of sexual identity. For these particular students, however, the easiest way to deal with this when discussing *Edward II* was to attempt to erase from their minds all notions of historical distance and difference which, for their reading of this text, made Edward's 'homosexuality' recognisable and, I would suggest, 'safe'. In exactly the ways that even the most cursory reading of Foucault's *History of Sexuality Vol 1* would have revealed to them as problematic (and it is one of the texts on the reading list for the module) they read Edward's 'gayness' as the fundamental feature of his identity: everything that he did and everything that happened to him was as a result of his identity as a homosexual, rather than as a man. In other words, he was *not* like them. Their masculine identity was defined against the representation they were exploring in Marlowe's play. They vociferously argued that Edward was gay so that they could set themselves against him; seeing his lack of political astuteness and military prowess as a clear sign of his homosexuality and the inevitable effeminacy that they attached to it. Disturbingly, then, the ending of the play (which, again, they read as entirely unambiguous, almost despite the text itself) was seen by them to be an entirely logical conclusion. The 'red hot poker' was no more than a symbol for the way Edward had lived his life and ruined his country. Other, women students, were equally vociferous in pointing out that the text does not support such unambiguous categorisation and that their research had suggested to them that homoeroticism and masculinity were not opposite in Renaissance culture but, as they argued, so the male students became even more entrenched in their views. The more the women attempted to deconstruct the notion of homosexuality, so the men clung more firmly to it. Edward was gay, he had a sexual relationship with Gaveston, that's why he was a bad ruler, that's why he was killed in the fashion he was. The notoriety of *Edward II* in the popular imagination made the play an ideal ground upon which these students could enact their masculine identity. Masculinity, for them, was straightforwardly synonymous with heterosexuality. If they had to drag the historical Edward hundreds of years out of his context and subject him to a categorisation that would not have been available at the time Marlowe's play was written, let alone when the historical figure of Edward II lived, they were prepared to do so. What powerful forces were at work on these men that drove them, so forcefully, to assert their own model of contemporary masculinity through their reading of the play and on the other members of the seminar? This is a question to which I shall return.

The discussion of Marlowe's play was tense and difficult at times; it is very difficult, as we all know, to encourage debate and discussion and at the same time attempt to keep the discussion from wandering into unpleasant and, in this case, potentially offensive territory. What I had not fully appreciated at the time, however, was how much the path these students had adopted in their approach to the first text was to compromise and threaten their sense of self as we moved into discussion of Lyly's play, *Campaspe*.

Edward II is a fairly canonical text in Renaissance studies these days; it has a well-established place in the performance repertoire and the plot is often thought by many students to be familiar to them (until they read or see the play!). As such, the play poses a real challenge in the teaching of issues such as gender, sexuality and history – students have many preconceptions about it which are difficult to break through – and this seminar proved to me that the distance and difference of early modern models of gender and sexuality (here masculinity and homoerotic desire) are made more threatening to traditional models of contemporary masculinity in the process of recognising that distance. The potential continuity between, and fluidity of, masculine identities in the Renaissance is replaced in our own time by a severing of different models and a policing of the new, apparently fixed boundaries of licit and illicit masculinities. This is what Eve Sedgwick has characterised as 'the potential unbrokenness of a continuum between homosocial and homosexual – a continuum whose visibility, for men, in our society, is radically disrupted'.[4] The strategy adopted by the male students in this seminar, then, was to make the difference between the homosocial and the homosexual as distinct as possible, and to erase for themselves and, I suspect, in the minds of their peers, any notion that they might potentially sit on the same continuum. Their keenness to pin down Edward's sexuality (and, therefore, identity), to make it familiar and recognisable in their own terms (gay, homosexual) in this well-known Renaissance tragedy was matched only by their reluctance to even contemplate doing the same for the protagonist of Lyly's relatively little known court comedy.

John Lyly's play, *Campaspe*, is about Alexander the Great and tells the story of how he falls in love with Campaspe, a woman captured during one of his military campaigns. During the course of the play, Alexander's love for Campaspe is criticised openly by his confidante, Hephestion, and covertly by his soldiers, who find there is no longer a role for them as all masculine activity (here, war!) has stopped for the duration of their general's dalliance. Indeed, the play describes how his love for Campaspe has an effeminising effect on Alexander and his world. In an exchange between two of his soldiers, Parmenio tells Clitus:

> I mislike this new delicacy and pleasing
> peace; for what else do we see now than a kind of softness
> in every man's mind...
> ...O Philip [Alexander's father], were thou alive to see this
> alteration – thy men turned to women, thy soldiers to
> lovers, gloves worn in velvet caps instead of plumes in
> helmets – thou would either die among them
> for sorrow or confound them for anger.[5]

The misogynist aspects of this play which clearly sees the love of men for women as a second rate, irrational kind of love with damaging social effects is shaped very much by the context of the 1580s and the attitudes of many of the influential men at the Elizabethan court who felt that a woman's rule had effeminised England and made her prone to invasion. The most pressing political debate at the time the play was written concerned the desire of men like Leicester and Burghley to go to war against Spain in support of the Protestant Low Countries and I argue that Lyly's play was designed as an intervention in this debate to support the views of the religious radicals. So, much of the play is concerned with promoting highly traditional views of masculinity which are characterised by activity – military strength, aggressive imperial expansion and invasion as opposed to Elizabeth's long sustained policy of peace (or passivity). None of this seemed to cause any particular difficulty for the students in the seminar except some of the women students became rather uncomfortable at some of the more explicitly misogynistic attitudes displayed. One moment in particular stands out in my memory as the students responded so differently. Hephestion, Alexander's 'confidante' berates his friend:

> And shall it not seem
> monstrous to wise men that the heart of the greatest
> conqueror of the world should be found in the hands
> of the weakest creature of nature – of a woman, of a
> captive?[6]

The shock of the women students at such an explicitly sexist attitude (and it never fails to surprise me that many women students are genuinely shocked by the extent to which Renaissance texts are often so deeply sexist) was countered by the laughter of the male students, whose enactment of their masculine identity at this point in the discussion appeared to assert their sympathy with the views of Hephestion. Alexander, unlike Edward II, was a 'proper' man and, although his love for Campaspe was foolish, it did not undermine his masculine status as such – for them. It seemed that for as long as the discussion focused strictly on issues of gender the male students were comfortable and engaged, able to defend Alexander as 'a bit of a lad'. They clearly saw in him something which they could recognise; a masculine 'type' with which they shared common ground.

The generally good-tempered, if at times polarised discussion of *Campaspe* took a turn when I introduced the points raised by Alan Bray's excellent article on male friendship in Elizabethan England which I had asked the students to read for the seminar.[7] Interestingly, it was now time for some of the women students to laugh. They looked at me knowingly, almost mockingly, and playfully teased me about wanting to uncover a 'gay' relationship between Alexander and Hephestion in the play. Despite the gentle teasing, several of the same women students needed no help from me and had produced some excellent readings of the play through their own research that recognised the operation of homoerotic desire in the play. In his discussion of the 'masculine friend', Bray notes that Elizabethan men were likely to share a bed and kiss each other publicly and that '[e]motional bonds...had their place alongside the physical links of friendship'.[8] However, the masculine friend had somehow to be clearly differentiated from its horrific 'other', the sodomite. What Bray's work shows us, though, is that while in theory the 'distinction between the two kinds of intimacy [friendship and sodomy] was then apparently sharp and clearly marked: the one was expressed in orderly "civil" relations, the other in subversive', in practice, [t]he signs of the one were indeed sometimes the sign of the other'.[9]

The distinction, then, between the masculine friend and the sodomite was not so very clear in the period or, as the women students attempted to show, in its cultural remains. What we have to do in our readings of Renaissance texts concerned with masculine identity, they concluded, is to be open to the *potential* that homoerotic desire may at all times be operating, even directly alongside heteroerotic desire and that neither of these expressions of sexuality were directly related to gender (here, masculinity). Alexander, then, loved both Campaspe and Hephestion, was tied by eroticised bonds of patronage to the painter, Apelles, to whom he finally 'gives' Campaspe as a wife, and through the eroticised bonds of warfare with his soldiers. Careful readings of the topography of the play were produced, where the off stage 'camp' of the soldiers and its symbolic significance as an all-male space during war time was explored. Extracts from Plutarch, Castiglione and Montaigne concerned with friendship were produced to support their argument. This discussion led us into a wider debate about hyper masculinity and the potential to read for homoeroticism in the contemporary sporting world. Rugby, I remember, came under particular scrutiny. The women students were altogether more assertive in their reading of *Campaspe* than they had been in their reading of *Edward II*. They had not been able to resist the traditional view of Marlowe's play and found it difficult to counter the views put forward by the male students although they very clearly did not comply with the view that Edward died as he'd lived. With *Campaspe*, however, they were encountering a text previously unknown to the whole group. They had done their research and, interestingly, played out their reading quite forcefully to the seminar and, perhaps more specifically, to the male students who had become increasingly quiet during this discussion. Their discomfort was palpable.

My own contribution to the discussion focused around the ways in which homoerotic desire could be seen to function as a socially orderly force and a means by which masculine identity could achieve some level of stability within the play, especially when we take into account the historical context of Elizabethan masculinity. The play could, I argued, be seen to call for a vigorous re-establishment of homosocial relations at the Elizabethan court and that this could include erotic relations between men who had for too long been bound up in a Petrarchan fantasy world where they had been divided endlessly among themselves in the shifting relations of factionalism. This, it seemed was too much for the male students to tolerate. To try and 'insinuate' that Alexander was 'gay' was one thing, but to then argue that this could be a 'good thing' for masculinity was just beyond what was reasonable. Nothing that had been said in the discussion so far could be directly evidenced by the text, it was suggested, and all the research was 'just' theoretical anyway. It was all, by implication, worthless.

The discussion was becoming rather heated between the students so I decided to intervene. The male students were, as I explained, very keen to recognise Edward II as 'homosexual' so, I thought, I would use their own approach to establish the possibility that even if they didn't think that Alexander could be discussed in terms of homoerotic desire, Marlowe certainly did. In what I thought was a neat (if rather well-rehearsed) moment of intertextual analysis, I asked them to look back at *Edward II* and find the reference to Alexander and Hephestion. In that play, Mortimer Junior is complaining to his uncle about the relationship between the King and Gaveston. Edward reveals his own view of their relationship when he asks Gaveston:

Knowest thou not who I am?
Thy friend, thy self, another Gaveston.[10]

For Marlowe's Edward, their relationship is entirely commensurate with the key, defining feature of masculine friendship in the period: equality between the partners. This view of the relationship was not the one taken by the male students, neither, as it happens, is it the view taken by the Mortimers in the play. However, where the students clearly viewed the homoerotic nature of the relationship as in some way threatening, Mortimer Senior reassures his nephew that there is nothing in it to cause concern:

The mightiest kings have had their minions:
Great Alexander loved Hephaestion,
The conquering Hercules for Hylas wept,
And for Patroclus stern Achilles drooped.[11]

Here, Mortimer Senior uses the pejorative term 'minion' to describe Hephestion which automatically suggests a sodomitical element to the relationship between him and Alexander because their rank, in Mortimer's account, is so incompatible that they cannot be counted as friends. In the play which the male students were convinced dealt explicitly with issues of 'homosexuality' then, the relationship between Alexander and Hephestion comes top in a list of classical homoerotic relationships, but is seen by Mortimer Senior as harmless in the overall scheme. I suppose the implication of what I was trying to point out was that they couldn't have it both ways – if they accepted the view that Edward was 'gay' and that the play's conclusion as they saw it somehow 'proved' this (despite Edward's own assertions that he loved Gaveston as a friend or 'another self') then why was it impossible to recognise the potential for homoerotic desire in the relationship between Alexander and Hephestion? The male students simply responded that 'it wasn't the same' and that 'we' (by which I think they meant the women students and myself) were 'reading too much into it'. This retreat into the equivalent of undergraduate infancy came as a surprise to me, as did the surly manner in which these male students left the room at the end of the session. It was to be the last time I saw them in a seminar on that module.

In the hurly burly of the seminar we perhaps don't have time to stop and think enough about why a particular student, or group of students, wants (or perhaps needs?) to resist a particular view or position. It is very easy to become seduced oneself by the fantasy that all this is 'just' theory and that it doesn't really matter above and beyond the intellectual exercise. What became clear after this seminar was that there was much more at stake than I'd ever realised.

Several hours after the seminar, and at the end of a long-working day, there was a knock on my office door. I was the last person left in the department on that particular day. The two male students I have been discussing came in and, despite my repeated requests that they should take a seat, they insisted on standing. It was also very obvious that they had both been drinking and they admitted to having been in the pub in order to 'pluck up the courage' (as they put it) to come and see me. They began telling me that they were not enjoying Early Modern Sex and Sexualities and that they didn't really want to take it in the first place; it was, apparently, the best of a bad bunch of modules on offer that semester. Their primary complaint was with the women students who, they felt free to say, 'talked rubbish'. They had not come to University, I was informed, to listen to a lot of housewives talking amongst themselves. I immediately told them that I found this attitude towards their fellow students disrespectful and unacceptable. This seemed to ignite their fury. As each of them spoke, the other made remarks under his breath and they made explicit reference to my wanting to 'find' homosexuality in texts where there was none (ironically, this was exactly what I was warning against in the seminar). *Campaspe*, it seemed, was a text about soldiers, war and the love between men and women, nothing more. Yes, *Edward II* was about homosexuality but, as they saw it, I had disregarded their contributions on this text because I didn't like the way it ended. The aggression in their demeanour and the attitudes they displayed made me feel threatened and I asked them to leave my office. They didn't, and kept repeating that I needed to recognise that I was being unreasonable in reading too much into these texts because of what I was. I asked them what they meant by this but they would not be any more specific. Eventually I insisted that they leave my office, as it was clear we could not have a sensible conversation while emotions were running so high on their part. At this point they left, muttering insults over their shoulders.

The ways in which these particular students had managed to defend their own views of traditional masculinity had required them to separate themselves off from the rest of the predominantly female student body against which they defined themselves, and to ally themselves with particular members of staff with whom they felt they could operate in a master/disciple relationship (even if the staff member did not share their views). In addition, they formed a very powerful bond with each other; always turning up to lectures and seminars together, always sitting next to each other and exchanging contemptuous looks as their peers made contributions to the discussion. This approach seemed to have worked for them, until they arrived in Early Modern Sex and Sexualities, when they were faced with an openly gay lecturer whose sexuality and, I suspect, relative youth, made it impossible for them to view me as a master of any kind. As it was also clearly too difficult for them to relate to me on friendly terms, they were at a bit of a loss. The curriculum of the module itself seemed to alienate them from the start, while at the same time empowering the women students who, in some cases, seemed to have a score to settle with these men.

The extent to which the male students felt driven to label Edward II as 'homosexual' in order to contain any threat posed by the nature of the topic we were studying is surprising, at least to me. They were deeply uncomfortable with the idea that as categories such as homosexual and gay did not exist in the Renaissance, people simply didn't define themselves in the way many do today, in terms of the gender of their object of desire. The implied fluidity of this model, which allows for the potential of homoerotic relations as a constituent part of homosocial relations, was clearly too much for them to accept. However, having firmly established in their own minds that homosexuality did exist in the Renaissance (as evidenced by *Edward II*) they set themselves up as the guards whose role it was to police the boundaries of who 'was' and who 'wasn't'. The greatest challenge to the integrity of the boundaries that they established came in our discussion of friendship and, looking back, I can begin to see why they found this as threatening as they clearly did. These men had formed a very powerful friendship that had seen them through their university careers so far; they remained 'untarnished' by the charge of effeminacy that could so easily have been their fate as male English undergraduates. However, in a discussion of Elizabethan models of masculine friendship that ranged over Aristotle, Plato, Plutarch, Castiglione and Montaigne, the very concept of masculine friendship itself was brought into relief and was placed under the microscope of that seminar discussion. The conclusion that 'male friendship in early modern England may have been openly and normatively homoerotic'[12] resonated too strongly as the male students themselves had worked so hard to eradicate historical difference in their reading. The model of masculinity that they so clearly feared and against which they had guarded themselves throughout their studies thus far, the effeminised man, the 'homosexual', was embodied in the figure sitting at the front of the room, in a position of authority, and was inviting them, challenging them even, at some deep level, to explore the very nature of the relationship that underpinned their identity as men in that room at that time: friendship. The irony is that, given the nature of psychosexual dynamics, none of us fully realised that that was what was happening!

I started this chapter with a long explanation of my own path into the teaching of English, and the enormous significance of the subject for my own personal history and identity formation. I can only guess at the extent to which that history has shaped my current investment in the subject that has since given me a living. How far has that history shaped not only my choice of research specialism, but also the curriculum that I teach each year? How far did my personal investment in this material further provoke the events that occurred in and after that Early Modern Sex and Sexualities seminar? How could I have handled it better? How far am I still engaged in a struggle to define myself against the traditional model of masculine identity defended and promoted by those male students? What part does my teaching and my professional identity play in this struggle?

The title of this chapter is intended to recognise the complex relations between the practice of teaching, the material we teach, who we teach and who we are. English is a subject more profoundly engaged with the processes of identity formation than any other. Every engagement with every text involves, at some level, the negotiation of our sense of self with the external world. When that engagement takes place in a public space, with a group of people, there is no telling how many personal stories could be circulating, how many narratives are being written and rewritten, challenged and affirmed. As George Steiner observes:

> The pulse of teaching is persuasion. The teacher solicits attention, agreement, and, optimally, collaborative dissent. He or she invites trust ... Persuasion is both positive – 'share this skill with me, follow me into this art and practise, read this text' – and negative – 'do not believe this, do not expend time and effort on that.' The dynamics are the same: to build a community out of communication, a coherence of shared feelings, passions, refusals. In persuasion, in solicitation, be it of the most abstract, theoretical kind ... a process of seduction, willed or accidental, is inescapable.[13]

The process of seduction outlined by Steiner recognises an erotics of pedagogy. It should come as no surprise, then, that encounters in the seminar will be more or less comfortable, depending on the individuals involved. What is important for us, as teachers, is to recognise the value, and indeed the necessity, of the refusals, to the maintenance of always precarious individual identities.

Notes

1. George Steiner. *Lessons of the Masters*. Cambridge, MA. and London: Harvard University Press, 2003. p. 27.
2. Ben Knights. *Writing Masculinities: Male Narratives in Twentieth-Century Fiction*. Basingstoke: Macmillan, 1999. p. 38.
3. Ibid. pp. 39–40.
4. Eve Kosofsky Sedgwick. *Between Men: English Literature and Male Homosocial Desire*. New York: Columbia University Press, 1985. pp. 1–2.
5. John Lyly. *Campaspe* and *Sappho and Phao*. G.K. Hunter and David Bevington. (Eds) Manchester: Manchester University Press, 1991. IV, iii, pp. 6–27.
6. Ibid. II, ii, pp. 61–65.
7. Alan Bray. 'Homosexuality and the Signs of Male Friendship in Elizabethan England' in Jonathan Goldberg. (Ed.) *Queering the Renaissance*. Durham and London: Duke University Press, 1994.
8. Ibid. p. 45.
9. Ibid. p. 47.

10. Christopher Marlowe. *Edward II* in Mark Thornton Burnett. (Ed.) *Christopher Marlowe: The Complete Plays*. I, i, pp. 141–142.
11. Ibid. I, iv, pp. 390–393.
12. Mario DiGangi. 'Marlowe, Queer Studies, and Renaissance Homoeroticism' in Paul Whitfield White. (Ed.) *Marlowe, History and Sexuality: New Critical Essays on Christopher Marlowe*. New York: AMS Press, 1998. p. 198.
13. Steiner. p. 26.

Works cited

Bray, Alan. 'Homosexuality and the Signs of Male Friendship in Elizabethan England' in Jonathan Goldberg. (Ed.) *Queering the Renaissance*. Durham and London: Duke University Press, 1994.

DiGangi, Mario. 'Marlowe, Queer Studies and Renaissance Homoeroticism' in Paul Whitfield White. (Ed.) *Marlowe, History and Sexuality: New Essays on Christopher Marlowe*. New York: AMS Press, 1998.

Knights, Ben. *Writing Masculinities: Male Narratives in Twentieth-Century Fiction*. Basingstoke: Macmillan, 1999.

Lyly, John. *Campaspe* and *Sapho and Phao*. G.K. Hunter and David Bevington. (Eds) Manchester: Manchester University Press, 1991.

Marlowe, Christopher. *Edward II* in Mark Thornton Burnett. (Ed.) *Christopher Marlowe: The Complete Plays*. London: Everyman, 1999.

Sedgwick, Eve Kosofsky. *Between Men: English Literature and Male Homosocial Desire*. New York: Columbia University Press, 1985.

Steiner, George. *Lessons of the Masters*. Cambridge and London: Harvard University Press, 2003.

4
Charlotte Dacre's Nymphomaniacs and Demon-Lovers: Teaching Female Masculinities

Ranita Chatterjee

'"Why, there is certainly a pleasure," with a fierce malignant smile, observed Victoria, "in the infliction of prolonged torment"' (Dacre 1997: 205). With this shocking confession, Charlotte Dacre's 1806 gothic novel *Zofloya: Or, The Moor* portrays its heroine's unbridled erotic tastes and miscegenation with a black lower-class Lucifer, named Zofloya, as threats to the emerging British Empire. Despite its didacticism, especially its attribution of all flaws in the daughter Victoria to her weak-willed mother Laurina, Dacre's novel relishes in Sadean scenes of seduction, torture, and violence. The novel begins with Laurina di Loredani's seduction by her husband's house guest, the German Count Ardolph. Ardolph is a libertine whose 'savage delight [was] to intercept the happiness of wedded love – to wean from an adoring husband regards of a pure and faithful wife' (1997: 43). The wicked Ardolph is so taken with Laurina's fidelity that he does not rest until he successfully seduces her and convinces her to leave her husband. As a result of her actions, her family disintegrates: her son Leonardo runs away from home, her husband dies in a duel with the Count, and her daughter Victoria is imprisoned by the Count in the home of a distant and strict Catholic aunt with a 'mercenary soul' (1997: 67). Victoria both escapes from her female oppressor, and marries her lover Berenza. Nevertheless, she continues to blame her mother for all the subsequent evil that befalls her. Although the novel is subtitled *A Romance of the Fifteenth Century* and is set in the morally corrupt aristocratic world of Venice, the novel's characters are recognizably late eighteenth-century Britons who wrestle with issues of female propriety and mothering akin to what Mary Wollstonecraft discussed in her 1792 *A Vindication of the Rights of Woman*. Given Wollstonecraft's equation of strong nationhood with virtuous mothering, Diane Hoeveler claims that in placing the blame for

Victoria's hellish nature on a promiscuous mother, *Zofloya* is a 'virtual parody of Wollstonecraft's works' (1997: 185).

Dacre's novel suggests that Victoria's own horrific imagination attracts Satan. Zofloya, a former slave and present servant of Victoria's husband, first appears to her in an intensely passionate dream as a humble, yet majestic figure willing to do her bidding. In Victoria's dream, Zofloya is adorned in angelic white and gold clothes, and an emerald bejeweled turban with a green feather. His bare arms and legs are also 'encircled with the finest oriental pearl', and his neck and ears are decorated with 'gold rings of an enormous size' (1997: 145). Not only is Zofloya a painstakingly orientalized (and thus feminized) Moor with knowledge of a variety of nefarious drugs, he also only appears to Victoria after she calls for him in her 'dark mind' (1997: 165). Moreover, he is associated with the most sensual feelings Victoria experiences: his voice is 'like the sweet murmuring sound of an Æolian harp, swept by the breath of a zephyr' (1997: 165). Victoria's female imagination, then, is associated with otherness, darkness, and danger because, as Adriana Craciun notes, it originates in 'physical sensation' (1997: 165–166, n. 1). Like his literary precursor Vathek (from William Beckford's 1786 oriental tale of the same name) and his infamous successor the Malay (from Thomas De Quincey's 1821 *Confessions of an English Opium-Eater*), Zofloya is clearly depicted as enjoying a non-normative 'oriental' sexuality. That he turns out to be the devil is no surprise. What is surprising is the scope of the upper-class Victoria's desires. With Zofloya's aid, Victoria slowly poisons her husband Berenza to death; imprisons, tortures, and brutally murders her rival and ward, the innocent orphan Lilla; and for one night, undergoes a metamorphosis to look like the deceased Lilla in order to sleep with her betrothed Henriquez, who is Berenza's loving younger brother and the object of Victoria's lust. After Zofloya helps Victoria to escape the authorities and extracts her unquestioned allegiance, she passionately gives her body and soul to him.

In her introduction to the novel, Adriana Craciun observes that 'Unlike the conventional woman in a demon lover ballad who is horrified to see her lover revealed as infernal, Victoria, like several of Dacre's poetic narrators, finds his supernatural and infernal origins arousing' (1997: 17). I argue that Dacre's gothic novel is unique in its depiction of the heroine's transformation from a 'beautiful and accomplished angel' (1997: 40); to an 'untameable hyaena [*sic*]' (1997: 75), glossed by Craciun as 'hermaphroditic' (1997: 75, n. 1); a woman 'wild with the furor' (1997: 144), glossed by Craciun as nymphomaniac (1997: 144, n. 1); and finally to a woman with 'bold masculine features' (1997: 211). Victoria's physical appearance grows more masculine and her skin becomes problematically darker as she progressively embarks on further evil deeds to satisfy her bloodlust. While one may interpret these bodily changes as corporeal manifestations of the soul's increasingly corrupt nature, I think we need to consider what these changes might suggest about the period's own notions about masculinity and femininity. Is Victoria a girl gone wild? Is she a woman behaving badly? Can we blame her mother for Victoria's unruly ways? Is Victoria so thoroughly poisoned by patriarchy's negative view of women as either angels or whores that she expresses her desires (which she should not even have) in terms of demonic activity? Or, as students often suggest, is she simply a woman behaving like a man? The portrayal of the sexually deviant and socially defiant Victoria befriending an exotic Moorish devil, though racist and orientalist, may signify the extent to which her libidinal power can neither be confined by the early nineteenth-century's nascent and limited conception of femininity, nor codified as anything other than nymphomania. Indeed, Dacre's novel is a remarkable exploration of the social production of racial and gender classifications. The classroom is precisely where these questions concerning how to read Victoria's gender get worked out and, significantly, with this novel, where alternative conceptions about *masculinity* emerge. After all, what does it mean to say that Victoria behaves *like a man*?

Despite the institutionalization of certain strands of post-1960s critical theory, what educators believe to be a dialogic space of learning may still be to our current English literary and cultural studies students a place of overwhelming terror. Fear and trembling aptly describe many of our students' experiences in the hegemonic arena of the college and university classroom. The age and experience of the teacher, as well as of the students, may also produce a similar, though muted, gothic feeling in the English literature professor. This may partly explain the unconscious adherence to well-rehearsed scripts of gender and pedagogic performance. Even in a playful Derridean challenge to the canon, be this in choice of texts, interpretative strategies, or alternative pedagogical practices, new lines of power are inevitably drawn and defended. For example, in queer studies, a field that strikes many as automatically subversive, a pernicious form of racial and gender hegemony may still dominate the discourse. As Susan Stryker and Judith Halberstam note, queer theories and queer activism with their focus on non-conformist and non-normative gender and sexual identities have the potential to explode the myth of binary gendered and sexual manifestations. Yet, in the academy, and especially in our pedagogical practices, though we acknowledge that gender is socially constructed, we tend to resurrect a two-gendered, two-sexuality model and ignore, or worse, forget about the existence of transgendered and transsexual individuals. For Stryker, what she calls 'transgender phenomena' 'bear witness to the epistemological rift between gender signifiers and their signifieds. In doing so, they disrupt and denaturalize Western modernity's "normal" reality, specifically the fiction of a unitary psychosocial gender that is rooted biologically in corporeal substance' (Stryker 1988: 147). The failure to explore the formation of transgender subjectivities also keeps masculinity firmly wedded to male bodies, especially white male bodies, in a sacrosanct union. Thus, in the West, ethnic masculinities are tenuously male, whereas gay masculinity is hyper-male as long as it is in a white body. In her critique of the new hegemony of white gay masculinity, Judith Halberstam argues that the 'future of queer studies ... depends absolutely on moving away from white gay male identity politics and learning from the radical critiques offered by a younger generation of queer scholars who draw their intellectual inspiration from feminism and ethnic studies rather than white queer studies' (Halberstam 2005: 220).

There is a similar phenomenon in theory classrooms. Speaking about ' "theory" as a practice, an educational genre, rather than a curriculum', Ben Knights claims that with its 'compulsive, almost theological allusion to a new canon of patriarchs (Nietzsche, Saussure, Heidegger, Gramsci, Lévi-Strauss, Althusser, Foucault, Lacan, Barthes, Lyotard, Derrida, Baudrillard and so on)', English studies has become 'a diglossic culture, ... where the 'high' language gestures towards mastery even while simultaneously denying its possibility' (Knights 1999: 45–46). Our students' anxieties often stem from having to learn an overwhelming new theory vocabulary that only the professor apparently knows how to use. Even if the theories are meant to empower the learner and reveal the ideological workings of power in the classroom, only those students who understand the theories can recognize their own agency. Critical theory classes and gender-aware spaces may potentially breed even more hostile subjects than the supposedly traditional non-theory classrooms. Both Halberstam and Knights conclude that these new 'theory' hegemonies produce pedagogical and scholarly models, whether in terms of race or gender or both, that reinstate earlier patriarchal forms of masculinity and gender hierarchies. 'What's a girl to do?' may be the most crucial formulation of the question of how to create a responsible and responsive pedagogy that encourages a heteroglossic exploration of texts within their historically specific gendered and sexualized contexts. In this essay, I will use my experiences in teaching the nineteenth-century gothic novel *Zofloya: Or, The Moor* by Charlotte Dacre to argue that we need to attend more to the historically changing performances of gender and sexuality, especially of alternative sexualities. In disassociating our contemporary socially constructed notions of masculinity and femininity from their rigidly maintained embodiment in biological male and female bodies, we may be able to challenge some of the ways patriarchy rears its ugly head over and over again in a variety of apparently subversive pedagogical contexts.

It has been almost two decades since Judith Butler first discussed gender as a performance that is, nevertheless, not voluntary and is strictly enforced 'within a highly rigid regulatory frame' (Butler 1993: 33). Butler concluded *Gender Trouble* with her now infamously misunderstood discussion of drag queens and how their performances expose the lack of an original femininity: misunderstood because Butler's critics incorrectly assumed that identifying a social construction, in this case femininity, as a performance liberated individuals to perform whatever gender however they chose. As Butler clarified later in *Bodies That Matter*, gender performance is not a 'willful appropriation and it is certainly *not* a question of taking on a mask' (1993: 7). If gender is a performance under social surveillance and the punishment is severe for not embodying one's gender as others see fit, then we must wonder why the parody of femininity in certain controlled settings can be so entertaining, whereas there are no such possibilities or venues for the corresponding parodic performance of masculinity. Why do discussions of masculinity, both within and without academia, fail to consider *female masculinity*? Despite our theory savvyness when it comes to the relationship between sex and gender in our various analyses of femininity, why do we insist on, or at least act like we believe in, an inherently natural bond between masculinity and biological male bodies? These are the troubling questions raised by Judith Halberstam's groundbreaking 1998 book *Female Masculinity*, where she describes the 'general disbelief in female masculinity' as a 'failure in a collective imagination: in other words, female-born people have been making convincing and powerful assaults on the coherence of male masculinity for well over a hundred years; what prevents these assaults from taking hold and accomplishing the diminution of the bonds between masculinity and men?' (Halberstam 1998: 15). Moreover, Halberstam argues that as long as we associate female masculinity with lesbianism or keep 'reading it as proto-lesbianism awaiting a coming community, we continue to hold female masculinity apart from the making of modern masculinity itself' (1998: 46). In addition to women making 'their own unique contributions to what we call modern masculinity', we should recognize female masculinity as a 'proliferation of masculinities' that multiplies in Foucauldian fashion the more we identify the 'various forms' (1998: 46). This very disbelief in the existence and contributions of diverse female masculinities enables the replication of patriarchal structures in our classrooms, no matter how subversive our curricula.

In our now predominantly female English literature classes, teaching gothic texts by women writers raises particular problems. Since gothic discourse is not only about power and its transgressions, but also explicitly about gender and sexual relations, our students, whether they have formally studied feminist theory or not, become gender-aware subjects in the classroom. Indeed, most students' initial responses to the gothic are predetermined by feminism which, as Laura Fitzgerald indicates, 'was instrumental in institutionalizing Gothic studies' (2004: 9). Generally, students have liberal feminist tendencies, that is, they believe in a superficial gender equality that does not address the systemic and institutional structures that produce inequities in the first place. Thus, students are eager to interpret female writers of the Romantic period as always challenging the gender status quo of the time, either in their texts or lives, precisely because these authors were women who chose to publish gothic works without a male pseudonym. In this case, students celebrate the text's content as radical, whether historically it is or is not, and miss the truly radical challenges to the very institution of gender at specific historic moments in some gothic texts, such as Dacre's *Zofloya*. Moreover, because of their belief in a transhistorical inherent connection between female bodies and femininity, and likewise, between male bodies and masculinity, these students can ignore, diminish, or exceptionalize examples to the contrary in their quest to interpret the works of women writers as somehow associated, however obliquely, with their own 'commonsensical' ideas of femininity. In large part, students' liberal feminist essentialist reading strategies for British Romantic works are not a disservice to the novels by Ann Radcliffe, Mary Wollstonecraft, and other women writers of the 1790s. These female writers used the gothic for sociopolitical commentary, specifically to expose the horrors of imprisonment in the patriarchal institution of marriage. That Mary Wollstonecraft's writings are an early example of liberal feminism also bolster's students' interpretations of many women writers in the Romantic period. Gothic scholars have even identified the key traits of 'female gothic' versus 'male gothic' texts, a binary guilty of ahistorical essentialism, if not also liberal feminism. For Diane Hoeveler, 'the typical female Gothic novel presents a blameless female victim triumphing through a variety of passive-aggressive strategies over a male-created system of oppression and corruption (alternately known as the patriarchy' (Hoeveler 1997: 107). In her *Art of Darkness: A Poetics of the Gothic*, Anne Williams explains that:

> Male Gothic derives its most powerful effects from the dramatic irony created by multiple points of view,...posits the supernatural as a 'reality',... has a tragic plot, ... specializes in horror, ... [and] focus[es] on female suffering, positioning the audience as voyeurs who, though sympathetic, may take pleasure in female victimization. Such situations are intimately related to its delight in sexual frankness and perversity, its proximity to the 'pornographic'.
>
> (1995: 102–105)

If Charlotte Dacre's gothic novel was presented through the victimized Lilla's point of view and, despite being tortured (albeit by a woman), Lilla escaped and married her fiancé Henriquez, we may be able to include her text in a female gothic tradition. However, *Zofloya* with its supernatural Moor and omniscient third-person narration of adulterous mothers and mother-figures, impotent husbands, feminized men, and masculinized women does not comfortably fit into the female gothic tradition. In fact, Dacre's novel is as violently misogynistic as the work of the infamous 'Monk Lewis'.

It is a scholarly commonplace to note that Dacre's text rewrites Matthew Lewis' 1796 *The Monk*. As Robert Miles notes, 'Charlotte Dacre's *Zofloya: Or, The Moor* (1806), is in two respects a female version of Lewis's *The Monk*: a woman, Victoria di Loredani, now occupies Ambrosia's role, while the sexual politics of the Gothic are viewed from a feminist perspective' (Miles 2002: 167). In a note, Miles explains his use of the term feminist: 'Dacre's novels make their bows towards conventional morality, but her complexly furnished heroines do not fit into these conventional boxes; issues of "gender politics," rather, are left open and it is in this qualified sense that I term her "feminist"' (2002: 219, n. 4). Although a productive description of 'feminist' since Miles implicitly acknowledges feminism's commitment to exploring the production of gendered subjects, his need to label Dacre's novel, even with qualifying caveats, as 'feminist' prevents us from considering the role of sexuality. In other words, binary *gendered* models fail to account for the diversity of gender and sexual expressions in the era, as

Foucault and others have shown, when gender and sexuality were being realigned along a binary essentialist model, namely the conflation of female bodies with femininity, male bodies with masculinity, and non-heteronormative bodies with perversity. Queer, then, might be a more precise term to describe Dacre's texts. Indeed, as Paulina Palmer notes, both 'Gothic and "queer" share a common emphasis on transgressive acts and subjectivities' (Palmer 1999: 8).

In the rest of this paper, I shall consider one pedagogical context in which these discourses of masculinity emerged: a small undergraduate senior honors seminar on experimental narratives of the British Romantic period. Like the early reviews of *Zofloya* that were generally ad hominem attacks, some accusing Dacre of being worse than the depiction of her devil, students initially had negative responses covering the spectrum from dismay to disgust. When asked to elaborate, all the students stated that they could not explain what they perceived to be a discrepancy between the author's female gender and her violent, pornographic text. I had expected this type of psychobiographic interpretation, whereby the author functions as the signified for the text's various signifiers, to be dismissed or, at least, challenged by our reading of a wide range of gothic texts written both by men and women, radicals and conservatives. I should note that I also taught Dacre's text in a mandatory graduate theory course that used *Zofloya* as a casebook for the application of several theoretical approaches (from deconstruction and Lacanian psychoanalysis to feminisms, queer theories, theories of race and ethnicity, and cultural studies). Although I do not have space in this paper to explore the pedagogical production of masculinity in this graduate seminar, let me briefly say that I had hoped that theory, especially our readings from Butler's *Gender Trouble* and Halberstam's *Female Masculinity*, would enable students to see the limitations of a psychobiographic analysis of Dacre's unconventional gothic novel. In both pedagogical spaces, the students' resistance to the idea of female masculinity amazed me. And this despite the novel's careful portrayal of Victoria as a defiant agent of a malleable conception of gender and race. Clearly, various extra-textual matters are at stake when we raise issues of gender and sexuality in the classroom.

The gender dynamics of any class affects how discussions of masculinity might play out. In my undergraduate honors class of 12 exceptionally articulate and bright students in their twenties, only four were self-identified men. Regardless of what we discussed, I could see that the young men wanted to appear sensitive to the concerns of their female colleagues, probably to ward off any suggestions that they might be as misogynistic as Dacre's Count Ardolph or her male critics. Consequently, my male students did not pursue some of their more intriguing interpretations. On the other hand, young women in the class struggled with appearing to be feminist for fear of being accused by the few self-identified feminists of patriarchal indoctrination. Additionally, I had one brilliant Moslem student who reminded us of the historical stereotyping of non-Anglo-Saxon men, such as Jews and Moors, as always already embodying a perverse masculinity. In this complex pedagogical atmosphere, I used close readings, some post-structuralist and queer theories, and historical documents on gender and sexuality to encourage my students to broaden their conceptions of masculinity. What emerged were numerous lively discussions of race, slavery, and Empire in relation to Zofloya's satanic non-normative masculinity. Because we had already discussed Beckford's oriental tale *Vathek* (1786), De Quincey's *Confessions of an English Opium-Eater* (1821), and Lord Byron's *The Giaour* (1813), the students had enough diverse models of male masculinity to recognize the orientalist and racist aspects of *Zofloya*'s portrayal of its Moorish devil. From the megalomaniacal desires of the Caliph Vathek, the criticism of patriarchal Moslem and Christian men in *The Giaour* (which is an Arabic word for infidels), and the opium-induced paranoid haze through which De Quincey imagines an encounter with a textbook pernicious non-Western other (the Malay), both my male and female students productively explored the influence of racial and imperialistic anxieties in the formation of male masculinity. The students were particularly adept at noticing the ways in which the masculinity of non-Western male characters is compromised by perceived feminine traits, such as the jewels that cover Zofloya, or the passivity of De Quincey's imaginary Malay. Furthermore, the students engaged in a nuanced discussion of the homoerotic dimensions of the male interactions in these gothic novels without automatically assuming its textual presence based on their knowledge of the historical authors. This class approached the topic of masculinity through Zofloya and the depiction of his 'oriental' sexuality, which they all agreed produced a non-normative compromised masculinity. That non-normative masculinity might also include the portrayal of Victoria did not initially occur to these students, especially the women who desperately sought to reconcile Dacre's historical feminine gender with her apparently 'male gothic' narrative.

One of the male students tried to suggest that because Victoria is abandoned by her mother after her ineffective father is killed, she models herself after the only powerful person she has known: at first, this is her mother's lover Count Ardolph. Later, Victoria's role model becomes the Satanic Zofloya. Donna Heiland also observes that 'within the world of the novel, the person she [Victoria] most resembles is not Lilla or any other woman, but Zofloya' (Heiland 2004: 46). My male student also argued that the three other significant male characters – Victoria's brother Leonardo, her husband Berenza, and his brother Henriquez – all exhibit a passive, perhaps effeminate, masculinity. In the class discussions that followed, we noted that curiously, all three men are the objects of a female gaze. This is explicitly the case with Leonardo. After Leonardo runs away from home, he has several adventures that involve eluding amorous adulterous mother figures, the most significant one with Berenza's former mistress Megalena Strozzi. Megalena's description of first seeing the young Leonardo sleeping rivals that of any male gaze:

> on his cheek, where the hand of health had planted her brown-red rose, the pearly gems of his tears still hung – his auburn hair sported in graceful curls about his forehead and temples, agitated by the passing breeze – his vermeil lips were half open, and disclosed his polished teeth – his bosom, which he had uncovered to admit the refreshing air, remained disclosed, and contrasted by its snowy whiteness the animated hue of his complexion.
>
> (Dacre 1997: 120)

As Robert Miles states, 'the iconography of the modest female is present' both in Megalena's depiction and in Leonardo's response to her questions (Miles 2002: 171): 'His cheeks became suffused with deepening blushes, and his eyes, with which he longed to gaze upon her, were yet cast bashfully towards the earth' (Dacre 1997: 121). Thoroughly eroticized, the 18-year-old Leonardo is easily seduced by the older, more experienced 'syren [sic] Megalena' (1997: 123) to do whatever she desires, particularly to exact revenge against Berenza who has moved on to a new lover. Megalena fabricates a false tale to justify why Leonardo should murder Berenza who, unknown to both, has made Victoria his new mistress. He hides in Berenza's bedroom until they have fallen asleep. As he raises his dagger, '[t]o a hand rendered unsteady by a confused consciousness of the meditated crime, was added the intense and over-powering horror of at once recognizing a sister, and burying in the same moment (as he believed) his dagger in her heart' (1997: 133). This is a more powerful scene when we discover that Leonardo forgets to retrieve the dagger whose hilt is engraved with the name 'Megalena Strozzi' (1997: 135).

Students had no problems reading this scene psychoanalytically, that is, they viewed Megalena quite literally as the phallic mother in her relationship with Leonardo, and were disturbed by the incestuous overtones of him stabbing his sister. However, they were less capable of articulating the possible relationship between Victoria and Megalena that Leonardo facilitates. Many of the students read the murder scene as two women fighting over one man. I asked the class to compare this portrayal with the homosocial one in Byron's *The Giaour* between Hassan and the infidel Giaour whose love for Hassan's courtesan Leila prompts the Ottoman overlord to kill her for her infidelity. Byron's poetic oriental tale emphasizes the intimacy of the two men bonded by hatred. In reconsidering Megalena's anger against Victoria once Leonardo explains the situation, many students began to read the novel's attempted murder scene as foregrounding the homosocial bonding and rivalry not between two men, but remarkably between two women (also noted by Heiland 2004: 44). However, at this point in our discussions, only the male student who suggested that Victoria models herself after Ardolph and Zofloya wrestled with my argument that female masculinity, instead of the limited concept of phallic femininity, might be a more productive way to read the character of Victoria who, unlike Megalena, is less invested in empowering her femininity than in adopting masculinity.

While most students did acknowledge the passive masculinity of Victoria's brother Leonardo and her husband Berenza, the women in the class did not want to interpret Victoria's adoption of masculine role models as anything more than the expression of a radical feminism. Furthermore, some students of both genders explained that because Zofloya first appears in Victoria's dream, we should read him as her evil doppelganger: that he is a satanic, orientalized Moor indicates the extent to which Victoria's desires for power are unconventional. Whether Zofloya is a figure for Victoria's desires or not, Dacre's text implies that the origins of Victoria's demonic imagination are specifically gendered social injustices against which writers like Mary Wollstonecraft and her literary circle fought. For Victoria survives the knife wound and is so highly regarded by Berenza for saving his life that he rewards her the only way he knows: by marrying her. That Berenza deemed her unworthy for a wife and kept her as a mistress until this life-saving event is never forgotten by Victoria. When she secretly vows revenge because Berenza did not initially want to marry but ravish her, Victoria's rage appears to be less against Berenza than against her society's gendered double standard for social conduct: men can have lovers and wives, but women may only be wives or whores. 'With what pleasure, with what delight, with an air how unembarrassed, did he *now* introduce, as his *wife*, to an elegant and respectable society, her whom he could have felt but a vain and inconsiderable triumph in introducing as his *mistress* to the gay and dissolute!' (Dacre 1997: 139). Only in this feminist reading may Victoria's later murder of the considerably younger daughter-figure Lilla be read as another revenge killing against the kind of woman society considers acceptable. But as we turned our attention to the two women, my students, especially the self-identified feminists, had more difficulty with a feminist interpretation.

To begin with, all the students recognized the novel's subversion of conservative Romanticist conceptions of femininity, such as passivity, affectionate mothering, female bonding, obedience to men, emotional weakness as in crying or fainting, and irrational childish behavior. Although Victoria's mother Laurina is a failure and is rightly blamed for not instilling higher moral principles in her daughter, she is also stereotypically feminine in her lusty desires and in her inability to resist temptation. As my students noted, Laurina simply moves from angelic mother to whorish adulteress. The descriptions of Lilla and Victoria replicate the angel/whore dichotomy less than a female–male opposition. Henriquez, whom Victoria tries to conquer with her feminine wiles and seductive arts, describes her in masculine not promiscuous terms. Compared with Lilla's

> trembling delicacy, her gentle sweetness, her sylph-like fragile form, ... [and] softloveliness, ... Victoria he viewed with almost absolute dislike; her strong though noble features, her dignified carriage, her authoritative tone – her boldness, her insensibility, her violence, all struck him with instinctive horror; so utterly opposite to the gentle Lilla, that when, with an assumed softness she [Victoria] deigned to caress her [Lilla], he almost trembled for her tender life, and compared the picture in his mind, to the snowy dove fondled by the ravenous vulture.
>
> (Dacre 1997: 196)

In class, the students were surprised that Henriquez's disgust did not arise from Victoria's promiscuity or marital infidelity (after all, she is married to his older brother). Rather, as my students noticed, Henriquez is horrified by Victoria's masculine traits: if she were a man, Henriquez's portrayal would hardly be considered negative.

Earlier in this honors class, we had discussed the potential lesbian undertones of Samuel Taylor Coleridge's poem 'Christabel' (1816) in which the evil Geraldine is described by Bard Bracy in a dream as a 'bright green snake' (Coleridge 2006: 537) wrapped around a dove, representing the innocent Christabel. While Coleridge's poem encourages us to read Geraldine as a phallic woman and, thereby, raises the spectre of homoeroticism (albeit problematically as lethal lesbianism), Henriquez's description of Victoria left these students with what they considered to be a jarring fusion of honorable masculine characteristics and a female body. In fact, as the novel progresses towards the climactic scene of Victoria repeatedly stabbing a scantily clad, starved and tortured Lilla, it became almost impossible for my class to see Victoria as a radical feminist fighting patriarchy. Perhaps 'the most bizarre scene', as Hoeveler rightly states, 'in the history of the female gothic' (Hoeveler 1997: 193), Lilla's death is both bloody and pornographic:

> Victoria, no longer mistress of her actions, nor desiring to be so, seized by her streaming tresses the fragile Lilla, and held her back. – With her poignard she stabbed her in the bosom, in the shoulder, and other parts: – the expiring Lilla sank upon her knees. – Victoria pursued her blows – she covered her fair body with innumerable wounds, then dashed her headlong over the edge of the steep. – Her fairy form bounded as it fell against the projecting crags of the mountain, diminishing to the sight of her cruel enemy, who followed it far as the eye could reach – those fair tresses dyed in crimson gore, that bleeding bosom.
>
> (Dacre 1997: 220–221)

Though the class assumed that Victoria is heterosexual, as with Megalena, they were able to discern the violent undertones of slasher lesbianism in the prolonged murder of Lilla. Even those male and female students toying with the notion of female masculinity were distressed by the novel's negative portrayal of non-normative masculinity (both in Zofloya and Victoria).

I suggest that Victoria's excessive rage over other more domesticated women combined with her confident pleasure in her own sexual prowess (portrayed as nymphomaniac) may be read as female masculinity that cannot express itself as anything but a pathologized masculinity. However, all students were dissatisfied with our analyses of Victoria. This was the case precisely because students could not relinquish their belief in an essentialist two-gender model. In other words, they had trouble with Victoria because they were unwilling, in Butler's terms, to 'trouble' gender, and, subsequently, to sever the bond between male bodies and masculinity, as Halberstam advocates. Following the lead of the few self-identified feminists who strove to interpret Dacre as a radical feminist of her times, none of the students articulated a queer reading of Victoria despite their collective close reading to suggest as much. At the end of the day, I believe these undergraduate students were more disturbed with what the novel's association of passivity with femininity and aggressive violence with masculinity implies about masculinity, whether it is embodied in so-called normative white male bodies, non-normative minority bodies, or non-normative female bodies.

Through our mutual professor–student heteroglossic exploration of discourses of masculinities in Charlotte Dacre's problematic gothic novel, what emerges are embittered and embattled masculinities that are no longer the sole preserve of male-born individuals. Moreover, our discussions of *Zofloya* expose the limitations of two-gendered essentialist models that cannot account for any kind of transgendered position. Masculinity, then, effectively gets relegated to a liminal position to which both females and males have access. Ultimately, this is Judith Halberstam's goal: to pry apart masculinity and male bodies and allow masculinity to occupy a fluid space. It is in the limited or contained dialogic space of fictional narratives as they are explored in the inevitably hegemonic classroom that masculinity remains an open issue and that female masculinity may emerge from the closet. In this queer space, reading for female masculinity empowers those students who wish to interpret Charlotte Dacre herself as feminist for transgressing the generic boundaries of what women writers could publish. In other words, by teaching Dacre's gothic novel in terms of the spectrum of masculinities, including foremost female masculinity, students can recover the radical feminist elements of an otherwise problematically misogynist female-authored text. In the hands of Dacre, the post-Sadean gothic may then function as an instrument for female liberation both for its author and its heroine. However, this liberation comes with a price. Dacre's gothic tale, if not read as queer gothic, requires renewed loyalty to the period's own xenophobic anxieties and discourses of racial and class hegemony.

Works cited

Butler, Judith. *Bodies that Matter: On the Discursive Limits of 'Sex.'* New York and London: Routledge, 1993.
——. *Gender Trouble: Feminism and the Subversion of Identity.* New York and London: Routledge, 1990.
Coleridge, Samuel Taylor. 'Christabel.' *Romanticism: An Anthology.* In (Ed.) Duncan Wu. Malden, MA: Blackwell, 2006. 639–655.

Dacre, Charlotte. *Zofloya, or The Moor: A Romance of the Fifteenth Century.* (Ed.) Adriana Craciun. Peterborough: Broadview P, 1997.

Fitzgerald, Lauren. 'Female Gothic and the Institutionalization of Gothic Studies.' *Gothic Studies* 6. 1 (May 2004): 8–18. 2004.

Halberstam, Judith. *Female Masculinity.* Durham and London: Duke University Press, 1998.

——. 'Shame and White Gay Masculinity.' *Social Text* 84–85 (Fall/Winter 2005): 219–233. 2005.

Heiland, Donna. *Gothic and Gender: An Introduction.* Malden, MA: Blackwell, 2004.

Hoeveler, Diane Long. 'Charlotte Dacre's *Zofloya*: A Case Study in Miscegenation as Sexual and Racial Nausea.' *European Romantic Review* 8.2 (Spring 1997): 185–199.

——. 'Teaching the Early Female Canon: Gothic Feminism in Wollstonecraft, Radcliffe, Austen, Dacre, and Shelley.' *Approaches to Teaching Gothic Fiction: The British and American Traditions.* (Eds) Diane Long Hoeveler and Tamar Heller. New York: The Modern Language Association of America, 2003. 105–114.

Knights, Ben. *Writing Masculinities: Male Narratives in Twentieth-Century Fiction.* New York: St. Martin's Press, 1999.

Miles, Robert. *Gothic Writing. 1750–1820. A Genealogy.* Manchester: Manchester University Press, 2002.

Palmer, Paulina. *Lesbian Gothic: Transgressive Fictions.* London: Cassell, 1999.

Stryker, Susan. 'The Transgender Issue: An Introduction.' *GLQ: A Journal of Lesbian and Gay Studies* 4.2 (1988): 145–158.

Williams, Anne. *The Art of Darkness: A Poetics of Gothic.* Chicago and London: University of Chicago Press, 1995.

5
Masculinity and Modernism: Teaching D.H. Lawrence[1]

Robert Burden

Introduction: The problem with teaching Lawrence

Teaching Lawrence and gender requires careful historical understanding. Female students who react to his anti-feminism, or male students who identify with his promotion of male leadership have to think beyond themselves – the situation of their own lives – and get back to the first contexts of Lawrence's writing. Like many writers of his generation, Lawrence registered shifts in gender coding. Indeed, he was particularly sensitive to them because his main concern was with the changing relationship between men and women. Before 1915 he supported wholeheartedly the 'feminization' of the culture. After 1915 he began to propose a 'new masculinity', a reassertion of degrees of patriarchy which by the end of the war took on more strident tones. Lawrence is an interesting case for gender studies because, as Hilary Simpson (1982) pointed out, his writing career 'spanned one of the most crucial periods in women's history', with its intense period of radical feminism up to 1914, and the anti-feminist reaction after 1918.[2] His 'post-war paranoia was not merely personal, but shared with many men of his generation'.[3] Furthermore, the sea change in sexual ideology was the more total in inverse proportion to the utter belief in the New Woman before the war, when Lawrence made categorical statements like: '(Men should) draw nearer to women, expose themselves to them, and be altered by them'.[4] The early Lawrence spent a lot of time in the company of radical women; and, the extent to which his modern women friends and lovers were also his literary collaborators is now much clearer.[5] After the war, Lawrence registers that general reaction to feminism which took the form of a belief that the changes had gone too far, that women had become too idealistic, too wilful, that they had succumbed to the general malaise of modernity in losing their 'natural feminine instinct' through mechanical adherence to the latest chic behaviour.[6] In terms of sexual politics, as recent feminist theory has so often argued, Lawrence is representative of the masculinist reaction of his day, striving to reassert itself at a time of post-war disillusion and dislocation.

In this chapter, I argue that Lawrence's masculinist doctrine undergoes degrees of deconstruction in fiction characterized by Lawrence himself as 'thought-adventure'.[7] Lawrence appears to test out the ideas expressed categorically in his essays and letters in his fiction. There is a consensus view that Lawrence promoted masculine supremacy in phallocentric and phallocratic fictions, especially in the so-called 'leadership novels' after the First World War where he appears to turn more explicitly against women. His writing from about 1918 expresses an 'hysterical masculinity', and one which is part of a general post-war reaction against the extent of female emancipation – appearing to express 'a male modernist fear of women's new power'.[8] Now, this consensus view has been variously challenged in recent criticism by claiming that it is precisely here, in these novels of the 1920s – *Aaron's Rod*, *Kangaroo* and *The Plumed Serpent* – that Lawrence was at his most experimental, his most modernist. The adventure of thought is read as an adventure of writing, in which the theories of masculinity are promoted in texts which in their play of linguistic and representational codes implicitly question fixed meaning and grand narratives, and traditional certainties of gender. In this chapter, I look at how to teach the characterological and textual instabilities in Lawrence's fiction that undermine the doctrinal assertions of male leadership, as he represents the post-war crisis of gender as a crisis of writing.

Hysterical masculinity and male leadership: Lawrence's masculinist doctrine

The new masculine anxiety is recalled by Lawrence in his late essay, 'The Real Thing' (1929):[9] 'Perhaps the greatest revolution of modern times is the emancipation of women...The fight was deeply bitter, and, it seems to me, it is won. It is even going beyond, and becoming a tyranny of women' (*P* 196). For Lawrence the sexual revolution has gone too far. Men have lost faith in themselves and have become submissive to the demands of women; demands that are not instinctive but willed, and therefore false. What began with men worshipping and glorifying women in literature, and then by the new cinema (so despised by Lawrence), has now ended up in a period (the 1920s) 'of the collapse of instinctive life-assurance in men', so that sex has become 'a great weapon and divider'. The new freedom for women has led to a greater unfreedom. So man's old self needs to die and be reborn into a renewed instinctive masculinity – a forgotten instinct. The 'real thing' is to 'feel right' by being 'in touch with the vivid life of the cosmos' (*P* 202).

This essay can, then, be taken as an example of Lawrence's most consistent principle, namely, the instinctive is the natural, and any attempt to change instinct by thought is an aberration. Lawrence writes of that modern woman, 'always tense and strung-up' who has 'less peace, less of that lovely womanly peace that flows like a river, less of the lovely, flower-like repose of a happy woman' (*P* 197).

Lawrence was not always so poetically sentimental. In 1918 he wrote in more categorical, programmatic terms to Katherine Mansfield:

> I do think a woman must yield some sort of precedence to a man, and he must take this precedence. I do think that men must go ahead absolutely in front of their women, without turning round to ask for permission or approval from their women. Consequently the women must follow as it were unquestioning.[10]

It is here that Lawrence's belief in the return to male superiority is first expressed. In the same year, 1918, he is writing the essays, 'Education of the People', soon to be followed by 'Democracy' (1919);[11] and, in 1921 *Fantasia of the Unconscious*, where he formulates in stark terms his critique of the ideals of liberal democracy, like equality – seeing it as unnatural, and an attempt at the kind of mechanical process of standardization in modern industry and mass society – and the traditional role of motherhood in the upbringing of children which he accuses of destroying the child by 'emotional and psychic provocation' (*P* 621). Maternal love is now a specific target for Lawrence, driven no doubt by a revision of his own case as represented in *Sons and Lovers* (1913). However, the denunciation of the idealization of the Mother as *Magna Mater* is also evident in *Women in Love*. The 'deadly idealism' of idolizing the mother – child relationship has lead to 'the grovelling degeneracy of Mariolatory!' (*P* ibid.). Lawrence insists that women are 'devouring mothers' dominating men, treating them as boys. Lawrence warns women to beware 'the mother's boy!'[12] In *Mr Noon* Johanna complains about those mothers' darlings, 'all Hamlets, obsessed by their mothers, and we're supposed to be all Ophelias, and go and drown ourselves'.[13]

Lawrence's post-war essays are, in Hilary Simpson's words, 'a violent and often sadistic attack on democracy and liberal idealism, in the ranting style that now begins to characterize Lawrence's writing'.[14] It is in this tone and style that Lawrence insists on a new masculinity which will abolish the kinds of gender relatedness sought in *The Rainbow* and *Women in Love*. Henceforth there will be a return to the hierarchical order of Patriarchy, but not simply in the senses analysed by Kate Millett (1969) in *Sexual Politics*. Lawrence's Patriarchy will be based on more ancient models close to the Old Testament Church Fathers, or a pre-Columbian 'natural' aristocracy (in *The Plumed Serpent*). It would not be the last time in the twentieth century that, in the general chaos of post-war dislocation, masculinist mythic solutions will be found for the problems of political realities.

The Great War has also played its part in ruining 'manhood': 'These are the heroes of the Great War. They went and fought like heroes, truly, to prove their manhood'.[15] But they did this from a wrong idea of manhood. Like 'heroic automata', they understood themselves within the given masculine codes of heroism, unquestioningly believing they were making the world safe for democracy. They 'never faced the strange war-passions that came up in themselves'. They believed the world would be the same again. For Lawrence, the opportunity for a new world has been missed:

> Out of the strange passion that arose in men during the war, there should have risen the germ of a new idea, and the nucleus of a new way of feeling. Out of the strange revulsions of the days of horror, there should have resulted a fierce revision of existing values... and the fierce repudiation of false values should have ripened the seed of a whole new way of experience, the clue to a whole new era.[16]

Post-war man is disillusioned, disoriented and deracinated. T.S. Eliot's 'hollow man' wanders in the wasteland of post-war England. Lawrence will take himself and his fictional protagonists abroad in search of alternative models of man – as political and spiritual leaders.

In 1925 Lawrence declared that: 'The reign of love is passing, and the reign of power is coming again'.[17] But we should be clear about what Lawrence means by 'power'. He differentiates between 'will' and 'power'. The Nietzschean 'will-to-power', as Lawrence understands it, is just 'bullying' – like the force imposed by the fascist dictator on the masses which Lawrence had witnessed in Italy, and which is emergent in *Aaron's*

Rod. Lawrence works through the problems of power and leadership in this and the two subsequent novels, *Kangaroo* and *The Plumed Serpent.*

Power is beyond the egotistical will, it 'comes to us...from beyond'.[18] It cannot be grasped through 'willing and intellectualizing', it is 'self-generated'.[19] It comes from 'living' which consists in 'doing what you really, vitally want to do: what the *life* in you wants to do, not what your ego imagines you want to do'.[20] Lawrence's theory of power derives from the idea of the charismatic leader common in political theories of the time[21] combined with the notion of a 'natural' aristocracy of prophetic artists or writers, like himself, who would lead the people by example into an era of cultural regeneration. The political version of this is played out in *Kangaroo*, an Australian staging of the political theatre of 1920s Europe. The process of a cultural regeneration through spiritual revivalism is dramatized in *The Plumed Serpent.*

Power can be destructive and creative. But in Lawrence's sense, argued for in his essays, true power is always instinctive; and, by implication, when responsibly used is creative: it always 'puts something new into the world'.[22] It is up to the new man to regenerate the culture in the 'reign of power'. In *Fantasia of the Unconscious* he blames the whole post-war cultural crisis on living 'from the head' instead of 'from the spontaneous centres' of the self.[23] His solution to the crisis is quite explicit:

> We can't go on as we are. Poor, nerve-worn creatures, fretting our lives away and hating to die because we have never lived. The secret is to commit into the hands of the sacred few the responsibility which now lies like torture on the mass. Let the few leaders be increasingly responsible for the whole.[24]

However, in order to make it absolutely clear that these few are men, Lawrence resorts to a reductionist conservative theory of sexual difference: women are naturally passive, men active; women belong in the domestic sphere, men in the public sphere;[25] women live by feeling, men by a sense of purpose;[26] man is the great adventurer with the passion of collective purpose.[27] Thus, Lawrence's new masculinity is based on old gender stereotypes.

Fortunately, Lawrence's women characters are not as one-dimensional as the doctrine seems to demand. It is in the fiction of the 1920s, contemporary with these discussions, that Lawrence takes the woman's question and the reaction to it in the form of the new masculinity on a series of 'thought-adventures'. What makes these works still interesting is the way they both assert and deconstruct the new masculinist doctrine. Knights (1999) sees in Lawrence's writing a paradox: 'that one of the most avowedly phallocentric writers is in fact engaged in a critical account of masculinity which inevitably raises questions about the nature of male being and male power'.[28]

Masculinity and literary modernism

There is of course a cultural history of masculinity in the early twentieth century, which provides a context for reading and teaching Lawrence. Middleton (1992) explains how men began to reflect on themselves as a gender, asking themselves and each other what it meant to be a man, after feminism had been raising consciousness about gender difference. Men turned their gaze inward and began questioning culturally constructed images of masculinity, the process from boyhood to manhood, manliness, and their position of power, social expectations and conventional responsibilities. The danger in such self-reflexivity is that men might succumb to fantasies of 'self-aggrandizement'.[29] Literary Modernism was very preoccupied with the issues of masculine subjectivity, and in a more self-conscious way than popular culture at the time. Lawrence belongs to this moment in the early history of twentieth-century masculinity. For him, as for others of his generation, the 'relation between subjectivity and power' was – as it still is – 'difficult to articulate'.[30] Man only became consciously gendered once patriarchy was questioned as the dominant mode of socio-cultural formation. Rethinking 'existing concepts of gender and identity in terms of the relations between society, reason and emotion'[31] enables a theorizing of masculinity as a preliminary to cultural change.

The First World War was a focus for the crisis in masculinity. Traditional codes of heroism and cowardice, patriotism and sacrifice, violence and pacifism could no longer be taken for granted. On the Western Front the new war machine was a transpersonal instrument of mass destruction. At home the force of changing social and cultural values were partly the result of the women's movement. State propaganda was no longer going unquestioned, especially in Modernist writing, which represented a subjectivity at odds with itself. Lawrence's *The Rainbow* has often been analysed in these philosophical terms.[32] As Middleton argues, in *The Rainbow* the history of consciousness is a gendered history, as the men characters struggle to form 'an inward gaze', while the women characters from the outset cope better with the pressures of modern subjectivity. For Middleton, the portrait of Will Brangwen 'is one of the first important analyses of modern masculine sexuality in

English writing'.[33] Traditional codes of manliness, virility and patriarchy are increasingly under threat in the novel from, in Lawrence's
words, 'woman becoming individual, self-responsible, taking her own
initiative'.[34] Anna's fight with and victory over Will, and Ursula's
destruction of Skrebensky, just as Gudrun's battle for supremacy with
Gerald in *Women in Love*, are all key instances of modern masculinities
succumbing to the new, independent-minded woman. And this type of
female character persists in Lawrence's 'leadership' fiction of the 1920s
as a radical voice, albeit in the margins of the text. I'm thinking here of
characters like Harriett Somers in *Kangaroo*, and Josephine Ford or the
Marchesa in *Aaron's Rod*. In *The Rainbow*, the men are supposed to learn
about their emotions and their sexuality from the women. Yet it seems
that the men will not change that easily because the old masculine
codes are deeply ingrained, and the pressures to be a man are sometimes overwhelming. Will Brangwen, the craftsman, devotes himself to
Gothic church art; Anton Skrebensky, the soldier, marries the colonel's
daughter and is posted to India; Gerald Crich, the captain of industry,
commits suicide. The more successfully 'feminized' man, Rupert Birkin,
already shows signs of the emergent new masculinity: first, as he feels the
need for a close relationship with a man – although the precise form
that should take is left teasingly ambiguous – and he thus foreshadows
the relationships between Rawdon Lilly and Aaron Sissons in *Aaron's
Rod*, Cooley and Somers in *Kangaroo*, and Ramon and Cipriano in *The
Plumed Serpent*; and, second, as he reacts violently to the power of a
woman's love, which he wants to destroy for ever because it is so wilful
and insistent. Birkin wants to get beyond the 'messiness' of sex, into a
more impersonal relationship; and in this he prefigures Aaron Sissons
walking out of his marriage and trying to live without sex altogether.

The problem of male intimacy first emerges in Lawrence's fiction in
the Gerald–Birkin relationship in *Women in Love*: they only get close
to intimate physical contact by staging a naked wrestling contest. In
Aaron's Rod, Lilly massages Aaron's sick body, in a bolder moment of
homoeroticism on Lawrence's part. Yet the role model is that of mothering the sick boy. Indeed, here where the men try to go it alone
without women, domesticity has only female models, and it is described
as such in text as the men take it in turns to be mother. Homosocial
bonding is a crucial focus in Lawrence's writing (even as early as *Sons and
Lovers* where Paul Morel bonds with his erstwhile rival Baxter Dawes).
However, Lawrence remains ambivalent towards homosexuality. There
is a tacit heterosexual imperative that runs through the fiction, and a

repressed homoerotic desire that sometimes threatens to express itself. As Jonathan Dollimore argues:

> running through it all is the problem, or the promise, of the homo-
> erotic. It is made to carry the burden of *Women in Love*'s deepest
> tension or contradiction: it is both the agent of death, reduction and
> degeneration, and the source of the deepest possibility of redemp-
> tion. The extent of Lawrence's ambivalence towards homosexuality
> is striking.[35]

Lawrence's writing in the period of Modernism coincides with key discussions on sexuality and gender difference in Freudian psychoana-lysis, the sexual theories of Edward Carpenter and Havelock Ellis,[36] Marie Stopes' *Married Love* (1916), as well as the assault on Victorian taboos and prudery in literature.[37] Carpenter promoted a more open recogni-tion of homosexuality, which in itself enabled the sexuality of women to emerge as a phenomenon and a discourse in its own right. Gender difference drew attention to the sexuality of men, but the discussion took long to emerge. Indeed, men developed a consciousness of their gender and sexuality because of the First World War, as the general transvaluation of values affected traditional masculinity too, making it visible and questionable.

Lawrence's work clearly belongs to the crisis in masculinity which really began in earnest in the early twentieth century and is still with us today. What is important, however, is to get the students to notice that Lawrence's search for a new language to express feelings and sexuality contrasted markedly with mainstream Modernism. T.S. Eliot founded a whole theory of literature on ways of containing emotions in an accept-able aesthetic form. If, like female sexuality, emotional outburst was dangerous then the 'objective correlative' would textualize it in such a way that the reader or spectator could experience it impersonally – at a safe, aesthetic distance. Lawrence rejected Eliot's neo-classicism for expressive theories first developed by the Romantics. His representations of moments of emotional crisis are closer to the Symbolists, and some-times to the Expressionists, both inheritors of the Romantic tradition of individual inner expressivity. Lawrence's writing is a locus for the expression of emotion, masculine or feminine, against the grain of the conventional gender designation of the emotional sphere as exclus-ively female. In *The Rainbow*, the principal male characters struggle to express their feelings, and need the female characters to help them do this. How would a mixed age seminar group – with different levels of maturity and abilities to express their sexuality openly (indeed in groups where usually the female outnumber the male students) – respond to Lawrence's demands?

Lawrence's 'male leadership' writing engages fully in the crisis of masculinity in the post-war world, telling stories of men questioning their lives with women, their sexuality, sexual difference, in fiction which tried to imagine masculinist alternatives to the cultural crisis. After they fail to go it alone, male characters tend to be involved in collective alternatives for men only – a political group planning to reassert itself on the public stage, as in *Kangaroo*; or a religious movement planning a return to a more authoritarian ritual order, as in *The Plumed Serpent* – public arenas where men's feelings can traditionally express themselves.

Lawrence draws attention to the gendered constructions of narratives. These fictions are themselves stories men invent and tell each other. They are stories of quest, travel, adventure, leadership. They allow men to imagine a superior place for themselves at a time of crisis in masculinity. Moreover, they are ancient, traditional masculine narratives. As Knights (1999) has argued, masculinity is more than gender difference, or male encoding; it is at the same time a way of telling stories.[38] And as we can see from a cursory glance at the critical reception of Lawrence, male and female critics have told different stories about Lawrence, just as older teachers appear to be more committed to the continuing relevance of his work. What they all should acknowledge, though, is that Lawrence's masculine stories are often framed in the ironies that destabilize their truth. And these ironies should enable us to question the force of the masculinist argument. He does this by giving women a debunking role in a world of idealist men, or by positioning women as focalizers with mixed feelings about male supremacy. For example, in *Kangaroo* (Lawrence's most explicitly political novel) Harriett Somers casts a shadow over men's idealism, and her husband's involvement:

> What is all their revolution bosh to me! There have been revolutions enough, in my opinion, and each one more foolish than the last. And this will be the most foolish of the lot. And what have *you* got to do with revolutions, you petty and conceited creature? You and revolutions! You're not big enough, not grateful enough to do anything real. I give you my energy and my life, and you want to put me aside as if I was a charwoman.[39]

In *The Plumed Serpent*, a western woman, Kate Leslie tries to understand the contradictions of Mexico, and is both repelled and later attracted to its macho culture. The one novel where the woman's viewpoint is marginalized is *Aaron's Rod*. Aaron Sissons' attempt to live without women is represented at the narrative level by his exclusive masculinist reading of the situation, often objectively and without moral scruples as he abandons his wife and children on Christmas Eve for an itinerant existence as a flute-player. It is a masculine story certainly appealing to male more than female readers, a solidarity already represented in the degrees of male bonding in the text. Yet, because Lawrence allows the women's voices in the text to undermine any doctrinal masculinist certainty, we can read the text against itself, and against Lawrence's less ambiguous essays, by repositioning what is marginal. The spirit of this critical female – even feminist – voice is already evident in *Mr Noon*, where Johanna's sister complains that 'all Englishmen are Hamlets, they are so self-conscious over their feelings, and they are therefore so false ... these men with their tragical man-hysterics!'[40]

Aaron's Rod has been traditionally read as doctrinally anti-feminist. But the text is not so consistently transparent. It offers us degrees of deconstruction at different levels. We should look to the margins of the text to decentre the masculinist ideology. A teacher might get the students to find answers to the following questions:

- How exclusive is the male perspective?
- How absolute are the dominant anti-feminist ideas?
- How certain is the Lawrence of the essays of the ground on which his new masculinity is built?
- Can we trust the tale?

There are two points of entry into this deconstructive reading of *Aaron*. First, the marginalized role and speech of the women characters which casts a shadow of doubt over all the masculinist assertions; second, the meta-narrative intrusions of the narrator which undermine the authority and reliability of the male stories. A different truth emerges, therefore, in the voices of those marginalized women characters, and the narrator who breaks through the otherwise exclusive perspective of the main protagonist.

In order for a novel to maintain the coherence of the ideology it represents it has to maintain a determinate silence on what might threaten to tell a different story.[41] *Aaron's Rod* is a *locus classicus* for the representation of an ideology – the new masculinity. However, it is questioned from outside that ideology by the critical voice of the feminine speaking from the margins of the text. Rereading the text through feminist theory which is already in the text demonstrates that the authority of the masculinist ideology is based on its exclusivity and its marginalization of the feminine – which might create an interesting dilemma for articulate women in the classroom. What is interesting about *Aaron* is that it already prepares the ground for the woman student or feminist critic through the women characters in the novel. Whilst the masculine ideology of Lawrence's post-war essays remains internally coherent and can only be accepted or rejected by the reader as a matter of belief, the novel with its play of narrative perspective already offers the reader the possibility of rejecting the dominant ideas it is trying to promote. In this respect the fiction demonstrates the limits of the ideas in the essays. And this gives students the licence to reread the essay and letters back through the fiction.

Aaron's wife is only seen from his view, in both senses as focalized and as ideology, except once when on his last visit home she has it out with him, accusing him of not being a man (with all its traditional connotations). Most significant, though, is when she says: 'You ran away from me, without telling me what you've got against me' (*AR* 125). He can only reply that he went because he had had enough. Her conventional way of seeing things wins our sympathy as it breaks the monopoly the man has on the truth – the new masculinity seems rather shaky as an ideology.

Josephine Ford, the representative modern, metropolitan woman-artist, is given the privileged role of focalizer at the opera through which we get biting satire of the sham representation of Verdi's Egypt. Lawrence marks her exceptionality by giving her 'some aboriginal American in her blood' despite her self-conscious arrogance (*AR* 46). She takes the initiative, inviting Aaron to dinner, gets him to talk about himself, and finds him inwardly indifferent to her, if not to everything (*AR* 65). She takes the lead sexually, seducing him in spite of his avowed refusal of women and love. Her view of him, and her behaviour establish a level of plausibility which undermines his version later that sex with her was the direct cause of his illness (we do not get the sex described). She represents the greatest threat to the new, vulnerable male. She is the second female character whose voice has refused to remain marginalized.

Lady Franks is the strongest figure of traditional feminine idealism. She is satirized for her belief in her work of reform, and the 'restoring of woman to her natural throne' (*AR* 147). She disapproves of Aaron's attitude to life, even though he can impress her with his music. Again we get a critical perspective, albeit from a representative type mostly at the receiving end of the masculinist attack. She reads him from her own firm ideological position.

The Marchesa is also a critical voice incensed by the general misogynistic attitude of the young men (*AR* 236ff.). Although she is seduced by Aaron's music, as he revives her singing and her sexuality with his phallic flute, it is she who scripts his role in her *opera buffa*, despite the sex-scenes being told from his privileged focalization. His earnest and deliberate dominance of her is undermined by her easy acceptance of his explanation that he cannot continue the affair because he is still attached to his wife. His lie is clear to us; but it matters less to her because the rules of the affair are what count. Her casualness is a symptom of her experience in the game of adultery with a younger man. This genre (with its implications of comic opera) offers the reader a completely different perspective in its value as light entertainment to that of Aaron's masculine seriousness. Indeed, we are shown by an older, wiser woman that he takes himself far too seriously. We are again made suspicious of his motives for giving up the affair. Furthermore, just as he turns her into the object of his desire, fetishizing her body in part-objects, so she for her part uses him as her 'fetish', a magic, phallic implement for her pleasure (*AR* 272–273). Although it is Aaron who becomes aware of this, and thus it could be read as yet another male fantasy, it seems plausible that it is the woman's view because of the way she sets up the affair and uses the younger man, with the utmost discretion.

These women's voices speak, each in their own way, from the margins, and give us a vantage point from which to read the masculinist ideology against itself. Students could look for the details in text and discuss the effectiveness of these voices: are they all effective enough to counter the masculine ideology? And are we now being told that it is not so easy to accept masculinity as a return to natural instinct, given its constructedness as a force to counter the perceived dominance of the New Woman? Don't motives for the male attitudes towards women appear in their contexts suspicious? Personal fears or war-affected weariness are often talked up into a frenzy of misogyny and idealist solutions, as they are in Lawrence's essays. Yet in the novel they seem to lead nowhere, except further away. Travel is the only remedy offered for the crisis of masculinity. The assumptions on which the masculinist ideology relies for its authority are questioned by what the women say and do in the text. These assumptions are also in doubt because of Aaron's inability or unwillingness to commit himself to Lilly as the new leader.

However, the decisive point is that the reversal of an opposition is no guarantee of a fundamental change. As Derrida insisted, all oppositions are violent hierarchies, the first term being in the position of power.[42] If for Lawrence the wilful woman was dominant in the post-war culture, then does not reversing the hierarchy give power back to the men? And does not the situation still remain one of power and subjugation? We need to go one step further and, by understanding the assumptions on which the binary of male–female relies, displace the power struggle by changing the terms of the social formation. How you do this is another matter. This does not invalidate the method of deconstruction – and importantly a method that should enable the students to challenge the masterful pedagogy of the Lawrencian teacher.

The role of the narrator (and the teacher), as distinct from the focalizing agents, is also a destabilizing one. Like the narrating persona of *Mr Noon*, only less anarchic, the narrator of *Aaron* breaks the flow of the story with meta-narrative comments: 'Our story will not yet see the daylight' (*AR* 39); 'Our story continues by night' (*AR* 45); 'Behold our hero' (*AR* 131). And in doing this, a different relationship is established with the reader (and the teacher with the students): a pact at a meta-narrative level demanding a satirical attitude to the fiction from the reader. We are thus at several removes from the dominant masculinist views of Aaron (as spokesman for the Lawrence of the essays and letters): first, through his distancing and estranging perspective; second, through the further distance created by the marginalized women's voices; third, through the doubts Aaron has about Lilly and the idea of being able to go it alone; and, last, through the self-conscious narrator. None of this will mitigate the force of the misogyny for those readers who, seeking to prove a case against Lawrence, will be offended. The question to ask, though, is why Lawrence writes a novel characterized by degrees of play and instability which undermines the authority of ideas he appears to believe in at the time? Did he want to pre-empt the attack from his women readers? Should we really trust the tale?

There are two other intrusions from the narrator which have more significance. The first is when he discusses how he has to represent Aaron's self-understanding in a way that Aaron could not. What is 'risen to half consciousness' in the character, is made explicit by the narrator in the form of commentary; but one that is also meta-commentary (*AR* 163). Aaron thinks deeper thoughts in music, while the narrator has to translate them into words. And here the narrator with the comic persona of the English tradition (dominant in *Mr Noon*) turns modernist too: 'If I, as word-user, must translate his deep conscious vibrations into finite words, that is my own business. I do but make a translation of the man. He would speak in music. I speak with words' (*AR* 164). Aaron is not as articulate with words as the narrator; and the 'gentle reader' should not 'grumble' at this fact, but merely decide whether the thoughts attributed to Aaron are plausible (*AR* ibid.). The second is just an aside, but a telling one. Aaron has written a letter to Sir William which contains the gist of Lawrence's current philosophy and the narrator comments: 'When a man writes a letter to himself, it is a pity to post it to somebody else. Perhaps the same is true of a book' (*AR* 264). If Lawrence felt in the early 1920s that writing was like sending a letter to yourself, then we are reminded that it must have been difficult for him to imagine a reader because of the continual difficulties he had getting his books published after the banning of *The Rainbow* in 1915. Moreover, this might account for the presence of characters as readers in his fiction since *Women in Love*, and the extreme frustration shown by his now infamous assault on the female reader in *Mr Noon*. And this is all a much more serious matter than just playful meta-narrative markers about the story's progress. It goes to the heart of the representationalist crisis of Modernism.

I suggest, then, that if Lawrence's novels of the 1920s are examples of this process of self-questioning, then we need to assess the extent of his critical stance towards the new masculinity which he promotes aggressively at the same time in his essays. A serious methodological point that arises from this approach is that we should be wary of reading the fiction exclusively through the essays. It might be more useful to read the essays and letters from the critical perspectives of the fiction – which might be simply done by handing out extracts for comments. This process should find the grounds for an effective challenge to monolithic readings of Lawrence's truth like those of the early feminist attack, which begins with John Middleton Murry's (1931) character assassination of Lawrence and reaches its high point with Kate Millett (1969).[43] To quote Knights once again:

> To set about re-writing male narratives was to risk rendering the whole subject unstable, so Lawrence's later programme was not simply a performance of a script supplied by his own neuroses, but a response to problems he had himself courageously opened up.[44]

Students should become aware of the extent to which, in Lawrence's fiction, gender becomes mobile as the characters move out of the traditional feminine and masculine spheres of self-definition, and travel in search of new identity. The rooted Brangwen existence of the opening of *The Rainbow* will give way to deracination for which the restless women are initially responsible. Aaron Sissons, Rawdon Lilly, Lovatt Somers and Kate Leslie – all as part-selves of a travelling author – are representations of the new mobile self in the writing of the 1920s. The first three characters are in flight from the feminized world of post-war England in search of a new masculinity. Kate Leslie is in flight from herself in a story which attempts to reverse the historical process of modernity and the feminization of culture. However, by imagining in *The Plumed Serpent* the consequences of a return to pre-Columbian patriarchy, and filtering the story through the critical views of a modern woman, Lawrence draws attention to the cultural constructedness of what is otherwise passed off as an ancient instinct. The female protagonist creates enough doubt through a modern, disarming irony to make the ground un-firm on which the new patriarchal grand narrative is founded. In Lawrence's fiction, gender difference was being destabilized in a narrative Modernism. The representation of masculinity and femininity in these novels undermines the reductionism of any ideologically narrow criticism, and should enable a critical perspective on the gender stereotypes on display in contemporary culture.

Summary

I have argued in this paper that Lawrence belongs to the ongoing discussion within Modernism of the politics of gender; but also that his fictional narratives are not monolithic expressions of doctrine, but instead the masculinist ideas in them are partly questioned by the texts which try to promote them. The critical women's voices create ironies. Lawrence is at his most sceptical in parts of *Aaron's Rod* and practically all of *Kangaroo*, his most adventurous writing. The doubts are played down in *The Plumed Serpent*, yet the deconstructive position of the principal female character teases out the contradictions in the text to an extent that the earlier feminist readings, for instance, could not achieve by exclusively concentrating on the sexual politics. What emerges is the recognition of a writing which, while seeking to express a doctrine of masculine supremacy in reaction to the perceived wilfulness of modern women and the general post-war cultural disintegration, represents degrees of modernist experiment. Thus it is that textual instabilities undermine the assertions of ideology. In this, the 'leadership' novels belong to the whole play of writing that began with *Women in Love*, and includes *The Lost Girl* and *Mr Noon*.

The textual instabilities, and the shifting relationship between the essays, letters and fiction, should impact on teaching the text: a less authoritarian approach to Modernism, gender and Lawrence. The students should not be allowed to wait for the truth from the one who is supposed to know;[45] nor should they hope that the canonical text has a single truth. But also shifting truths and textual instabilities should not be allowed to lead to interpretive anarchy but encourage the open-minded investigation of writing in open-endedness and its different genres.

Methodologically speaking, I would first point out that reading the essential oppositions against their assumptions is a strategy of re-appropriating the text in an understanding that goes beyond its own self-understanding, and, at the same time challenging those readings which are parasitic on that self-understanding. Second, I've read the text of *Aaron's Rod* as self-deconstructing, as a self-conscious play of writing that always already rehearses the critical disputes of its reception.[46] In doing this, I'm working with the assumption that monologic, narrowly ideological reading is deconstructed by the play of meaning in the text, by the destabilizing strategies of writing. As Derrida asserted:

> some works which are highly 'phallocentric' in their semantics [he has Joyce in mind], their intended meaning, even their theses, can produce paradoxical effects, paradoxically antiphallocentric through the audacity of a writing which in fact disturbs the order or the logic of phallocentrism or touches on limits where things are reversed: in that case the fragility, the precariousness, even the ruin of order is more apparent.[47]

Notes

1. An earlier version of this paper without the pedagogic discussion was published in Simonetta de Filippis and Nick Ceramella (eds), *D.H. Lawrence and Literary Genres* (Napoli: Loffredo Editore, 2004).
2. Hilary Simpson, *D.H. Lawrence and Feminism* (London: Croom Helm, 1982), 15.
3. Ibid.
4. Letter to Arthur McLeod 2 June 1914, respectively. Cited in Simpson, op. cit., 16.
5. Cf. Simpson's last chapter. The collaboration was not changed by the war. *The Boy in the Bush* (1924) was a reworking of Mollie Skinner's text; and Lawrence had plans to write a novel with Mabel Dodge Luhan called 'The Wilful Woman', a fragment of which is extant (1922).

6. The term 'feminism' had a largely pejorative sense in the 1920s, as it entered more common usage. As Buhle explains, 'its meaning [was] encapsulated in the pejorative "careerism." Feminism came to signify masculinism, and little else'. Mari Jo Buhle, *Feminism and its Discontents* (Cambridge, Massachusetts and London: Harvard University Press, 1998), 13.

7. *Kangaroo* (London: The Penguin edition of the Cambridge D.H. Lawrence, 1997), 279.

8. Marianne Dekoven, 'Modernism and Gender' in Michael Levenson (ed.), *The Cambridge Companion to Modernism* (Cambridge: Cambridge University Press, 1999), 174.

9. Reprinted in *Phoenix: The Posthumous Papers of D.H. Lawrence* (London: Heinemann, 1936). All page references for this and other essays, which appear in *Phoenix* are to this edition, and will be indicated by (*P*) in text.

10. 5 December 1918 in *The Selected Letters of D.H. Lawrence* compiled and edited by James T. Boulton (Cambridge: Cambridge University Press, 1997), 163.

11. Both not published until 1936.

12. 'On Being a Man' (1923) reprinted in *Reflections On the Death of a Porcupine and Other Essays* (1925), edited by Michael Herbert (Cambridge: Cambridge University Press, 1988), 216.

13. *Mr Noon* (London: The Penguin edition of the Cambridge D.H. Lawrence, 1996), 124.

14. Simpson (1982), op. cit., 93.

15. 'On Being a Man', loc. cit., 219.

16. Ibid., 221.

17. 'Blessed are the Powerful' in *Reflections on the Death of a Porcupine*, op. cit., 321.

18. Ibid.

19. Ibid., 322.

20. Ibid., 323.

21. For the sources of Lawrence's political ideas, see Rick Rylance, 'Lawrence's Politics' in Keith Brown (ed.), *Rethinking Lawrence* (Buckingham: Open University Press, 1990); Peter Fjagesund, *The Apocalyptic World of D.H. Lawrence* (London and Oslo: Norwegian University Press, 1991); Anne Fernihough, *D.H. Lawrence: Aesthetics and Ideology* (Oxford: Clarendon Press, 1993).

22. 'Blessed are the Powerful', loc. cit., 323

23. *Fantasia of the Unconscious and Psychoanalysis and the Unconscious* (London: Penguin, 1971), 83.

24. Ibid., 88.

25. Ibid., 97.

26. Ibid., 102–103.

27. Ibid., 109–110.

28. Ben Knights, *Writing Masculinities: Male Narratives in Twentieth-Century Fiction* (London: Macmillan, 1999), 89.

29. Peter Middleton, *The Inward Gaze: Masculinity and Subjectivity in Modern Culture* (London: Routledge, 1992), 9.

30. Ibid., 10.

31. Ibid., 12–13.

32. Cf. Michael Bell, *D.H. Lawrence: Language and Being* (Cambridge: Cambridge University Press, 1991); Anne Fernihough (1993), op. cit.; Fiona Becket, *D.H. Lawrence: The Thinker as Poet* (London: Macmillan, 1997).
33. Ibid., 75.
34. Letter to Edward Garnett 22 April 1914.
35. Jonathan Dollimore, *Death, Desire and Loss in Western Culture* (London: Allen Lane/Penguin, 1998), 270–271.
36. Edward Carpenter, *Civilization, its Cause and Cure* (London: Swan Sonnenschein 1889); Henry Havelock Ellis, *Studies in the Psychology of Sex, 7 volumes* (1897–1928, revised edition, 1936).
37. For a well-informed study see Sally Ledger, *The New Woman: Fiction and Feminism at the Fin de Siècle* (Manchester: Manchester University Press, 1997).
38. Ben Knights (1999), op. cit.
39. *Kangaroo* op. cit., 162.
40. *Mr Noon* op. cit., 196.
41. This is the classic Althusserian argument best exemplified by Pierre Macherey in *A Theory of Literary Production* (London: Routledge, 1979. First published 1965). Edward Said also redeploys it in *Culture and Imperialism* (London: Chatto and Windus, 1993).
42. Cf. Jacques Derrida, *Positions* (3 interviews) (London: Athlone Press, 1981. First published 1972).
43. John Middleton Murry, *Son of Woman* (London: Jonathan Cape, 1931); Kate Millett, *Sexual Politics* (New York and London: Virago, 1969).
44. Ben Knights op. cit., 84.
45. 'le supposé à savoir' – Lacan's critique of the analytic situation where the analysand's expectation of the analyst's authority is denied. The question of knowledge and authority in teaching might be further investigated through the Lacanian model. But this would require another paper.
46. For more detailed discussion of masculinity in Lawrence's leadership writing, see Robert Burden, *Radicalizing Lawrence* (Amsterdam: Rodopi, 2000) Chapters 4 and 5.
47. Jacques Derrida, 'That Strange Institution Called Literature: An Interview with Jacques Derrida', in *Acts of Literature*, edited and introduced by Derek Attridge (New York and London: Routledge, 1992), 50.

Works cited

Primary literature

Boulton, James T. (ed.) *The Selected Letters of D.H. Lawrence*. Cambridge: Cambridge University Press, 1997.
Lawrence, D.H. *Aaron's Rod*. London: The Penguin edition of the Cambridge D.H. Lawrence, 1995. First published 1922.
Lawrence, D.H. *Kangaroo*. London: The Penguin edition of the Cambridge D.H. Lawrence, 1997. First published 1923.
Lawrence, D.H. *Fantasia of the Unconscious and Psychoanalysis and the Unconscious*. London: Penguin, 1971. First published 1923.
Lawrence, D.H. *Mr Noon*. London: The Penguin edition of the Cambridge D.H. Lawrence, 1996. First published 1984.

Lawrence, D.H. *Phoenix: The Posthumous Papers of D.H. Lawrence*. Edited by Edward D. McDonald. London: Heinemann, 1936.
Lawrence, D.H. *Reflections on the Death of a Porcupine and Other Essays*. Edited by Michael Herbert. Cambridge: Cambridge University Press, 1988. First published 1925.

Secondary literature

Becket, Fiona. *D.H. Lawrence: The Thinker as Poet*. London: Macmillan, 1997.
Bell, Michael. *D.H. Lawrence: Language and Being*. Cambridge: Cambridge University Press, 1991.
Buhle, Mari Jo. *Feminism and its Discontents*. Cambridge, Massachusetts and London: Harvard University Press, 1998.
Burden, Robert. *Radicalizing Lawrence*. Amsterdam: Rodopi, 2000.
Dekoven, Marianne. 'Modernism and Gender' in Michael Levenson (ed.), *The Cambridge Companion to Modernism*. Cambridge: Cambridge University Press, 1999.
Derrida, Jacques. *Positions* (3 interviews). London: Athlone Press, 1981. First published 1972.
Derrida, Jacques. 'That Strange Institution Called Literature: An Interview with Jacques Derrida', in *Acts of Literature*, Edited and Introduced by Derek Attridge. New York and London: Routledge, 1992.
Dollimore, Jonathan. *Death, Desire and Loss in Western Culture*. London: Allen Lane/Penguin, 1998.
Fernihough, Anne. *D.H. Lawrence: Aesthetics and Ideology*. Oxford: Clarendon Press, 1993.
Filippis, Simonetta de and Nick Ceramella (eds). *D. H. Lawrence and Literary Genres*. Napoli: Loffredo Editore, 2004.
Fjagesund, Peter. *The Apocalyptic World of D. H. Lawrence*. London and Oslo: Norwegian University Press, 1991.
Knights, Ben. *Writing Masculinities: Male Narratives in Twentieth-Century Fiction*. London: Macmillan, 1999.
Ledger, Sally. *The New Woman: Fiction and Feminism at the Fin de Siècle*. Manchester: Manchester University Press, 1997.
Middleton, Peter. *The Inward Gaze: Masculinity and Subjectivity in Modern Culture*. London: Routledge, 1992.
Millett, Kate. *Sexual Politics*. New York and London: Virago, 1969.
Murry, John Middleton. *Son of Woman*. London: Jonathan Cape, 1931.
Rylance, Rick. 'Lawrence's Politics' in Keith Brown (ed.), *Rethinking Lawrence*. Buckingham: Open University Press, 1990.
Simpson, Hilary. *D.H. Lawrence and Feminism*. London: Croom Helm, 1982.

6
Gender and Narrative Form[1]

Ruth Page

Texts, technology and gender

The practice of responding to texts stands at the heart of the student's learning experience on an undergraduate degree in English studies. Despite its critical status, analysing reader response is less than easy and might involve any number of influential factors. Early studies in feminist literary criticism considered the role that a reader's gender might play in textual response, and how practices of reading might entail a political (specifically feminist) dimension.[2] Now, some 20 years on, there is still some way to go in addressing questions of gender and reader response. As Johnson points out, changes in language and gender research have challenged the focus on the study of women alone to incorporate analysing the construction of masculinities.[3] The kind of texts that readers might encounter both within and outside their academic study is also shifting, with the evolution of digital culture.

The development of digital texts is highly significant. It brings into sharp focus the potential influence of medium in the reading experience. In particular, it provides an alternative to print culture, which Douglas describes as so dominated by familiar conventions that 'we can never hope to clarify precisely what happens during the transaction between reader and text'.[4] Instead, both the technology and the alien conventions of an electronic reading environment present the opportunity to scrutinise reader response from a fresh perspective. The discussion of reader response that follows in this chapter is thus embedded in wider debates about technology, textuality and gender.

Studies that explore the relationships between gender and technology present a complex and contradictory picture. On one level, technology (in general terms) has been characterised by masculine dominance and sexism. On another, amongst the manifold forms and uses of technology, hypertext in particular has been attributed with feminist potential. Indeed, the multiplicity of hypertext is a form of textuality which can be used to open up co-existing contradictions and provide spaces from which marginalised perspectives on gender can be expressed. Landow returns to Cixous's description of écriture feminine, in which textual boundaries are ascribed with ideological significance, and univalence and closure understood as patriarchal restriction which women's writing must overcome. Given hypertext's multiplicity, Landow goes as far to debate 'whether hypertext fiction and, indeed, all hypertext is in some way a feminist sort of writing'.[5] As such, the political application of hypertext has been exploited by researchers like Sullivan, who, working in pedagogical contexts use hypertexts as part of an educational programme to create the possibility for reader-viewers 'to interrogate their positions within dominant ideological regimes of representation' especially where these ideologies are understood as patriarchal.[6]

For the most part, it is feminist researchers and practitioners who have made use of hypertext to examine the construction of specifically women's identities and writing, as does Love, for example.[7] While this may be for good reason, such emphasis is not unproblematic, for it leaves the issue of masculinity largely uncontested. The outcome is that it is too easy to assume 'masculinity' to be a single, monolithic construct that does not need to be questioned in relation to textual medium or form. However, formulating questions about masculinity and texts needs to be handled with precision and sensitivity. Within the existing research literature, the equation of hypertext, écriture feminine and feminism seems to be based upon a theoretical correlation which in turn conflates issues of form, content and medium. It is also necessary to disentangle the terms used to discuss 'gender' in this context. Thus biological sex can be distinguished from gender as a social construct, both of which are separable from political positions such as feminism or patriarchy.[8] Given the metaphorical nature of Cixous' work which has influenced so much of the theoretical discussions of technology, textuality and gender, there is an increasing need for empirical data which examines what actually is, both in terms of use of technology and reader response more generally. The data and analysis discussed in the rest of this chapter are a first step towards this end, exploring the potential connections between form, medium, biological sex (of the reader) and representations of gender.

Data sample and methodology

The analysis discussed here examines the responses of 96 readers to a collection of stories called *Fishnet*.[9] The readers were all undergraduate students at higher education institutions in the United Kingdom. Forty-seven of the readers were male and forty-nine were female. The study was carried out in three stages, with these readers divided into groups according to subject of academic study and whether they read the hypertext or the print version of the stories. This is summarised in Table 6.1.

The main focus in this chapter will be on the readers taking part in an English studies programme, with only brief comparisons made with those who were part of a Faculty of Computing, Technology and Engineering.

Fishnet is an amateur piece of writing by Charles Sundt. It might best be described as transitional rather than native hypertext in that *Fishnet* was originally written as eight separate, conventional stories about the same set of characters that the author later integrated together into one overarching web. As such, *Fishnet* does not contain many of the characteristics of more sophisticated experimental hypertexts such as multimedia effects (sound, image or animation) and readers can only comment on rather than contribute to the story text. However, readers are free to navigate their way through the hypertext in various ways. The underlying principle is that the reader treats *Fishnet* as if it were a series of stories being screened simultaneously that they can switch between at will.

The rationale for choosing *Fishnet* was twofold. First, in its simplicity, it facilitated a fairly crude analysis of the mechanics of hypertextual reading by the analyst tracing which kinds of links the readers followed. Second, in its transitional nature, it offered a transmedial comparison of print and hypertext versions of the 'same' story, as the original print versions of the stories were also available from the same website. In this way, the potential influence of medium on reading response in

Table 6.1 Details of readers

Academic subject	Hypertext/print	Male	Female	Total
English	Hypertext	14	28	42
English	Print	11	15	26
Computing	Hypertext	22	6	28
Total		47	49	96

this study could be explored, at least in part. As I have discussed in my earlier work, numerous other factors may be important too, not least of which is the reader's evaluation of the narrative content. In this case, they deemed *Fishnet* to be 'poorly written', which in some cases led to their disengagement from the text.[10]

The English studies readers were asked to respond to *Fishnet* during their class time as part of a module 'Narrative Analysis'. Although the use of technology within the class was unusual, the students were familiar with the practices of close reading that the task set demanded. They read through the hypertext, recording their responses in a reading log which charted the pathway that they navigated and their qualitative comments about the experience. They then wrote a short creative piece which extended the original storyweb in some way. The students from Faculty of Computing undertook exactly the same task. Finally, a third group of English studies readers were given a print version of the short stories. They were not asked to complete a reading log, but carried out the creative writing task only.[11]

The mechanics of reading

The first area of reader response I examined was the pathways that the readers took as they navigated through the hypertext. The structure of *Fishnet* offered two polarised alternatives for navigating the storyweb. Readers could click on numerical hyperlinks, which enabled them to follow one storystrand consistently, or use the lexical hyperlinks, which switched them into a different storystrand. The pathways generated by following the different types of links contrasted sharply. The numerical links could create a strongly linear sequence like a conventional print narrative, often with a defined beginning, middle and end. In comparison, the lexical links produced an associative pathway, with little narrative coherence at all.

On the surface, these options share similarities with gendered descriptions of reader response. For example, the linear sequence is not unlike Carolyn Dinshaw's metaphorical description of 'reading like a man' which provides 'a single, univalent textual meaning fixed in a hierarchical structure',[12] or Peter Brook's analysis of the 'male plot of ambition' which mirrors the reader's sequential progression through conventional narrative dynamics.[13] In contrast, the fragmentary and open-ended characteristics of the associative pattern of reading are suggestive of the Cixous description of écriture feminine which 'bursts partitions, classes and rhetorics, orders and codes, must inundate, run through'.[14]

However, gendering reading response in this way is limited, for these analogies rest upon an abstract equation of sexual and textual response which threatens to universalise both femininity and masculinity and fails to explain how these metaphors might be related to actual reading practices.

The data gathered in this study challenges these metaphorical associations of gender and textual response. Critically, neither the binary distinction between linearity and association nor its unequivocal mapping onto gender values could be sustained. Both the male and female readers used *both* types of links as they navigated through the text, although with differing emphases. Furthermore, no two readers took exactly the same pathway, reflecting the individualised nature of the reading experience. At its most rudimentary, this suggests that the explanatory power of biological sex as a sociological variable is limited, and throws the gendering of reader response itself into further doubt. However, comparing the readers' pathways was a useful first step in uncovering other differential patterns of response. With that in mind, the readers' pathways were analysed and then compared according to the number of numerical hyperlinks taken. This indicates the extent to which they recreated conventional narrative structures, where the greater the proportion of numerical links, the higher the degree of perceived linearity. The results of this analysis are presented in Table 6.2.

At first glance, the figures seem to suggest that there is some difference in the pathways that the male and female readers took through the hypertext. Male readers used the numerical links and created conventional narrative sequences more frequently than did the female readers, who instead made greater use of the lexical hyperlinks. However, the qualitative comments that the students made about the experience suggest that biological sex is not in itself a determining factor in this aspect of reader response, nor did they describe their reading experience in explicitly gendered terms at all. Instead, the choice of reading pathway seems to be associated with the reader's expectation of hypertext as a medium. Several of the male readers explained their navigation

Table 6.2 Proportion of linear steps taken by readers (%)

	Female readers (%)	Male readers (%)
Average	26	42

as a result of their frustration with *Fishnet* as a hypertextual structure. One student wrote:

> But after I discovered that the lexias had no connection I read the story I liked best in a traditional linear way. The format while at first seems clever, becomes redundant.

Another commented,

> The interactivity of the experience is rather pointless. I can imagine a button labelled 'Take me to another random page please!' doing pretty much the same job and producing an experience of similar quality.

The decision to reconstruct a conventional narrative thus seems to result from the reader's search for relevance in the reading experience, rather than an essentialist impulse to read in a 'masculine' way.

The extent to which these navigational choices might be interpreted as a gendered process remains open to debate. Indeed, it is striking that it was only the male students in this group who expressed their frustration with the hypertext. This could be explained by their greater familiarity with digital texts, which they described as including e-journals, weblogs and more sophisticated hypertextual narratives. By way of contrast, none of the female students claimed to have any experience of using technology in such forms. Thus it is the readers' differential experiences of technology and their subsequent expectations of hypertext as a medium that resulted in their choices to navigate the text in a particular way. In the case of this sample of readers, the degree of technological familiarity varied according to sex, where the male readers showed greater technological expertise than the female readers. This correlation seems to support early stereotypes of digital technology as a masculine domain, and thus might function indirectly as a resource for enacting 'masculine' behaviour. However, more recent research indicates that patterns of technological usage do not support this stereotype, and I do not wish to claim that the difference found here is in any way fixed or universal. Despite the stereotypical gendering of technology as 'masculine', in this sample, there is little explicit evidence that the technological expertise was understood by these students as a way of performing their masculinity. However, it does seem to bear further influence on the ways in which the readers conceptualised gender identity as expressed in their rewritings of the hypertext version of *Fishnet*.

Gender in the storyworlds

The readers' responses to the hypertext were also analysed in the light of the creative writing they undertook which extended the original storyweb in some way. These narrative fragments are understood as what David Herman terms 'storyworlds'.[15] Storyworlds are special kinds of mental models created when readers interpret narratives. Critically, storyworlds do not treat narratives as textual products alone. Rather as mental models, the reader's interaction with them is inextricably linked with their experience of real world contexts (albeit in a complicated fashion which is less than easy to pin down). In this sense, the analysis of representation is not limited to textual concerns alone but may have wider implications for understanding these readers' conceptions of gender identity.

I am most interested in characterisation as a storyworld element. Following Herman's work, I use Halliday's system of transitivity choices to examine who does what to whom.[16] I am particularly interested in the most frequently occurring participant role: that of 'Actor'. This is the 'do-er' role associated with Material processes of external action. In the following example, the Actor is underlined.

He clenched his fists, squeezing the small grains of tobacco deeper beneath his nails.

(Male reader, hypertext version)

The Actors were analysed according to the ways in which they were marked for gender. The characters' gender could be lexically signalled, so that the reader interpreted them as masculine, feminine, human but without clear marking of gendered status, gendered in a shifting or plural sense (for example as transgendered individuals) or non-human characters (either abstract or concrete). The results of this analysis are given in Table 6.3.

The results show that there is no clear pattern of difference in the characterisation based on the biological sex of the reader. Instead, there are many points of similarity. For example, the proportion of characters that were given a non-human identity was almost identical for the students rewriting the print version of the stories (16.9 per cent for the male readers, 17 per cent for the female readers). Where differences did occur, these were not systematically distributed. Just as with the reading pathways, there is no evidence here from which we might gender reader response in some essentialist manner, be that derived from the biological sex of the empirical reader or from the abstract figure implied by metaphorical

Table 6.3   Gendered characteristics of Actors and Sensers (as %)

	Actor (masculine)	Actor (feminine)	Actor (unspecified)	Actor (trans-gendered)	Actor (non-human, abstract)	Actor (non-human, concrete)
Hypertext male reader	25.3	6.1	15.2	2.0	8.6	6.6
Hypertext female reader	28.0	10.9	10.6	0	7.7	2.6
Print male reader	15.1	22.6	6.6	0	7.5	9.4
Print female reader	22.8	15.4	6.6	0	7.4	9.6

allusions to 'reading like a man'. That said, the representational choices in these storyworlds remain significant as suggesting a range of ways in which gender identity was conceptualised by these students.

The characterisation in these storyworlds indicates that the readers of both the hypertext and print versions primarily constructed fictional gender identities that were either clearly masculine or feminine. Indications of gender include naming choices, linguistic details such as pronouns (which in English inflect for gender in the third person singular), or use of culturally recognised patterns of behaviour, such as clothing choices. The pattern of binary difference remains a powerful norm which regulates the characterisation choices for both male and female readers, and for both text types. A typical example of this characterisation is given below.

> Carly picked up the snowdome and it cracked. She began to cry because it was the only thing she had left that her father had bought her. 'It's cheap tat.' Said her evil cousin, 'he probably paid 10 pence for it.' With that, Carly attacked her cousin and slashed his throat with a piece of the glass snowdome. As her cousin lay dying on the carpet, Carly shook with fear. 'He should never have said anything about my father,' she cried and threw herself on Paul's dead body.
>
> (Female student, hypertext version)

In itself, this choice is not unremarkable, especially given that the normative pattern of representation was also found in the source texts (both print and hypertext). What is more interesting is that the textual medium seemed to play an influential role on gender representation, particularly as seen in the human characters who did not fit into a binary classification of masculinity or femininity.

One representational choice was to create characters that were not distinctly marked for gender at all. It is striking that the male students who rewrote the hypertext version of *Fishnet* used this type of characterisation more than anyone else. Usually, these storyworld participants were represented as a generalised group, or as individuals who were not described with enough detail to infer a gendered identity, as in the examples given next.

> The rich and poor were meant to live as equals. But as time went on, some became more equal than others. The ones who were once poor always remembered how the rich had treated them before. So when the time came, the poor before moved into the great houses while the rich before were left out in the cold.
>
> (Male student, hypertext version)

> The meaning of life is something that has been thought about by many people, but each person only thinks about it once. It takes this one chain of thoughts for an intelligent person to realise there is no meaning to life, except to create more life.
>
> (Male student, hypertext version)

One effect of this type of characterisation is to make the storyworlds appear less personalised. The characters of the storyworld seem less vivid, and in some cases are backgrounded further still through the use of passive constructions or nominalisation, as underlined in the example below.

> When one wants a child, one donates sperm or eggs at the enfant-clinique and within a year your child, <u>DNA altered according to your taste</u>, is ready for <u>collection</u>. Single-parent families, 400 years ago <u>seen as the scourge of society</u> are now the norm.
>
> (Male student, hypertext version)

Overall, in comparison with both the print-derived storyworlds and the hypertext worlds written by the female readers, the creative responses of the male readers to the hypertext seemed to de-emphasise the precise detail and agency of the characters.

Although inevitably more speculative, it is also important to explore the reasons that might lie behind representational choices. On the surface, it is tempting to suggest that there are some similarities here with the storytelling styles of men in other contexts. Argamon *et al.* found salient differences in the written style of women and men, particularly as realised through the linguistic choices used to present people and objects. Specifically, women writers tended to use grammatical and lexical choices which created greater personalisation than did the men who used less specific forms of reference as a 'depersonalization mechanism'.[17] Similarly, Barbara Johnstone analysed a sample of Midwestern American storytellers, observing that in men's storyworlds:

> People fill roles in the story, but rarely have individual identities. The male protagonists in men's stories act alone, they do not rely on other people, though they do often rely on things – which are often described with the level of detail women use for people.[18]

Against this wider background, the less-detailed characterisation created by the male readers is symptomatic of a stereotypical view of masculinity as impersonal and less socially oriented, ultimately opposed to a model of femininity which emphasises community. Brady Aschauer explains that these 'masculine' characteristics have been seen as resulting from gender-specific patterns of socialisation and the male child's psychoanalytic detachment.[19] However, as Johnson points out, to perpetrate this stereotype may be in some cases both misleading and politically suspect.[20] Indeed, it is dubious at the least to abstract the findings from one set of data and then superimpose them onto another. Despite the echoes in this stylistic difference across mode and context, I do not want to suggest that superficial parallels in findings necessarily correspond to parallels in causation.

On the basis of the data in this study, I would want to strongly resist a simplistic correlation between biological sex and storytelling style and to argue instead that other factors may be highly significant. Indeed, it is not exclusively male readers who created non-gender-specific characters, and in the case of the readers responding to the print version, the women and men used this type of characterisation equally (6.6 per cent each). Given that the difference occurred most prominently in relation to the hypertext version, this hints that one possible influence that might explain the variation in characterisation is the medium in which the students read the original story.

The group of male students who responded to the hypertext narrative were distinctive in that they had the greatest experience of texts using new technology. Their subsequent expectations of hypertext's potential lead to them navigating through the text in a particular way. I suggest that these medium-specific expectations also coloured the representational choices in their creative writing. One dimension of this is the gendered schemata that are particularly associated with the electronic environments in which fictional hypertexts are situated.

Virtual reality and online communication available through the Internet, computer games, the World Wide Web and other digital developments provide environments where the norms of gender identity can be challenged. As Roberts and Parks put it:

> The virtual worlds of the Internet give people unparalleled control over the construction and presentation of their identities. Gender-switching is perhaps the most dramatic example of how people exercise this control.[21]

From this perspective, digital technology, be it through virtual reality, online communication or fictional hypertext, carries the potential to deconstruct fixed gender identity. I suggest that the greater the experience of these electronic environments, the more likely it might be that the reader draw upon these gendered associations and carry this into the characterisation of their storyworlds. Indeed, it is striking that it was the male readers of the hypertext version (that is, those who had the greatest technological expertise from those in the School of English) who uniquely created fictional participants that deconstructed binary gender categories. Examples of these characters included individuals who switched gender, or otherwise merged human and machine in cyborg-like imagery, as in the following examples.

> Lobe by lobe the brains of the experimenters were extracted and transferred to the mainframe of the global network server. From vile to phile. Gender was now genuinely an attitude and penises were 'add ons' at the 'online' peripheral outlet.

> It seemed natural since he did not remember any of his previous lives. That was probably for the best since when 'Joseph' hit puberty things started to go very wrong. You see poor Joseph has been christened Georgina and now had to cope with the advances of boys at school.

Although it was only the male readers from the school of English who created characters like this, it is clearly not the reader's biological sex that motivates such a choice. None of the male readers responding to a print version of the stories created gender-switching characters. Furthermore, female readers who did have more experience of digital texts from the separate group of students from the faculty of computing produced storyworlds with similar characterisation.

> 'We'd then have to spend hours in front of the mirror every morning.'
> 'And period pains, childbirth, hormones,' Rob went on. 'In fact, that's a heavy price to pay. Guess we're going to have to be more sympathetic towards Erika and Karen?'
>
> (Female Computing student)

Characterising fictional gender identity in more fluid, multiple forms is thus open to readers of differing sex and who construct their gender in various ways. Crucially, the results of this analysis point to the influence of hypertext as generating particular gendered schemas, and suggests that this form of technology might open up alternative possibilities for exploring gender, both masculinity and femininity in broader and more plural terms.

Even while the rewritings of the hypertext seem to offer a platform from which a binary categorisation of gender can be deconstructed, it is important not to promote this as unqualified emancipation. First, the examples of gender switching were by far in the minority of the characterisation (only 2 per cent of the Actors in the hypertext-derived writing). Second, even when transgendered possibilities were presented, the policing effects of heteronormative gender identification are still in force. To cross defined gender boundaries beyond normative masculinity is presented by the students in their writing in negative terms as something 'embarrassing' or a 'heavy price to pay'. It is clear that within these storyworlds, the gender representation created by these students legitimates identities which keep within the cultural norms of masculinity and do not move beyond this in any far-reaching or sustained manner.

Summary

The point we have reached is that the results of the analysis indicate that it is not the biological sex of the reader that is the primary influence in their response to the text, either in the case of the pathway they navigated through the hypertext or in their creative writing carried out subsequently. Instead, the data also showed important points of similarity between the male and female readers' responses, along with intracategory variation. A simplistic model of gender difference in reader response is untenable in the face of this empirical evidence. In turn, there appears to be little (if any) evidence to suggest that reading patterns themselves can be gendered in some essentialist manner. To 'read like a man' is a metaphor, and in the light of this study, cannot be substantiated as a distinctively 'masculine' practice in any clear way.

Instead, I have suggested that there are other influential factors at work here. The role of the textual medium is particularly important, where the readers' expectations of hypertext as an interactive form seemed to play a part in their navigational choices and also contributed to the way they characterised gender in their storyworlds. For this group of students, their expectations of the medium were related to their previous technological experience, which differed between the male and female students. This gender difference must be understood as context-specific and certainly not immutable. In my earlier work, I carried out a fuller comparison with the students from a Faculty of Computing, Engineering and Technology, showing that academic discipline also shaped the ways in which readers responded to digital texts.[22] The young women from the Faculty of Computing also had high expectations of digital texts' potential, indicated here through the way they chose to conceptualise fictional gender identity.

What then might this mean for the use of technology and texts in the context of English studies in the United Kingdom at this point in time? First, it is important to recognise the potential influence of medium on reading experiences. On one level, the limited technological experiences articulated by the young women in the group from the School of English indicates that there is much more that can be done to familiarise students with the wealth of narrative texts and genres being exploited in digital media. On a deeper level, there is also more that can be done to explore the opportunities that narratives in new media present for asking questions about gender, identity and power. Earlier research has already indicated the possibilities that the multiplicity of hypertext holds for deconstructing monolithic gender perspectives, especially when employed by women for feminist ends. This multiplicity need not be applied to questions of femininity alone, but also used to challenge a unified concept of 'masculinity'. Given that it was the young men in this sample who were most familiar with technology, they might be particularly well placed to open up this possibility.

One application of this study then, is to recognise and reiterate Takayoshi's point that 'teachers would be wise to use the Web as more than a glorified research database and realize its revolutionary potential for dismantling stereotypes about technology and girls',[23] to which we might also add, stereotypes about boys, men and masculinity. As Mullany points out, this is particularly important as elements of cyberspace can be used to reproduce exaggerated conceptions of masculinity that strengthen dichotomies, rather than deconstruct them.[24]

That said, the use of hypertext to challenge gendered stereotypes is not without its constraints. First, the use of multiplicity, especially in hypertextual forms, does not simply equate to a gendered revolution. The medium in which a narrative is constructed must also be seen in relation to its subject matter and purpose, neither of which need to entail explicitly gendered meanings. Moreover, textual multiplicity and non-linear reading patterns need not result in a meaningful reading experience. When multiplicity results in disorientation and frustration (as it did for at least some of the readers in this study) then this might lead to readers disengaging with the text altogether, in which case we might question its political potential at all. Indeed, textual changes which deconstruct gender identity need not lead to real world changes in understanding gender – either masculinity or femininity. Roberts and Parks point out that what happens to gender identity in virtual environments does not necessarily influence real world behaviour. They argue that gender switching 'should be viewed as experimental behaviour rather than an enduring expression of sexuality, personality or gender politics'.[25] Similarly, the gender deconstruction in the storyworlds created by the male readers need not break a binary view of gender in a lasting manner, nor bear any influence on their own 'real world' gender identity.

This study has indicated the ways in which a group of students responded to a hypertext narrative. There may be limited evidence to suggest that 'masculinity' as one half of a gendered binary is a salient variable in the reading experience, but this does not mean that gender need be dismissed from our discussions of reader response and technology. Even within the limits I have laid out, narratives using new media may also offer new ways of exploring masculine identities. How those identities are then performed outside the text within the classroom and beyond will remain to be seen.

Notes

1. An earlier version of this chapter was presented at Narrative, An International Conference (Ottawa, April 2006), supported by the British Academy grant OCG-42352. I am grateful for the ensuing critiques that helped reshape some of the concepts discussed here. Parts of the initial stages of the study reported here are also discussed from an alternative perspective in Ruth Page, *Literary and Linguistic Approaches to Feminist Narratology* (Basingstoke: Palgrave, 2006).
2. J. Rivkin, 'Resisting Readers and Reading Effects: Some Speculations on Reading and Gender', in *Narrative Poetics: Innovations, Limits, Challenges*, ed. James Phelan (Columbus: Ohio University Press, 1987), 11–22.
3. Sally Johnson, 'Theorising language and masculinity', in *Language and Masculinity*, ed. Sally Johnson and Ulrike H. Meinhof (Oxford: Blackwell, 1997), 8–26.
4. Jane Yellowlees Douglas, *Print Pathways and Interactive Labyrinths: How Hypertext Narratives Affect the Act of Reading* (Unpublished PhD thesis, New York University), 3.
5. George P. Landow, *Hypertext 2.0, Revised and Amplified Edition* (London and Baltimore: John Hopkins University Press, 1997), 206.
6. L. L. Sullivan, 'Wired Women Writing: Towards a Feminist Theorization of Hypertext', *Computers and Composition*, 16 (1999), 46.
7. J. Love, 'Elecriture: A Course in Women's Writing on the Web', *Kairos*, 7 (2002), *Available*: http://english.ttu.edu/Kairos/1.3/archival/3.html. (Accessed July 2004).
8. I will use the terms 'male' and 'female' to refer to the biological sex of the readers and 'masculine' and 'feminine' when talking about the cultural markers of gender identity. As postmodern feminists have pointed out, the distinction between sex and gender is itself false and neither should be understood as binary oppositions. However, given that the readers in this study identified themselves as 'male' and 'female', I will retain the distinction in this discussion.
9. Charles Sundt, *Fishnet* (2004). *Available*: http://www.angelfire.com/ny5/ *Fishnet*/index.html. (Accessed July 2004).
10. Page, *Literary and Linguistic Approaches*, 103–106.
11. The students reading a print version of *Fishnet* handwrote their creative retellings on paper. The students reading a hypertext version used a mixture of word processing and handwriting to create their versions. The mode of production for the creative writing did not correlate with any differences found in the textual response.
12. Carolyn Dinshaw, *Chaucer's Sexual Poetics* (Wisconsin: University of Wisconsin Press, 1989), 28–29.
13. Peter Brooks, *Reading for the Plot: Design and Intention in Narrative* (Cambridge, London: Harvard University Press, 1984), 39.
14. Hélène Cixous, 'Sorties: Out and Out: Attacks/Ways Out/Forays', in *The Feminist Reader: Essays in Gender and the Politics of Literary Criticism*, ed. C. Belsey and J. Moore (London: Macmillan, 1989), 113.
15. David Herman, *Story Logic. Problems and Possibilities of Narrative* (Lincoln and London: University of Nebraska Press, 2002).

16. M. A. K. Halliday, *An Introduction to Functional Grammar*, 2nd edition (London: Edward Arnold, 1994).
17. S. Argamon *et al.*, 'Gender, genre, and writing style in formal written texts', *Text*, 23 (2003), 331.
18. Barbara Johnstone, *Stories, Community and Place* (Bloomington and Indianapolis: Indiana University Press, 1990), 75.
19. A. Brady Aschauer, 'Tinkering with Technological Skill: An Examination of the Gendered uses of Technologies', *Computers and Composition* 16 (1999): 13.
20. Johnson, *Language and Masculinity*, 18.
21. L.D. Roberts and M.R. Parks, 'The Social Geography of Gender-Switching in Virtual Reality Environments on the Internet', in *Virtual Gender: Technology, Consumption and Identity*, ed. E. Green and A. Adam (London: Routledge, 2001), 265.
22. Page, *Literary and Linguistic Approaches*, 94–115.
23. P. Takayoshi, E. Huot and M. Huot, 'No Boys Allowed: The World Wide Web as a Clubhouse for Girls', *Computers and Composition* 16 (1999): 105.
24. L. Mullany, ' "Become the Man that Women Desire": Gender Identities and Dominant Discourses in Email Advertising Language', *Language and Literature* 13 (2004): 303.
25. Roberts and Parks, *Virtual Gender*, 266.

Bibliography

Argamon, S., Koppel, M., Fine, J. and Shimoni, A. R. 'Gender, Genre, and Writing Style in Formal Written Texts'. *Text* 23 (2003): 321–346.

Brady Aschauer, A. 'Tinkering with Technological Skill: An Examination of the Gendered uses of Technologies'. *Computers and Composition* 16 (1999): 17–23.

Brooks, P. *Reading for the Plot: Design and Intention in Narrative*. Cambridge, London: Harvard University Press, 1984.

Cixous, H. 'Sorties: Out and Out: Attacks/Ways Out/Forays'. In *The Feminist Reader: Essays in Gender and the Politics of Literary Criticism*, edited by C. Belsey and J. Moore, 101–116. London: Macmillan, 1989.

Clark, C. L. 'Hypertext Theory and the Rhetoric of Empowerment: A Feminist Alternative'. *Kairos*, 7 no. 3 (2002). *Available*: http://english.ttu.edu/kairos/7. 3/binder2.html?coverweb/clark/page1.html. (19 July 2004).

Dinshaw, C. *Chaucer's Sexual Poetics*. Wisconsin: University of Wisconsin Press, 1989.

Douglas, Jane Yellowlees. *Print Pathways and Interactive Labyrinths: How Hypertext Narratives Affect the Act of Reading*. Unpublished PhD thesis, New York University.

Halliday, M. A. K. *An Introduction to Functional Grammar*, 2nd edition. London: Edward Arnold, 1994.

Herman, D. *Story Logic. Problems and Possibilities of Narrative*. Lincoln and London: University of Nebraska Press, 2002.

Johnson, S. 'Theorising Language and Masculinity'. In *Language and Masculinity*, edited by S. Johnson and U. H. Meinhof, 8–26. Oxford: Blackwell, 1997.

Johnstone, B. *Stories, Community and Place*. Bloomington and Indianapolis: Indiana University Press, 1990.

Landow, G. P. *Hypertext 2.0, Revised and Amplified Edition*. London and Baltimore: John Hopkins University Press, 1997.

Love, J. 'Elecriture: A Course in Women's Writing on the Web'. *Kairos*, 7 no. 3 (2002). *Available:* http://english.ttu.edu/Kairos/1.3/archival/3.html. (19 July 2004).

Mullany, L. ' "Become the Man that Women Desire": Gender Identities and Dominant Discourses in Email Advertising Language'. *Language and Literature* 13 (2004): 291–305.

Page, R. E. *Literary and Linguistic Approaches to Feminist Narratology*. Basingstoke: Palgrave Macmillan, 2006.

Rivkin, J. 'Resisting Readers and Reading Effects: Some Speculations on Reading and Gender'. In *Narrative Poetics: Innovations, Limits, Challenges*, edited by J. Phelan, 11–22. Columbus: Ohio University Press, 1987.

Roberts, L. D. and Parks, M. R. 'The Social Geography of Gender-switching in Virtual Reality Environments on the Internet'. In *Virtual Gender: Technology, Consumption and Identity*, edited by E. Green and A. Adam, 265–285. London: Routledge, 2001.

Sundt, C. *Fishnet. Available:* http://www.angelfire.com/ny5/Fishnet/index.html. (19 July 2004).

Sullivan, L. L. 'Wired Women Writing: Towards a Feminist Theorization of Hypertext'. *Computers and Composition* 16 (1999): 25–54.

Takayoshi, P., Huot, E. and Huot, M. 'No Boys Allowed: The World Wide Web as a Clubhouse for Girls'. *Computers and Composition* 16 (1999): 89–106.

7

Bois will be Bois: Masculinity and Pedagogy in the Gay and Lesbian Studies Classroom

Dennis W. Allen

During the spring semester of 2006, at the large land-grant American university where I work, I taught a regularly offered course for senior English majors entitled 'Special Topics in Lesbian and Gay Studies'. The topic this time was Assimilation, and the class investigated the ongoing process of incorporating gays and lesbians into mainstream society, reviewing the history of the lesbian and gay civil rights movement and then addressing such issues as gay marriage and the commercialization of gay culture. Readings for the course consisted of books and articles by popular authors (Mark Simpson, Sidney Abbott, and Barbara Love) and academic queer theorists (Shane Phelan, Michael Warner) ranging from the 1950s to the present, as well as four films intended to showcase changing perspectives on lesbian and gay identity, including *The Children's Hour* and *Latter Days*. As is usually the case in such classes, about half of the 29 students were straight, the other half gay, lesbian, or bisexual, and the gender breakdown was roughly the same as that of other senior-level courses in the English Department (60 per cent female and 40 per cent male).

Now, when I began thinking about my essay for this collection, my initial reaction was that this class, like most Gay and Lesbian Studies courses, was not an ideal example to use in analyzing the gendering of the classroom and reflecting on the relations between masculinity and pedagogy, if only because such courses complicate those issues. Despite nearly 20 years of Queer Theory, which has insisted on the need to make a conceptual distinction between gender and sexual orientation, there is still a nearly universal tendency not only in the general population but also in the scholarly community to assume a correlation between the two. Although we didn't talk about masculinity or femininity very often in this particular class, much of the class discussion implicitly rested on unarticulated assumptions about the nature of the genders themselves and on the notion that there is a direct link between an individual's sexual orientation and the extent of his or her compliance with gender norms. They rarely said it out loud, but most of the people in the class, gay and straight, assumed that gay men are 'naturally' more feminine and gay women more masculine than their straight counterparts, even though there were people sitting in the classroom who disproved this notion. If the relations between masculinity and pedagogy are complex and difficult to unravel, adding sexual orientation to the equation makes matters even harder to sort out.

And yet, I think this additional complexity can be very helpful in refining our understanding of how masculinity functions in the classroom, if only because it forces us to reconsider our notions of masculinity itself. One of the recent developments in Gender Theory is to recognize that it is really not possible to speak of a single 'masculinity' or 'femininity', even in a specific culture at a specific time. In addition to a society's dominant or hegemonic gender definitions at any particular cultural moment, there are always variants, gender presentations that are differently inflected: influenced by race, age, class, cultural beliefs, and, yes, even sexual orientation (Gardiner 2002: 11). These variations are present, if often unnoticed, in every classroom, but, because of our cultural expectations of a link between 'sexual deviance' and gender non-conformity, they emerge into visibility in the Lesbian and Gay Studies course in a very clear way. In other words, it's in such classes that we are not only more likely to notice the queeny gay man or the butch lesbian but also to contemplate what their existence implies for our understanding of masculinity in general.

In addition to calling our attention to the multiplicity of gender, the Lesbian and Gay Studies classroom can also provide an additional insight into the nature of masculinity. Once we notice that there are multiple forms of masculinity evident at any given moment, some of which do not even correspond to biological sex, then it becomes easier to realize that gender is not particularly coherent or static, that what constitutes the masculine can not only vary among the individuals in a given space but can also change over time, both for the culture and the individual. Because masculinity does not exist transcendentally but only in its enactment by individuals, then masculinity – any version of masculinity – is not so much a thing or a quality as a process, which means that it can mutate or drift or even fail. Sometimes the butch lesbian isn't so butch; sometimes the jock-y fraternity boy isn't either.

What I'd like to do in this essay, then, is to explore both of these insights a little further to see what they can tell us about the gendered identities of the individuals in the classroom and then examine their implications for our understanding of the gendering of the pedagogical situation itself. As I hope to show, although the pedagogical model underlying English Studies derives from a particular set of masculine ideals used to construct the discipline as a whole, the multiplicity of identities and genders in any given classroom and the fact that pedagogy is a process that sometimes fails to reflect those ideals suggest that both masculinity and pedagogy may be more complex and less stable than current sociological studies of gender and the classroom sometimes indicate. As a result, I will argue, if we're concerned with guaranteeing gender equity in the classroom, then we have to realize that masculinity is not simply a pre-existing fact that enters the college classroom. Instead, it is a diverse set of identities and behaviors that are continually being enacted, revised, and negotiated there.

Boys will be bois

As it happened, the Assimilation class was like a Noah's Ark of contemporary American college students: there seemed to be at least two of every conceivable type. There were sorority girls and fag hags who looked exactly like sorority girls but whose worldview was diametrically opposed to theirs. There were drag queens and 'straight-acting' gay men and 'straight-acting' straight men and some lesbians who acted like the 'straight-acting' men and some straight men who didn't. There were straight women who 'read' as butch lesbians and 'alternative kids' of both sexes, always already just queer, whose gender was subcultural ('emo girl', 'slacker dude') and whose sexuality was often ambiguous. These variations in the class members' self-presentations were a matter of interest to the students because, as is always the case in such classes, everyone was very curious about everyone else's sexual orientation. Their usual strategy, following the cultural expectations about the relation of gender and sexual orientation that I've already mentioned, was to try to 'read' sexual orientation from an individual's gender presentation. What the students discovered, as the semester progressed and various individuals publicly announced their sexual orientation, is that it is almost impossible to determine, just by looking at someone, who they might want to sleep with. The latter point was very nicely illustrated by one of the sorority girls near the end of the semester, who related, in detail and much to the other students' amusement, which of her classmates she had initially misclassified in her personal assessment of who was what.

I was curious about who was what too, of course, but the gender variation evident in the classroom was also interesting to me because it confirmed Judith Halberstam's assertion that the categories in our binary gender system are so broad and general that, in order to make sense out of the multiple versions of masculinity that operate in any given culture at any given time, we all use what Halberstam has called 'nonce taxonomies', those informal categories that give us more conceptual specificity in assessing other people's gender presentations (Halberstam 1998: 27). Thus, there were, of course, people in the class who were perfect illustrations of hegemonic masculinity, which is defined in the academic literature as characterized by strong ego boundaries and an aggrandizing sense of self (Knights 1999: 5) and by behavior that is active, aggressive, quarrelsome, and attention-seeking (Kimmel 2000: 154). I'll simply add, drawing from the marketing niches used by advertising, that it is also supposed to be characterized by a relative lack of concern with grooming and fashion.

Yet the class also provided examples of two of the alternative masculinities recognized by the advertising community: metrosexuals (a form of 'consumption masculinity' in which male identity is defined by what one owns, specifically through the construction of the self as a model of taste and grooming) and slacker/Generation X guys (characterized by an ironic distance from mainstream culture, including the ideal of hegemonic masculinity) (Clarkson 2005: 238 243; O'Barr and William 2004). And, because the class was half lesbian, gay, and bisexual, there were some additional variations less widely recognized in academia or at Saatchi and Saatchi. There were 'straight-acting' gay men, who were indistinguishable except in their sexual orientation from whichever variant of masculinity they were enacting, and soft butches (lesbians who, while recognizably female, were otherwise straightforward incarnations of hegemonic masculinity and who thus provided a nice commentary on the assumption that gender must be linked to biological sex), not to mention a couple of types unique to gay male culture: bois (slightly feminine younger gay men), and queens (recognizably male, but with a camp re-presentation of stereotypical 'feminine' qualities).[1]

I will return to the implications that this proliferation of masculinities has for our understanding of the relations of masculinity and pedagogy and for the gendering of the pedagogical situation itself. For the moment, I'd simply like to note that it reveals the crudeness of the analytic lens evident in some of the sociological literature on gender and the educational system. Even as astute an observer as Michael Kimmel, who has published extensively on historical variations in conceptions of masculinity, loses some of his normal subtlety when discussing pedagogy. For example, summarizing previous research on gender bias in the classroom, Kimmel notes: 'Teachers call on boys more often and spend more time with them. They ask boys more challenging questions than they do girls, and wait longer for boys to answer' (2000: 154). While I'm sure these findings are true, the difficulty here is that the unconscious tendency in such studies to revert to biological sex (boys, girls) rather than gender as the taxonomic fulcrum oversimplifies the picture. What we also need is more refined analyses that take into account the co-existence of multiple versions of masculinity and femininity and that also assess the impact of variations in the relation between an individual's sex and his or her gender. Teachers may indeed call on boys more often than girls, but it also seems important to discover whether elementary school teachers call on tomboys more often than the girls whose role model is Hillary Duff or whether college professors pay less attention to the male art majors than to the sports management majors. Is sex the primary determinant of 'teacher attention' or do teachers respond (also or instead) to gender, to masculine behavior regardless of sex? Does the correlation (or lack of it) between a student's sex and his or her gender affect the teacher's treatment of the student? One of our initial conclusions, then, can be that more empirical research needs to be done on such issues if we want a more complete picture of the gendered classroom.

Lonesome cowboy

There are additional limitations to how some of the sociological literature analyzes gender in the classroom beyond this lack of attention to variations in gender presentation. Often, such research implicitly assumes that gender is relatively coherent and consistent although, to understand what is wrong with this assumption, we will first have to take a look at the student in the Assimilation class that I will call Bob. Bob was a straight man who was almost a textbook example of a particularly extreme form of hegemonic masculinity. In part because he was extremely bright and well-informed, personable, and often very funny, and in part because he was very self-assertive (his part time job outside of school was as a bouncer), Bob consistently took a lead role in class discussion, often setting the terms for the day's debate and orienting the other students' responses so that they spent a good deal of a number of class periods reacting to his statements. Just to round out the picture, I'll add that, in the course of the semester Bob managed to hit on every straight woman in the class. If Bob was thus a clear example of one valued form of masculinity in our culture, in the classroom he became, in a sense, the Beta, perhaps even the Alpha, male in the room.

Attention-seeking and self-aggrandizing, Bob would thus seem to be the consummate proof that classrooms revolve around and reward traditional masculine behavior, and yet Bob's self-presentation ultimately suggests some limitations in sociological analyses of gender in the classroom. Even while such analyses insist that gender characteristics are culturally constructed (so that men are not, then, 'naturally' self-assertive), these studies often unconsciously present the gender of individuals and gender itself as essentially fixed. To take only one example, Sadker *et al.*, looking at gender inequity in instruction, note that: 'Not only do male students interact more with the teacher but at all levels of schooling they receive a higher quality of interaction', defined as clearer and more precise comments from teachers than the female students receive (2000: 213). Perhaps because, once again, gender is rendered synonymous with sex here, this reads both the genders themselves and an individual's gender as completely formed and self-evident, as 'facts' or causes which then produce certain effects in the classroom. While gender is thus involved in a dynamic situation (since boys then get an educational advantage both in terms of learning and 'self-esteem'), gender itself is understood as a relatively stable binary of cultural roles, and an individual's gender, inculcated at an early age, is implicitly presented as more or less coherent, unitary, and static.

We can, however, look to Judith Butler for a slightly different take on what the social construction of gender might mean, specifically her assertion that, if masculinity is culturally constructed, then there is no ground upon which it is based except its construction, the continual performance of it that creates it. As such, masculinity (both in general and for the individual) has no internal coherence since it is founded on enactments of the ideal rather than on a transcendental essence. Even more apposite for our purposes is Butler's insistence that gender performances MUST be repeated in order for gender to exist and that there is always the possibility that the gender in question will be repeated differently or that it might not be repeated at all (Butler 1991: 21). In short, Butler suggests that, rather than being coherent or consistent, sometimes masculinity can fail.

And that brings us back to Bob. Bob's classroom persona was predicated on a highly defined sense of self, which provided the basis, actually the authoritative ground, for most of his assertions. Thus, Bob was invaluable in the classroom because many of the things he said were both controversial enough and presented in a sufficiently authoritative manner that they forced the other members of the class to challenge him, producing an in-depth discussion of the issues involved. When, for example, he insisted that the best course of action for gays and lesbians was to assimilate to the dominant culture since this was inevitable in any situation when minorities have to deal with a majority, he provoked a variety of strongly argued responses: that the majority sometimes had to adapt to minority cultures, that gays and lesbians had a rich subculture that it would be a shame to lose, and so on. Significantly, even some of the students who agreed with his opinions reacted negatively to how forcefully he presented them. In short, Bob's statements came, or appeared to come, out of sense of self that was strongly defined, confident, and that was to be understood, at least in a discursive context, as the site of knowledge or truth. In other words, Bob was demonstrating the independence, the individualism, and the ability to defend his own beliefs that we expect from a hegemonic male (Kimmel 1997).

And yet... what was finally striking on this as on other occasions was that, however adept Bob was at defending his position, the intense reaction that he provoked always seemed to surprise and bother him so that he would say to me privately, after class or before the next class, things like 'Perhaps I shouldn't have said that' or 'Maybe I shouldn't have taken this class'. I would reassure him, of course – I liked him and he really was invaluable – but the salient point is that he would have these doubts in the first place, that he would worry about the other students' reactions not only to his opinions but to him. I take these to be the moments when, in a certain way, his continual performance of hegemonic masculinity failed, precisely because the self on which that performance was based could not, ultimately, stand apart, independent and individualistic and self-validating, regardless of what anyone else thought. He couldn't live up to that impossible ideal (and, if he could have, it probably would have made him a jerk); instead, his sense of himself required external confirmation, some feedback from the outside that validated his worth, if only (or perhaps especially) from the professor. To put it another way, in the *High Noon* that the class sometimes became, Bob couldn't quite sustain the role of Gary Cooper.

The head of the class

I could provide other examples of mutations or failures of expected gender performances in the class: the straight woman who defied conventional gender expectations for women by being almost as self-assertive, aggressive, and verbal as Bob or the 'boi' who would talk to me privately about his perceived lack of success at that role, but I'd like to go on and address the implications of the notions that masculinity is both plural and incoherent. How does this more complicated picture of gender revise our understanding of the ways in which the classroom is gendered, of the relations between masculinity and pedagogy? Previous work on the gendering of the classroom sees it as an overtly patriarchal space. Writing in 1997, Michael Kimmel argues that the college classroom illustrates the inequality of gender both because male professors can conform to gender expectations while successfully pursuing their careers while female professors cannot and because of the different, and essentially unequal, life experiences of the male and female students in the room, including such factors as women's substantially more frequent experience of sexual harassment (Kimmel 1997). Although Kimmel's essay is useful in helping us to see how the classroom functions as an extension of patriarchal society, the essay, unfortunately, does not really analyze the pedagogical process itself.

Ben Knights, examining the gendering of the field of English Studies as a whole, provides a more subtle and specific analysis of the ways in which masculinity shapes what goes on in college classrooms. Knights notes that both the formation of English as a discipline and the pedagogical models it employs were a reaction by male professors to the perception that language and literature were essentially 'feminine' interests. In response to a fear of the affective, of subjectivity, and of the threat of male feminization, English Studies was thus constructed throughout the twentieth century as a complex assertion of male mastery. This insistence on masculinity, Knights argues, is evident on a number of levels: in the stress on the critic's objective detachment, in the field's emphasis on intellectual difficulty (initially, in the selection of the canon under New Criticism and in the emphasis on theory in more recent years), in an agonistic style of intellectual interchange, and in a classroom practice that has been predicated on the bonding of a small (male) elite with the (male) professor. As a result, any analysis of the pedagogical conventions of English classes cannot ignore the patriarchal underpinnings of the discipline. As Knights succinctly puts it, in a formulation that is particularly apt for courses in Gender Theory or Gay and Lesbian Studies: 'New knowledges transmitted through unexamined forms of pedagogy will inevitably fossilize and fail to bring about any lasting change' (Knights 1999: 36).

Now, if we take this admonition seriously, and I think we should, then we need to do more than simply select texts or discuss topics in class that provide a critique of patriarchal privilege. Instead, we need to rework the implicit gendering of the pedagogy itself, and that involves thinking a bit more about where and how masculine privilege inheres in the classroom. Since Knights' focus is on the discipline as a whole, he does not address in detail the ways in which pedagogy enacts a certain ideology of masculinity. We can, however, use his insights to begin to understand what Frederic Jameson would call 'the content of the form' of pedagogy in English Studies, the underlying belief system that shapes that pedagogy. If we look back at Knights' list of the twentieth-century masculinist ideals used to define the discipline, one way to view conventional pedagogical practices is that they are implicitly intended to create a classroom that is parallel to or isomorphic with the hegemonically masculine male of the era. Just as that male is thought to be coherent and unified, with strongly defined ego boundaries, and a aggrandizing sense of self, the classroom ideal that emerges might best be understood metaphorically as itself a corporate being that is constructed as 'male': intellectually serious, internally organized, goal-directed (in its focus on the acquisition of knowledge), structured hierarchically around the instructor as 'the head' of the class. Think F. R. Leavis...lecturing.

I'm certainly no F. R. Leavis for any number of reasons, but the Assimilation class, because its infrastructure derived from the conventional pedagogical assumptions of the discipline, implicitly invoked a gendering of the classroom as 'male' in the sense outlined above. This wasn't so much because there was a man standing at the front of the room but because of subtler factors: because it was a 'serious' course for senior majors, a theory component was included in the readings to give the course some 'depth'; there were rules designed to insure that the students' attention was focused on intellectual matters and that the class was free of distractions (e.g. no reading the newspaper or doing the crossword during class); class discussions were moderated by the professor, who called on people and sometimes provided commentary, which insured that the teacher remained the focal point of the class; and the classroom ideal, for both the teacher and the students, was a detached, unemotional inquiry into the issues, no matter how controversial some of them were. It could easily be argued, then, that despite its sometimes radical content, the Assimilation class was as patriarchal in its form as any other. Except that I'm not so sure that all of them necessarily are. Knights, discussing the gendered subject position offered to us by literary texts and conventions of reading, also argues for a process of reflexive or estranged reading of the male identity retailed in such texts, and I think we might also 'read' the college classroom 'against the grain', looking for the incoherencies and failures in what appears to be, in theory at least, a fairly seamless masculine pedagogical practice.

On a fairly obvious level, one of these incoherencies is that the classroom itself is always a plural site on a number of levels. Although the disciplinary model that we've been discussing stresses the teacher as the focal point of activity in the room, another look at the college classroom suggests that such models are only partially true, especially in discussion-based classes in the Humanities where, given the current stress on 'critical thinking', the students are supposed to develop, articulate and defend their own individual positions on the texts and issues addressed in the class. In the Assimilation course, because there were no clear answers to the basic question posed by the class ('Should gay people assimilate to mainstream culture?'), in the course of the semester, various students became advocates for particular positions on the topic. One of the butch lesbians always took an assimilationist stance that centered on gay marriage; one of the straight women consistently argued a queer perspective that rejected most social institutions, including marriage. Thus, in terms of the course content itself, there were multiple sites of 'intellectual truth' in the room, only one of which was centered on the teacher. Even more importantly, because of this, much of the class discussion involved the students responding to each other rather than to anything the professor had said. As a result, the professor's traditional role as moderator made him the center of the discussion in only the most nominal sense.

Moreover, precisely because the classroom is a complex social field, it's important to remember that there are always multiple levels of interaction and various agendas at play in the room. While the professor may tend to assume that the primary goal in the classroom is instruction, the students' motivations, both individual and collective, are more complex. Some students simply want to fulfill the basic course requirements and collect three more credits toward graduation; other students are looking for intellectual interchange and become genuinely involved in a particular class; some students fluctuate between these two poles. Moreover, while the students often react to each other intellectually, the classroom for them is also a complex social, emotional, and sometimes even romantic field. Bob wasn't the only one who was 'mac-ing' that classroom; one of the bisexual women went through a series of crushes on several of the other women in the class. Moreover, if identity is continually enacted, then on any given day the students will be performing aspects of their identities, including gender and sexual orientation, not merely as a simple continuation of previous performances but also as a complex reaction to the texts under discussion, the identity performances of the other students, and others' responses to their own performances. Rather than being a unitary entity, then, any classroom is the site of multiple points of view, academic and personal goals, and social interactions. To put it another way, if the classroom itself can be compared metaphorically to a man, it would have to be a man with multiple personality disorder.

Even more important than this obvious pluralism, however, is the fact that pedagogy is not a thing but a process. And this means that, like masculinity itself, conventional pedagogy (and its patriarchal underpinnings) must continually be enacted in order to exist. And that, as I've already noted, means the continual possibility that it will fail. Now, I'm not really thinking here about failures of the teacher's authority – like the long running and highly comic battle I had with two women who insisted on working the Sudoku puzzle during class – if only because I'm a bit reluctant to gender authority itself as male, which simply assumes gender stereotypes in the process of attempting to critique them. Rather, I'm thinking about the eruption of alternate identities and complex forms of interaction in class discussion, something that is particularly clear in a Lesbian and Gay Studies class. It's at such moments that the patriarchal underpinnings of the pedagogical model of English Studies are challenged in a more serious way than when students won't put the Sudoku puzzle away. Two examples, both conveniently bearing on questions about the nature of masculinity itself, should help to make the point clear.

Example 1: During a discussion of *Brokeback Mountain,* one of the bois in the class (we can call him 'Chad') concluded his analysis of the film's representation of gay men with an apparent digression intended primarily for comic effect. He found Jake Gyllenhaal's performance unrealistic, he said, because Jake didn't fully convey how painful anal intercourse can sometimes be for the recipient. If Jake believed in method acting, Chad argued, he should have practiced at home with a dildo first so that he could have made the right noises during the sex scenes.

Now, on one level, Chad was simply trying to get a laugh and to shock some of the straight people in the room, and he succeeded admirably in both of those goals. But it was clear, to me at least, that there was more going on here: Chad was also implicitly articulating a gay male perspective, specifically a boi perspective. If some of his classmates were taken aback by the sexual explicitness of the comment, its true shock value lay in the fact that it completely skewed their views of male sexuality or how a man would think or what a man would want. Although I know Chad hadn't read Queer Theorists such as Lee Edelman or D. A. Miller, and while I'm not sure he was entirely conscious of it, he was thus making the same point about gay male identity that they've made: in contrast to hegemonic masculinity's emphasis on well-defined boundaries, both for the ego and the body itself, its fear of penetration on a number of levels, Chad was articulating a version of masculinity that was more porous, more open, at least corporeally, to an osmotic relationship with others, even if that sometimes hurts. Moreover, the classes' discussion of gay and lesbian and queer perspectives on various issues was usually pursued, following academic conventions about intellectual interchange, on a certain level of conceptual abstraction that often worked, in effect, to erase the corporeality of gay identity. It was precisely the sexual explicitness of Chad's comment, which directly insisted on the details of the gay male body and its sexuality, that did more than any argument about gay marriage to provide some of the straight students with a clear understanding of a gay man's view of the world. Finally, it seems salient that Chad's reading of *Brokeback* was that 'homosexuality ruined everyone's lives', a message that he lamented in 'the most important gay film of our generation'. Although I would call this a misreading of the film's complex perspective on the subject, it is a telling one, for Chad's implicit sense that homosexuality is socially disruptive not only shaped his understanding of the film but also influenced his classroom behavior. A boi is supposed to be a little bit outrageous, a little bit disruptive, so that Chad's comment not only articulated but enacted his sense of his sexual identity. In other words, it was precisely at the moment when he was shocking people that Chad was not only presenting things from a boi's perspective but also actually *being* a boi.

Example 2: One of the texts for the class was a 1994 essay by Mark Simpson about metrosexuality ('Metrosexuality: Male Vanity Steps Out of the Closet'), identifying the phenomenon and discussing it as the result of attempts by marketers to extend the consumption of fashion and grooming products beyond the gay community to straight men. During class discussion of the essay it was soon clear that most of the class was comfortable with the larger implications of the article: that masculinity has multiple forms and changes over time. For example, the sorority girls in the class got Simpson's point immediately because, I learned from them, the metrosexual alternative to hegemonic masculinity was rife among fraternity boys. Bob, on the other hand, was having none of it. He insisted that such alternate masculinities represented inadequate variations on 'real men' and rigorously defended his own hegemonic view that a man should be a bit scruffy. Besides, he said, he did grooming too: 'I get up in the morning and I look in the mirror, and I want to vomit because I'm so ugly, and then I shower and shave'. At this point, one of the straight girls ('Toni') turned to him and said, from across the room: 'That's not grooming; that's just hygiene'. Once again, the entire class cracked up.

Now, leaving aside Bob's rather bizarre remark about what we might call his 'auto-bulimia' (which seemed calculated to insist on his masculinity by asserting his ugliness but which was also another moment where his normal self-confident masculinity seemed to falter a bit, looking for reassurance), this struck me as a fairly complex moment that actually enacted the classes' more abstract debate about varieties of masculinity. If, on one level, Toni was simply trying to clarify terms and definitions and thus distinguish between two types of masculinity, on another level her remark was also a critique of Bob's version of masculinity. While she presented it comically – she was also trying for a laugh – her response overtly suggested that Bob's view of proper masculine behavior might be wrong, at least so far as grooming is concerned. Even more importantly, in the context of the semester as a whole it was possible to see the comment as a not so subtle putdown that reflected a certain exasperation on her part with Bob's tendency to speak *ex cathedra* and dominate class discussion. If the content of the class discussion was about varieties of masculinity, I'd argue that the remark was the point when one form of masculinity was being rejected, contested as much by the action of the remark itself as by its content. In short, this was the moment when Toni finally said 'no' to Bob's performance of the hegemonically masculine.

Both of these examples are, of course, moments when the normal proceedings of traditional pedagogy failed: one student was sexually explicit, another one got a bit testy with one of her classmates. But I consider these aberrations in classroom decorum as fortunate in a way, as important symptoms of a deeper incoherence in the pedagogical ideal of the discipline of English Studies, moments where, like masculinity itself, the class revealed itself as plural and unstable. Classrooms are not always centered on the teacher or on intellectual issues nor are they always dispassionate or unemotional. They are also sites where, as with Chad, individuals are not only articulating but enacting (often, articulating by enacting) alternate forms of identity and where, as with Toni and Bob, the relations between various definitions of masculinity, of gender, are continually contested and negotiated, sometimes even more through the form of the discussion than through its content. Because the Assimilation class was explicitly presented as a site where alternate forms of identity were clearly acceptable, such moments may have been more obvious there, but I can say from experience that incidents like these occur in every class. If we want to understand and rework the gendering of the classroom then this involves more than simply insuring that girls and boys are called on equally. We also need to pay attention to and validate those 'digressive' moments in the classroom when the multiplicity of both pedagogy and gender become evident. At the end of the semester, 'Keri', one of the sorority girls, gave me her informal assessment of the course. 'It was a good class', she said, 'But we got off the subject a lot'. I agreed with her completely about the first part of her statement. As to getting off the subject, though, I don't think we ever did.

Note

1. While most people are familiar with the concept of the 'queen', 'boi' is an identity category in lesbian and gay subculture that is substantially less familiar to the general public. Originally coined to designate young masculine lesbians (or 'tranny bois'), the term quickly mutated, following a logic of parallelism, to apply to slightly feminine younger gay men as well. The fact that the difference between a boi and a queen is largely a matter of degree rather than kind confirms that gender presentations are extremely varied and that even subcultural nonce categories merely present artificial but culturally recognizable segments of what is actually a continuum of behaviors.

Works cited

Butler, Judith. 'Imitation and Gender Insubordination'. In *Inside/Out: Lesbian Theories, Gay Theories*. Ed. Diana Fuss. New York: Routledge, 1991. 13–31.
Clarkson, Jay. 'Contesting Masculinity's Makeover: *Queer Eye*, Consumer Masculinity, and "Straight-Acting" Gays'. *Journal of Communication Inquiry*, 29 (2005): 235–255.
Gardiner, Judith Kegan. 'Introduction'. In *Masculinity Studies and Feminist Theory*. Ed. Judith Kegan Gardiner. New York: Columbia University Press, 2002. 1–29.

Halberstam, Judith. *Female Masculinity*. Durham: Duke University Press, 1998.

Kimmel, Michael. *The Gendered Society*. New York: Oxford University Press, 2000.

——. 'Integrating Men into the Curriculum'. *Duke Journal of Gender Law and Policy*, 4 (1997). http://www.law.duke.edu/journals/djglp/articles/gen4p181.htm

Knights, Ben. *Writing Masculinities*. New York: St. Martin's Press, 1999.

O'Barr and William M. 'Roundtable on Advertising and the New Masculinities'. *Advertising & Society Review*, 5 (2004). http://muse.jhu.edu/cgi-bin/access.cgi?uri=/journals/asr/v005/5.4roundtable.html

Sadker, Myra, David Sadker, Lynn Fox, and Melinda Salata. 'Gender Equity in the Classroom: The Unfinished Agenda'. In *The Gendered Society Reader*. Ed. Michael Kimmel with Amy Aronson. New York: Oxford University Press, 2000. 210–216.

8
Invisible Men: Reading African American Masculinity

Rachel Carroll

In her 1990 article 'Fear of the Happy Ending: *The Color Purple*, Reading and Racism', Alison Light critically reflected on the experience of teaching a text authored by an African American woman in the context of a course on 'women's writing' and in a pedagogic situation in which students and tutors were all white. Light recorded that 'as tutors we were surprised that the discussion did not lead into the issue of racism, and at the ways in which it did not';[1] the 'fact' of Walker's and her protagonists 'blackness', did not in itself guarantee that 'race', as a contested issue, would be addressed. This chapter will reflect on the racial and gendered construction of African American masculinity in the context of the teaching of African American writing as a literary tradition: that is, it will explore the teaching of masculinity as a gendered identity in a context where the contesting of racial constructions of identity is foregrounded. It will explore what might be termed the curricula construction of racial and gendered identity as represented in, and as produced by, counter canons of literature. The premise of this discussion is that it is not simply the racial or gendered identities of tutors or students that produce the ways in which a text is understood; the curricula and pedagogic contexts within which the text is placed have the potential to make possible certain readings and to preclude others.

The identifications and appropriations which are at work in a pedagogic situation – between tutor, student and subject matter – are as complex, contingent and contradictory as the identities of its subjects. The study of African American writing, and its contribution to a historic struggle for liberty and equality, can inspire impassioned student engagement. Such an identification can be both problematic and productive. It may be problematic where it contains an evasion of a more troubling sense of implication in the histories of racial and colonial power; it may be productive, however, where it is expressive of a student's transformed sense of his/her own relationship to history and identity. Indeed, the provisional and imaginative occupation of the space of a historical and cultural 'other' can effect a meaningful estrangement from one's own lived identity. The pedagogic situation is in a sense a performative space and it is the 'staging' of the encounter with the subject which may determine how, and with what effect, positions of power, knowledge and authority are occupied. What will be staged below is a contextual reading of African American masculinity designed to make possible an understanding both of the complex implication of race and gender and of the uneven allocation of patriarchal masculinity. A reflection on the identification of Alice Walker's *The Color Purple* as 'woman's text' within a canon of women's writing will act a starting point from which to revisit constructions of racialised masculinity within the canon of African American male writing. I will conclude with a more sustained consideration of a poet whose work has received limited critical attention; a reading of Etheridge Knight's representations of masculinity, written within the historical context of the Black Power movement, is offered as a productive contribution to the ongoing curricula construction of counter-canons and histories.

Curricula constructions of African American masculinity

The complexity of the context of Alison Light's 1990 article is worth exploring in some detail. Alice Walker's 1982 novel *The Color Purple* is possibly the African American text with which non-African American readers are most familiar whether directly, or indirectly through the Steven Spielberg's popular if controversial 1985 film adaptation. With the expansion of courses dedicated to the study of 'women's writing', a genre inaugurated by Anglo-American feminist literary criticism, *The Color Purple* became canonised as a key text. Indeed, in the British context and period in which Light was writing, where courses dedicated to women's writing were becoming commonplace but where courses dedicated to African American writing (outside of American Studies programmes) were less common, *The Color Purple* may well have been the first, and in some cases only, African American text which students encountered. Studied within this curricula context, as a 'women's text' within the genre of 'women's writing', Walker's novel offers a representation of the patriarchal oppression, both economic and sexual, of women and of successful resistance to that oppression through self-expression. What this context risks, however, is the occlusion of the specific experience of African American women as subjects constructed through racialised as well as gendered historical contexts and cultural discourses. In its focus on the dynamics of an African American community, *The Color Purple* belongs to an African American literary tradition characterised by the foregrounding of African American perspectives rather than a reactive response to the imperatives of white racism. However, studied outside the context of this tradition, this strategic displacing of the privileged white gaze may pass unseen and the historical context of racism, which is one enabling condition for the double oppression of black women, may remain invisible. The curricula construction of *The Color Purple* as a woman's text may inadvertently contribute to the invisibility of the racial construction of the gendered identity of women (whether white or not-white); however, it may also inadvertently perpetuate the racial construction of gendered identity for African American men. While the female African American protagonists of *The Color Purple* are universalised as 'women' in feminist terms, the racial identity of the men who oppress and abuse them is not: what may problematically remain, then, is a *woman*'s testimony to her oppression and abuse by *black* men. The way in which the representation of these men is constructed through patriarchy as a *racialised* history and discourse is not examined; on the contrary, racist stereotypes of black men as sexually predatory and abusive may be inadvertently animated.

Critical reflection on teaching *The Color Purple* emphasises the danger of occluding the racial construction of African American women's gendered identity; it seeks to make white (female) feminists more conscious of the relationship between femininity and race, but leaves unexamined the implication of race in the construction of masculinity. What is invisible here is the status of African American masculinity as both a racialised and gendered construction of identity and the ways in which it can, as such, be enlisted to perpetuate patriarchal constructions of gender or mobilised to challenge them.

Much work in masculinities studies has sought to make visible the 'invisibility' of masculinity as a normative and universalised subject position; the trope of 'invisibility' has also been deployed in critical white studies to denote the unexamined status of whiteness which it seeks to contest. Writing in the introduction to their 1996 collection, *Representing Black Men*, Marcellus Blount and George P. Cunningham observe that 'African American men as gendered, rather than racial, subject, rarely if ever provide a strategic site for interrogating constructions of gender and sexuality within contemporary theory';[2] the 'invisibility' of masculinity as a gendered construction of identity is here specifically obscured by the historical and racialised construction of African American identity as constituting a problematic 'visibility'. The pedagogic context for a contextual understanding of the construction of African American masculinity will need both to 'make visible' the invisibility of masculinity and to contest the problematic visibility of race. The historical formation of African American masculinity demonstrates the way in which patriarchal prerogatives, while nominally universal, have been unevenly and unequally distributed to male subjects. Hence, an exploration of the impact of historical and cultural contexts, and more specifically of the experience and legacy of American slavery, is essential in enabling an understanding of the construction of African American masculinity as a racial and gendered subject position. Kobena Mercer and Isaac Julien's comments, in their key text 'Race, Sexual Politics and Black Masculinity: A Dossier', make explicit the relationship between patriarchy, masculinity and race:

> Whereas prevailing definitions of masculinity imply power, control and authority, these attributes have been historically denied to black men since slavery... In racial terms, black men and women alike were subordinated to the power of the white master in the hierarchical social relations of slavery and for black men, as *objects* of oppression, this also cancelled out their access to positions of power and prestige which are regarded as the essence of masculinity in a patriarchal culture. Shaped by this history, black masculinity is a highly contradictory formation as it is a subordinated masculinity.[3]

This reflection makes possible an important insight into the contradictions and inconsistencies of patriarchal masculinity. The asymmetry at work in the relationship between racial and gendered identity for African American men in a patriarchal context is captured by Robyn Wiegman when she refers to the 'contradiction that resides within all patriarchal relations': namely that 'empowerment based on maleness is not automatically conferred but can be, and frequently is, quite violently deferred'.[4] In a patriarchal culture where power is gendered masculine and powerlessness feminine, empowerment and disempowerment are experienced as gendered properties even where the distribution of power is determined not only by gender but also by constructions of race. Consequently, the historical struggle of African Americans to remedy what can be described as the 'violent deferral' of their rights as American citizens is implicated in gendered discourses of identity in complex ways.

The teaching of the African American literary tradition currently takes place in a contemporary context where African American expressive culture is an integral feature of a globalised mass culture; however, the latter has also been instrumental in the circulation of contentious representations of African American masculinity, including those identified with gun, gang or drug cultures. In such a context, it is perhaps all the more imperative to foster a more complex understanding of the politics of appropriation of normative gendered discourses. bell hooks is one critic who has written powerfully about the internalisation of patriarchal ideology by African American men:

> If black males are socialized from birth to embrace the notion that their manhood will be determined by whether or not they can dominate and control others and yet the political system they live within (imperialist white-supremacist capitalist patriarchy) prevents most of them from having access to socially acceptable positions of power and dominance, then they will claim their patriarchal manhood, through socially unacceptable channels.[5]

hooks' polemic is compelling and persuasive, but its import is perhaps contingent on its audience; that is, whether her readership is identical or other to the 'they' to which she refers. If the pedagogic situation does not endeavour to enable an understanding of the complex and conflictual relationship between patriarchy and race, there is perhaps a danger that such a critique might be too readily incorporated into an essentialising presumption that 'black males' are somehow more prone to patriarchal positioning: a presumption recursively confirmed by the availability of cultural representations of African American men as violent, criminal and sexually oppressive. I want now to turn to some key texts in the African American canon (oral, autobiographical, fictional and poetic) and to suggest how a focus on their relationship to normative gendered discourses might enable an appreciation of the historical and contemporary complexity of the relationship between race and gender.

An appeal to normative, and hence patriarchal, gendered roles has historically played a significant role in African American discourses of emancipation: as Wiegman has written '...both feminist-abolitionist and early African-American writings were overwhelmingly concerned with the slave as a gendered being, finding in the possibilities of sexual difference a rhetorical strategy for marking the African (-American)'s equal humanity'.[6] Wiegman questions the presumption that patriarchal discourses can only have conservative or reactionary effects: when appropriated by African American counter-discourses, a gendered role which is otherwise normative can become subversive. In the context of the teaching of gendered identity, an apprehension of sexual difference as 'rhetorical strategy' effectively casts into relief the constructed nature of all gendered positions. Hence, Sojourner Truth's celebrated retort to a white abolitionist audience at Akron, Ohio in 1851 – 'ain't I a woman?' – both mobilises *and interrogates* a gendered discourse in support of her rights as a woman and as an African American.[7] As a speaking subject who is marginalised both by race and gender, Truth's relationship to the dominant racial and patriarchal discourses of femininity – the 'cult of true womanhood' – is necessarily ironic. However, different kinds of complexity are evident in the relationship of a male speaking or writing subject to dominant gendered discourses in which 'manhood' promises a citizenship equated with masculinity. Michael Kimmel has written that the 'quest for manhood – the effort to achieve, to demonstrate, to prove masculinity – is one of the animating experiences in the lives of American men, as well as the history of the United States'.[8] The historical claim to 'manhood' on the part of African American male subjects explicitly challenges the racial construction of citizenship but in doing so potentially subscribes to its gendered formation as masculine. Key texts in what Stephanie Brown and Keith Clark describe as 'the great patri-narrative of African American men's literary genealogy'[9] depict the struggle by African American men to attain 'manhood' understood as synonymous with citizenship. In *The Narrative of the Life of Frederick Douglass: An American Slave* (1845), Douglass is inadvertently empowered as an African American by the actions of his white mistress Mrs Auld, who teaches him to read and write; his realisation of the power of the written word acts as a formative moment both in the context of his narrative and in the formation of an African American literary tradition. However, pivotal in a different way is Douglass's account of his confrontation with his overseer, Mr Covey; in physically overpowering a white man, Douglass is arguably contesting his 'feminisation' as a man by slavery and asserting his prerogatives as a masculine subject. 'Manhood' is the prize at stake in this battle and Douglass's overturning of Mr Covey's racially sanctioned masculine authority authorises his right to freedom in a way that his entry into written language, as enabled by his white mistress, cannot. The implications of the internalisation, as opposed to appropriation, of the patriarchal ideology inherent in American political philosophies of citizenship and freedom are exemplified in Richard Wright's 1940 novel *Native Son*. The novel's protagonist, Bigger Thomas, can be thought of as a literary manifestation of an African

American masculinity which has become a recurring trope in contemporary culture; the black man as hostage to patriarchal definitions of masculinity who seeks to remedy his disempowerment by transgressive appropriations of anti-social power (see hooks above). It is in the context of the historical demonisation of African American male heterosexuality as predatory and violent that Bigger Thomas accidentally smothers the daughter of his white employer. Wrongly suspected of the rape of a white woman but subsequently actually guilty of the rape and murder of a black woman, Bigger finds himself empowered by assuming the pathologised identity which a racist discourse has prepared for him. The problematic potential contained within this 'rhetorical' appropriation of normative discourses of gendered identity is articulated by Abdul R. JanMohamad:

> The fundamental premise of *Native Son*, which Wright entirely fails to examine critically, is that the protagonist can become a 'man' through rape and murder and overcome the racialization of his subjectivity... the phallocratic order can foreclose effective forms of resistance and can position some black males in such a way that they are incapable of asserting their 'manhood' against racism except by replicating phallocratic violence against women.[10]

Sojourner Truth's oratory, Frederick Douglass's autobiography and Richard Wright's fiction have been the focus of extensive critical attention by scholars working in African American studies; I want to conclude with a more sustained reading of an author whose work has not received the same kind of critical attention. The poetry of Etheridge Knight was written within the context of the Black Power movement and its rhetorical appropriations of militant masculinity but is interesting for the ways in which it critically explores the disempowered state of African American masculinity as a gendered as well as a racial condition without making recourse to recuperative or compensatory modes of patriarchal masculinity as its remedy.

Violent spaces: Modes of masculinity in the poetry of Etheridge Knight

The Black Power movement's appropriation of modes of militant masculinity to express its political agenda continues to have iconic power and currency, as seen in the popularity of Spike Lee's 1992 biopic *Malcolm X* and the commodification of the imagery and discourse of Black Power which accompanied it. The potent and provocative public image of the movement was one of the black male body as autonomous, disciplined and armed. The performative power of this mode of masculinity can be attributed not only to its reiterative enactment on public stages but also to its citational relation to previous historical constructions of African American masculinity: more specifically, in its refutation of the African American male subject as 'feminised' or 'emasculated'. As Wiegman has suggested '... it was precisely the elision between material and symbolic feminization that underwrote a great deal of Black Power rhetoric in the 1960s and 1970s, begetting the turn in popular culture towards images of a powerfully masculine black male'.[11] While this performative masculinity has the potential to subvert the dominant racial modes of masculinity which it cites, it equally has the potential to perpetuate patriarchal modes of masculinity. This tension is identified by Erika Doss who recognises an attempt to 'recuperate the socially constructed masculine attributes of power, militarism, independence, and control that had been denied subordinated black men since slavery' but also questions the way in which such strategies 'reinscribed the most egregious forms of patriarchal privilege and domination, from machismo and misogyny to violence and aggression'.[12] Most problematic, perhaps, is the employment of a rhetoric of sexualised power and violence, in which women (both black and white) are explicitly reduced to objects over which white and black men compete; the rhetorical force of Eldridge Cleaver's infamous invocation of rape as a weapon of racial insurrection in his 1968 autobiography *Soul on Ice* can be historicised, but cannot justify any rationalisation of the material and historical reality of women's experience of sexual violence. It is important to note that the phallic sexualisation of libertarian politics is a phenomenon common to counter-cultural movements of the late 1960s; however, in a context in which radical racial politics were being given an explicitly gendered, and arguably patriarchal, mode of expression, Etheridge Knight's poetry is especially interesting for its reflective and affective representation of modes of masculinity other then the empowered or the militant.

Knight's poem 'Hard Rock returns to Prison from the Hospital for the Criminal Insane'[13] explores the appropriation of patriarchal modes of masculinity, revealing it to be not perhaps not so much recuperative as compensatory. 'Hard Rock' centres on the acting out on a masculinity which is racialised and embodied in specific ways. As Arthur Flannigan Saint-Aubin writes:

There was a time when the black male was a non-person, when his body was not his own possession, a time when his subjectivity, his self-representation, and his representation by others emerged from this non-possession. At the same time, however, he *was* his body; that is, he was recognised and valorized for his physicality.[14]

Hard Rock manifests a form of African American masculinity closely identified with a male body attributed with hypermasculine properties; namely, the productive powers of the labouring body (which have historically been exploited) and the phallic powers of the sexualised body (which have historically been demonised). Hard Rock simultaneously evokes, perpetuates and avenges a certain stereotype of the African American masculinity as reducible to sheer materiality. The masculinity which is staged through this performance is characterised by an ability to inflict significant harm on other men and by the capacity to endure considerable pain; it is staged in scenes of Hard Rock's power over other men and the reiteration of his impenetrability by power. The 'scars' [2] on his body 'prove' [2] his masculinity; the 'lumbed ears' [3], 'welts' [3] and scar that 'plow[s]' [5] though his temple and hair testify to the impact of this testing of his manliness. Hard Rock's monumental masculinity can be considered compensatory in the way in which it symbolically, if not actually, avenges the disempowerment of African American men: 'our Destroyer, the doer of things/We dreamed of doing but could not bring ourselves to do' [34–5]. Moreover, this compensatory action is a collective currency, distributed through prison legend by 'the WORD' [7], and providing the shelter of the 'cloak/of his exploits' [15–16]. Hard Rock avenges the history of injustice carried in his appellation as a 'black son of a bitch' by a 'hillbilly' [24] by becoming the 'crazy nigger' [20] mythologised by his peers; he mobilises a dehumanising stereotype in order to exorcise the power which it carries. However, the 'emasculation' of African American men by racism in patriarchal culture is forcibly reasserted in the narrative of the poem. Both prison and the 'hospital for the criminal insane' are disciplinary institutions; in this context, medical technology is not a curative but punitive in its effects. Hard Rock's 'geld[ing]' [12] by surgical lobotomy and the forcible administration of electro-convulsive therapy returns his body to the status of an animal whose value is determined by its managed productivity. The performance of hypermasculinity becomes a cautionary spectacle when Hard Rock is 'turned loose... to try his new status' [11–12] and his 'tam[ing]' is publicly 'tested' [23]. The possibility that his 'new status' may signal the adoption of a new more subtly coded performance, that of 'being cool' [32] can be understood as an attempt to recuperate a measure of individual and collective dignity from his highly gendered humiliation; that is, one of the 'variety of attitudes and actions that serve the black man as mechanisms for survival, defense and social competence' and which act as 'facades and shields ... As black men fight to preserve their dignity, respect and masculinity'.[15] The failure of the attempt to read Hard Rock's mutilated body as a testament to heroic resistance is suggested in the final lines of the poem in which the captive bodies of African American men are depicted as historically inscribed: 'The fears of years, like a biting whip,/Had cut deep bloody grooves/Across our backs' [36–38].

If in 'Hard Rock' the speaker assumes a vicarious relationship to a performative and compensatory masculinity, then in 'The Violent Space (or when your sister sleeps around for money)' the speaker's relationship to dominant modes of masculinity can be characterised as deferred and displaced. In this poem competing modes of masculinity – the paternalist and the predatory – are evoked over the objectified body of an African American woman but the male speaker allies himself with the feminised body of the woman both as a child and as her sibling. Two bodies are captive in the 'The Violent Space': the addicted male body of the speaker and the sexually possessed body of his sister. The foregrounding of the male speaker's embodiment as giving rise to forms of vulnerability, powerlessness and dependency makes possible a sense of continuity between his marginalised masculinity and her exploited femininity. The sub-title of the poem implies a reputed identity by which the sister who 'sleeps around for money' is implicitly constituted by others as promiscuous and as herself economically exploitative: that is, as the agent of a transgressive feminine sexuality not as the object of an exploitative male heterosexuality. Her loss of name to the 'nameless void' [27] is the effect of its circulation and the compromises to which it subjects her identity: from 'the Virgin Mary' [24], to the eponymous subject who is offered consolation in the gospel standard 'Oh, Mary don't you weep' [28], to the juke joint Mary enjoined to 'shake your butt' [29]. The 'exchange [of] notes' [1–2] – whether commercial, musical or written – throughout the poem positions the African American female body as the object of exchange. The desire of the speaker to protect his sister from sexual exploitation, and his powerlessness to realise this desire, raises issues to do with the racialised distribution of patriarchal prerogatives: '... one of the salient historical features of racism has been the assumption that white men – primarily those who are economically powerful – possess an incontestable right of access to black women's bodies'.[16] The desire of an African American man to reclaim the sexualised and objectified body of an African American woman could be interpreted as the assertion of patriarchal right. However, this would be to deny the affective complexity of a desire which is not simply reducible to its patriarchal construction. This affect occasions a reflection on feelings of powerlessness expressed in questioning refrains – 'What should I do?' [20], 'what do I do' [32] and 'I am not bold' [35] – culminating in an admission of an inability to 'take hold' [35] of the 'weight' [36] of the white male body which bears down on an African American woman's 'black belly' [36]. Moreover, rather than compete to take the privileged place of the white male body the speaker expresses a sense of sharing his sister's place 'alone now/In your pain'. The admission of vulnerability is reinforced by the evocation of childhood subjectivities, with the speaker still occupying the position of sibling to his diminutive 'lil sis' [18] and as incapable of casting out the and 'demon[s]' [22; 30; 35] of sexual exploitation as of ever outrunning the fear of 'the Bugga man' [6; 13; 23].

The 'violent space' to which Knight's eponymous poem alludes might be understood as representing the contested and conflictual space of racialised masculinity: that is, a space which witnesses the complex relationship between subordinated and patriarchal masculinities, and the ways in which empowered forms of masculinity are internalised, appropriated or refused. If the 'violent space' indicates the forcible exclusion of African American men from the privileges of patriarchal heterosexuality then the motifs of emptiness, absence and the void in Knight's poetry suggests that it is not a space which the poems seek to reclaim or colonise. Historically, racial constructions of African American masculinity have taken contradictory but mutually reinforcing forms; disempowered but accommodated in its 'feminised' and 'emasculated' form or pathologised and demonised in its phallic and masculine form. African American counter-discourses, from abolitionist through accommodationist to Civil Rights and Black Power discourses, have had to negotiate with discourses of racial identity which are thoroughly implicated in discourses of gendered identity. I have tried to demonstrate how a contextual and gendered reading of African Americans texts might enable a pedagogic context in which the subversive appropriation of dominant modes of patriarchal masculinity can be appreciated: that is, a curricula context in which such negotiations with gendered norms are not simply dismissed as only or inevitably reactionary or regressive. Equally, such a context is designed to enable a recognition of the ways in which a refusal of empowered forms of masculinity is not necessarily reducible to a state of powerlessness; that is, to appreciate the significance of a refusal to make recourse to recuperative or compensatory modes of patriarchal masculinity.

This chapter began with some reflection on the way in which a pedagogic context may produce and stage the complex identifications and appropriations which it contains; this was not to dismiss the significance of the racial and gendered identities of the tutors and students who populate this context but rather to suggest that racial and gendered identifications do not simply or exclusively originate in their subjects. I would like to conclude this chapter with a reflection on the location of issues of race, masculinity and patriarchy in the curriculum. In the curricula context of a course on masculinities – or indeed in the context of a collection of critical essays on masculinity – the study of African American masculinity might seem to offer an exemplary 'case study'; the cultural and historical construction of masculinity is impossible to overlook in contexts where the prerogatives of masculinity are not automatically conferred on all biological males but are explicitly denied to some biological males on the basis of race. However, such a conscription of the study of African American masculinity in the service of the study of masculinity would be to mobilise a problematic power relation whereby African American masculinity is required to 'do the work of race', so to speak, in the name of gender. In the same way that the location of 'gender' within the curricula space of 'women's writing' might serve to perpetuate the invisibility of masculinity as a gendered construction of identity so might the exclusive location of 'race' within the space of non-white cultural formations serve to perpetuate the invisibility of 'whiteness' as racial construction of identity. Pedagogic reflection of the kind pioneered by Light has offered insights into the complexities and paradoxes attendant on white students' identifications with African American subject positions. Rather than merely problematise students' affective investments, perhaps the most productive outcome of such reflection might be to examine the ways in which the curricula might enable students (and tutors) to reflect constructively on the racial and gendered construction of their own subject positions.

Notes

1. Alison Light, 'Fear of the Happy Ending: *The Color Purple*, Reading and Racism', *Plotting Change: Contemporary Women's Fiction*, ed. Linda Anderson (London: Edward Arnold, 1990) 87.

2. Marcellus Blount and George P. Cunningham, 'Introduction: The "Real Black Man?"', *Representing Black Men*, ed. Marcellus Blount and George P. Cunningham (London and New York: Routledge, 1996) x.
3. Kobena Mercer and Isaac Julien, 'Race, Sexual Politics and Black Masculinity: A Dossier', *Male Order: Unwrapping Masculinity*, ed. Rowena Chapman and Jonathan Rutherford (London: Lawrence and Wishart, 1988) 112.
4. Robyn Wiegman, *American Anatomies: Theorizing Race and Gender* (Durham and London: Duke University Press, 1995) 12.
5. bell hooks, *We Real Cool: Black Men and Masculinity* (London and New York: Routledge, 2004) 57–58.
6. Wiegman, *American Anatomies* 44.
7. An account of this speech is anthologised in *Call and Response: The Riverside Anthology of the African American Literary Tradition*, ed. Patricia Liggins Hill (New York: Houghton Mifflin, 1998).
8. Michael Kimmel, 'Integrating Men into the Curriculum', http://www.law.duke.edu/journals/djglp/articles/gen4p181.htm (17 August 2005).
9. Stephanie Brown and Keith Clark, 'Melodramas of Beset Black Manhood? Meditations on African American Masculinity as Scholarly Topos and Social Menace: An Introduction', *Callaloo* 26:3 (2003) 733.
10. Abdul R. JanMohamad, 'Sexuality on/of the Racial Border: Foucault, Wright, and the Articulation of "Racialized Sexuality"', *Discourses of Sexuality: From Aristotle to AIDS*, ed. Domna Stanton (Ann Arbor: University of Michigan Press, 1992) 108.
11. Wiegman American Anatomies, 15.
12. Erika Doss, 'Imaging the Panthers: Representing Black Power and Masculinity, 1960s–1990s', *Prospects* 23 (1998) 493.
13. As anthologised in *Call and Response* 1998. The poems discussed here were first published in Knight's 1968 collection *Poems from Prison*.
14. Arthur Flannigan Saint-Aubin, 'Testeria: The Dis-ease of Black Men in White Supremacist, Patriarchal Culture', *Callaloo* 17:4 (1994) 1061.
15. Richard Majors quoted in Flannigan Saint-Aubin 'Testeria' 1059.
16. Angela Y. Davis, 'Rape, Racism and the Capitalist Setting', *The Angela Y. Davis Reader*, ed. Joy James (Oxford: Blackwell, 1998) 136.

Works cited

Blount, Marcellus and George P. Cunningham. 'Introduction: The "Real" Black Man?' *Representing Black Men*. Eds Marcellus Blount and George P. Cunningham. London and New York: Routledge, 1996.
Brown, Stephanie and Keith Clark. 'Melodramas of Beset Black Manhood? Meditations on African American Masculinity as Scholarly Topos and Social Menace: An Introduction'. *Callaloo* 26:3 (2003) 732–737.
Davis, Angela Y. 'Rape, Racism and the Capitalist Setting'. *The Angela Y. Davis Reader*. Ed. Joy James. Oxford: Blackwell, 1998.
Doss, Erika. 'Imaging the Panthers: Representing Black Power and Masculinity, 1960s–1990s'. *Prospects* 23 (1998) 483–516.
Flannigan Saint-Aubin, Arthur. 'Testeria: The Dis-ease of Black Men in White Supremacist, Patriarchal Culture'. *Callaloo* 17:4 (1994) 1054–1073.

hooks, bell. *We Real Cool: Black Men and Masculinity*. London and New York: Routledge, 2004.

JanMohamad, Abdul R. 'Sexuality on/of the Racial Border: Foucault, Wright, and the Articulation of "Racialized Sexuality" '. *Discourses of Sexuality: From Aristotle to AIDS*. Ed. Domna Stanton. Ann Arbor: University of Michigan Press, 1992.

Kimmel, Michael. 'Integrating Men into the Curriculum'. http://www.law.duke.edu/journals/djglp/articles/gen4p181.htm. (17 August 2005).

Liggins Hill, Patricia (Ed.). *Call and Response: The Riverside Anthology of the African American Literary Tradition*. New York: Houghton Mifflin, 1998.

Light, Alison. 'Fear of the Happy Ending: *The Color Purple*, Reading and Racism'. *Plotting Change: Contemporary Women's Fiction*. Ed. Linda Anderson. London: Edward Arnold, 1990.

Mercer, Kobena and Isaac Julien. 'Race, Sexual Politics and Black Masculinity: A Dossier'. *Male Order: Unwrapping Masculinity*. Eds Rowena Chapman and Jonathan Rutherford. London: Lawrence and Wishart, 1988.

Wiegman, Robyn. *American Anatomies: Theorizing Race and Gender*. Durham and London: Duke University Press, 1995.

9
Lifelong Learning in the Lifelong Poem

Chris Thurgar-Dawson

> And then went down to the ship, Set keel to breakers, forth on the godly sea [...]
>
> — Ezra Pound, *The Cantos* 1, ll.1–2[1]

> AS IF BECAUSE OF FATHER I WENT DOWN TO the soft forced notions of boats went as wax before repleteness in summer's heat [...]
>
> — Lisa Robertson 2001, 365[2]

> Silly humans, always filling in the blanks.
>
> — Susie, Cropcirclers Blog, 15 May 2006[3]

Extensive written and oral discourses already exist about my two key topics in this chapter: masculinity and the contemporary long poem. There is even a growing body of work, certainly in the international academy, which tentatively links and explores the two topics. What is lacking, however, and what this chapter seeks in its own way to address, is pedagogic reflection on how more meaningfully to learn from, teach and deliver such material. I should state at the outset that this chapter draws heavily on two specific teaching moments: the first belongs to Professor Cairns Craig who delivered the Long Poem MA module at the University of Edinburgh, United Kingdom in 1992, and the second goes to Prof. PhDr. Jaroslav Macháček at Palacký University in the Czech Republic who enabled my own Modern Long Poem module in 1995–1996. Part 1, below, focuses on masculinities in various contemporary long poem texts themselves. Part 2, concerning experiential pedagogy, is derived from the modules named above. Since I use long poem examples in most of the modules I teach – including those which address transformative writing in the creative/critical mode – my general argument stems from the strong belief that the contemporary long poem is a valuable and underused student resource in the exploration of male, not to say 'epic', identity.

Not to say 'epic' identity: Masculinity and the contemporary long poem

The quotations from Pound and Robertson which act as epilogues to this chapter tell of one mode of interrogation in which a (loosely speaking) postmodern long poem replies to a modernist one. The modernist one in this case is certainly not speaking in its own voice either – but is a roundabout reply to *Odyssey* XI, with a nod to two Medieval Latin translators, Andreas Divus of Justinopolis and Georgius Dartona of Crete.[4] We can suppose that the latter pair were themselves writing back to the set of Greek authors known as Homer, via a string of Romance intermediaries and pseudo-secular soothsayers: '[s]illy humans, always filling in the blanks'. Well yes, but us or them, and is there another option? But actually the most enlivening quotation of the three is Susie's, whom I have taken out of context in order to model her point. It reads in full:

> Silly humans, always filling in the blanks. I never thought about instinctual narrative tendencies. I do remember someone once pointing out that the whole gamut of education was to build and bridge connections between things that we otherwise might not notice. And I liked that notion at the time. But now, I'm thinking that we make up a lot of the stuff that we teach, even what we learn we make up. But I like stories
>
> (Susie, Cropcirclers Blog, comment posted 15 May 2006)

This opens up a question familiar to neurologists and behavioural psychologists: do we perceive first and then narrate, or do we instinctively build our perception into an immediate narrative, because humans are hard-wired to do so and simply have no choice? Are we primarily 'seeing' and 'visualising' creatures or 'narrating' and 'story-making' ones? But we need some more context and are still guessing at the real topic of conversation, the trigger for Susie's informal pedagogic message.

The physical object under discussion is the second edition of Sharon Thesen's *The New Long Poem Anthology* (Robertson 2001), which has become something of a standard work in the field, replying as it did to Michael Ondaatje's original *Long Poem Anthology* (Ondaatje 1979) and indeed to its own first edition which appeared to some acclaim in 1991. Susie, a student teaching practitioner, is making a message board comment on an original posting by 'Kaleidoscope' entitled 'Experiencing Reading/Writing the Long Poem'. Kaleidoscope is clearly a poet herself and the relevant part of her original posting is here:

> Thanks to Erin Mouré, who last year suggested that I write 'friends' for my poems, and who lead me toward reading long poems, I'm presently reading Sharon Thesen's 2001 *The New Long Poem Anthology* which includes such wonders as Anne Carson's 'The Glass Essay' and Jeff Derksen's 'Interface.' These two long poems are the beginning of a change in my poetic sensibility. What were once skimpy little lyrics (apologies, older poems...) are evolving into pages of startling material. Writing in this form is teaching me about the end. Thesen points out '... it is easy to see how both the resistance to end and the desire to continue [...] are the essential experiences of life itself.' The end can be anywhere, but if I keep pushing it off (in poetry we can choose to push off the end) I'm constantly surprised.
>
> (Kaleidoscope, Cropcirclers Blog, comment posted 15 May 2006)

In her stark admission that 'writing in this form is teaching me about the end', Kaleidoscope voices, perhaps unwittingly, one of the commonest concerns of the critical debate about the long poem, a debate stretching back to Ted Weiss, Rosenthal and Gall, Robert Kroetsch and the now infamous Long-liners Conference in 1985.[5] If the long poem is by default about delay, deferral and 'the resistance to end' (occupying the position of both symbolic ritual and ritualised symbol), then this appears in some sense to be a threat rather than a liberation to masculinity. Playing with this threat – ultimately the threat of death from which no man can save either his family or himself – becomes a generic prerequisite of this procrastinating form, a form described by Hamlet's players as 'poem unlimited', by Pound as 'the tale of the tribe' and by Poe as 'a flat contradiction in terms [...] mere size'.[6]

Certainly the role of man as saviour–warrior, of male subjectivity itself as at once embattled, questing, nation-forming and heroic is central to the epic tradition in western poetry and western culture until the end of the eighteenth century. In various ways it was the long poem itself which was the cause of this situation. Nor was it Wordsworth's *Prelude* that heralded a key change in sensibility; throughout the seventeenth century extended poetic texts were produced which already held masculinity in some disarray.[7] Nevertheless is was not until the twentieth century that publishing itself could allow the serious marketing and dissemination of long poem sequences and extended forms that challenged the bastions of epic masculinity with any force. While texts by H.D., Marianne Moore, Gertrude Stein, Amy Lowell and Laura Riding may have paved the way for overdue regenderings of the genre, and undoubtedly led to transitional texts by writers such as Barbara Guest, Lorine Niedecker, Kathleen Raine, Elizabeth Jennings and Elizabeth Bishop, it was not until truly postmodern times that the women's long poem and extended sequence had significant impact in replacing (more accurately, re-placing) male epic poetry. Indeed, if the 1980s have been recognised for various Thatcherite cultural and nuclear shifts in power relations, not to mention the concomitant rise of the 'New Man', they have not been recognised as the time in which female authorship of the epic *qua* took over from the male. Suddenly Diane Wakoski, Leslie Scalapino, Susan Howe, Kathleen Fraser and Lynn Hejinian in America found themselves matched by Daphne Marlatt, Phyllis Webb, Betsy Warland and Lola Lemire Tostevin in Canada. Even in the United Kingdom Anne Stevenson, Sally Purcell, Penelope Shuttle and others were joining the epic rewrite. Clearly, epic masculinity in English poetry was losing key ground, though as we shall see in the following three extracts, the crisis in traditional constructions of what it meant to be manly needed little help from across the gender divide.

The first example is the oldest: it is Ed Dorn's *Gunslinger*, published as a whole in 1975 and reissued with a new introduction by Marjorie Perloff in 1989.[8] *Gunslinger*, written in 4 books over 7 years remains one of the great poetic achievements of the last century but is known today to only a handful of academics and students of American literature. In it, Dorn simultaneously traces the decline of the myth of the American West alongside the debilitating processes of emasculation itself. He performs this through the thinly disguised figure of Howard Hughes (known as 'Robart') who also travels West on his specially adapted railroad carriage. It is a narrative of the utter failure of capital economy, of the parody of those popular forms which bribe and cajole consumer society, and finally of the triumph of language over substance in what Dorn announces as his 'ABSOLUTE LINGUATILT SURVEY SITE' (G 141). It is also an extended piece of often supra-real writing which charts like no other the highs and lows of the mescaline years of the sixties, as the key characters travel in their marvelous 'constellation' towards their ultimate destination, the 'hill-of-beans' in California. If the anti-hero of the piece is Gunslinger himself, referred to variously as Slinger or Zlinger, the hero of the poem is the 'bombed Horse' who takes on the voice of the philosopher Heidegger and becomes something of an ontological creature. The rest of the posse include Taco Desoxin, Tonto Pronto, Champagne Lil and the pseudo-medical man, Dr Jean Flamboyant, all of whom employ a creative panoply of voices and identities as befits their current situation on their stage-coach headed West. Parodying such historical landscape tropes as the American dust-bowl, the Californian gold rush, the Texan oil fields and Hollywood itself, the characters' Waynesque trot towards the setting sun becomes an important and vivid rewrite of American cultural politics in the second half of the twentieth century. The sixth and final member of the team is a character whose proper name is 'I', which leads among other things to the syntactically playful lines, 'I is dead, the poet said/poet that ain't grammatical' and in many ways typifies the crisis of the modern male, as argued here by Erik Cohen:

> [...] modern men are often alienated from the centre of their society or culture. Some of them may not be seeking alternative centres: their life, strictly speaking, is meaningless, but they are not looking for meaning, whether in their own society or elsewhere. For such people, travelling in the mode just described, loses its recreational significance: it becomes purely diversionary – a mere escape from the boredom and meaninglessness of routine
>
> (Cohen 1979: 185)[9]

But *Gunslinger* deconstructs masculinity more effectively in the narrative of Robart (Hughes) himself. At every turn, stereotypical social constructions of masculinity are established, upended, reestablished, faked, faded and lampooned. Hughes' famous last years on the ninth floor of the Desert Inn Hotel, Las Vegas provide the appropriate backdrop to a story that has seen him scale the heights of Trans World Airlines and plumb the depths of the Spruce Goose. He becomes, in Dorn's text, the ultimate symbol of self-crippling masculinity in a society that has learned neither to care for, nor to notice its symptomatic and metonymic victims. If Dorn's long poem is what it claims to be, that is, 'SUBLIME/STARRING THE MAN' (*G* 123), then the man it stars has indeed been found, but he was not (yet again) the man we were looking for.

Robert Kroetsch provides the second interrogation of masculinity here. Kroetsch is the perfect example of the Canadian long poet. He makes the right wrong moves, he uses the expected unexpected forms, he has made resistance to narrative an art form in an art form that resists all narration; blending biography with deconstruction, he abhors genre yet writes paradoxically within it. All this he does from a uniquely Canadian perspective and with no small amount of style. Indeed, he claims that to write like this is, uniquely, the Canadian perspective: the recuperation of an all-but-unnamable, settler identity. In addition he provides, as the contemporary critic of the long poem has come to expect, a marvelously complex assemblage of theories to cover all aspects of his poetic practice. *Completed Field Notes* (1973–1989),[10] in 3 books and 20 sections, complete with contents page, prologue and author's note end-piece, is a comprehensive lesson in self-regarding Canadian masculinity:

> a series of related poems that would in devious ways seek out the forms sufficient to the project (I leave it nameless) announced by Wordsworth and Whitman and rendered impossible by the history and thought and art of the twentieth century. Since the eloquence of failure may be the only eloquence remaining in this our time, I let these poems stand as the enunciation of how I came to a poet's silence. And I like to believe that the sequence of poems, announced *in medias res* as continuing, is, in its acceptance of its own impossibilities, completed. (author's note, *CFN* 269)

This author's endnote which claims, significantly, that 'the eloquence of failure may be the only eloquence left in this our time' is both central to the argument of this chapter and a useful point of entry stylistically. The prose here is oppositional, corrective, balanced. It is the kind of writing that constantly seems to be seeking its double, its *doppel*, its other. We move from the nineteenth to the twentieth century, from the expectancy of naming a 'project' to 'nameless', from 'eloquence' to 'failure', from 'enunciation' to 'silence', from 'continuing' to 'completed'. Such oppositional progress is highly ratiocinative in its structure, displaying the same contrapuntal strategies which form such an important part of the main body of the poetic text itself. The words seem to lie in wait for their partners, to anticipate their semiotic other, and it is this anticipation which drives the text forward as much as the weighted metrics of traditional poetic texts. As George Woodcock has observed, '[i]t is a two-steps-forward-one-step-backward kind of poetry'.[11] The writing desires simultaneously to affirm and deny the male voice in the same instant of enunciation and this schizophrenic challenge informs *Field Notes* at every turn. It lies deep at the heart not only of the split absence and presence of the linguistic sign, but also deep within what it means to set down the male identity of the Canadian (anti-)hero:

> Canadians seek the lost and everlasting moment when chaos and order were synonymous. They seek that timeless split-second in time when the one, in the process of becoming the other, was itself the other. The city of such dreams is unrealizable; the poem of the occasion becomes the unendable long poem.
>
> (Kroetsch, *The Lovely Treachery of Words*, 68)[12]

For Kroetsch, this sense of 'space all over the place'[13] is written on a gendered landscape. It is the Prairie space of his Alberta childhood, and the 'vast but contained environment [of] endless land and towering skies'[14] of the Northern Territories where he worked on inland riverboats from 1948 to 1951. This is 'the geography of middle space', where 'the very act of speaking announces space' (*LTW* 36, 164) and which Kroetsch contrasts so openly with the capitalised West in these extracts from his 'Upstate New York Journals':

> *Sunday, October 31, 1971 ...*
> The old/new struggle in the capitalistic West: land as
> earth and land as commodity. The connection lost,
> we find it. My deep longing of recent days for the
> west of my blood and bones. My ancestral west, the
> prairie west, the parklands. (*LTW* 141)

> *Sunday, January 14, 1973 ...*
> In the west we are possessed of a curious rhetoric. A
> rhetoric that goes back to religion and politics, to the
> outcry, to the curse, to the blessing, to the plea, to
> the song. Not to the educated man, imagining himself to
> be reasonable. (*LTW* 146)

The writing of this opposition which compares the masculinity of the urban, metropolised West with the masculinity required by the vast open landscape of the 'prairie west' had no poetic tradition in Canada until the 1960s. At that time a community of 'Prairie Poets' gradually appeared from various western provinces, all with the common aim of in some way recuperating the lost 'curious rhetoric' of which Kroetsch speaks. Apart from Kroetsch himself, the work of Eli Mandel, John Newlove and Dale Zieroth was instrumental in beginning to re-place the Canadian west in a form that was neither fictive in its handling of quintessential maleness nor necessarily naturalistic. The Canadian realist novel which had in many ways made its home on the prairies ('This fiction makes us real' as Kroetsch has said), seemed in no position to deal with the socio-economic changes which were remorselessly turning paternalistic prairie smallholdings into the horizonless voids of multinational agribusiness. For that task the Prairie Poets had to 'seek out the form suitable to the project', a project which has been strenuously continued since then in the work of a new generation of western poets: Andy Suknaski, Roy Kiyooka, Glen Sorestad and others. It was a task that belonged, Kroetsch felt, 'Not to the educated man, imagining himself to be reasonable' but to an authentic masculine voice that became masculine only by disavowing any notion of successful masculinity in the first place.

Since men, rather than women have been seen characteristically as the namers, the sex which has the power over the linguistic signifier, sometimes referred to as a 'pact of nomination', my third example comes from Edward Kamau Brathwaite's second New World Trilogy, republished as *Ancestors*.[15] The naming process lies at the heart of this long poem and to understand the trilogy fully in terms of linguistic annunciation, it is necessary to understand the nation language concept of 'Nommo'. For this I refer to Brathwaite's extended essay 'The African Presence in Caribbean Literature' written between 1970 and 1973,[16] since it provides the clearest explanation of the cultural reference behind the technique. Again I want to underline the fact that this is a specifically gendered concern relating to the Barbadian sociolect and to Brathwaite's insistence in writing poetry that is appropriate to the failing man's dialogue with his local environment: '[w]hat I am saying is that the choice of word (nommo) dealing with experience in and out of the *hounfort*, must be appropriate to the place and the experience' (*R* 227).

'Nametracks' as the title itself suggests, links the ideas of linguistics and naming with those of tracking and leaving a ground-trail, a male tribal role. This is evident in the way the text trails down the page swerving from side to side but also in the difficulty faced by the 'ogrady' figure to name the slave poet. In fact, in the movement of the punning and repetitive letter-swapping it is as much, perhaps, nametricks as nametracks. Again we can read close parallels with male characters in other long poems. Ed Dorn's *Gunslinger* faces exactly the same fear of being 'described' in Book One of his eponymous poem, 'Are you trying/to "describe" me, boy?' (*G* 25) while the Canadian Trickster figure in *Completed Field Notes* connects us to an acknowledged but hidden and unnameable Arcadian mythology. However, whereas Kroetsch and

Dorn see their task as one of unnaming and whilst Walcott is on record in many places for his project of initiating an 'Adamic naming', Brathwaite deals almost exclusively with the powers and dangers involved in the process itself of re-naming, a process which is ever subject to variform strategies of veiling, disclosing, doubling and secreting to which the contemporary long poem is both particularly suited and justly renowned. Coming full circle, the whole concept of male fame is itself linked to the idea of reiterating or re-sounding a name, thus for example the French word for famous, *renommé*, the 're-named'.

Brathwaite, too, recognises the travelling masculine internationalism of this power of language, a power which in the West is very much in question today, having gradually replaced an oral tradition or 'auriture' with a scriptural one, 'écriture'. Erring on the side of caution, it is fair to say that the feminist challenge to the denotative inefficacy of the word has been a largely twentieth-century phenomenon. Significantly, in 'The African presence in Caribbean literature', Brathwaite asserts that 'a certain kind of concern for an attitude to the *word*, the atomic core of language . . . is something that is very much present in all folk cultures, all pre-literate, pre-industrial societies' (R 236). In his desire to resubmit to us the full pre-existing Benjaminian aura of the Word as Sign, Brathwaite follows a long line of Modernist poets and proves himself to be the only true Modernist (albeit a late Caribbean Modernism) of this chapter. We think of Eliot's 'that is not what I meant at all', of Pound's 'it coheres all right/even if my notes do not cohere', of Beckett's 'I can't go on, I'll go on', of H.D.'s 'undecipherable script', and above all, perhaps, of David Jones's life-long 'utile' project to lift up valid signs, 'things that somehow are redeemed'. Such recognition of the failure of a male language to signify, of the poem, literally, to mean, is nevertheless part and parcel of Brathwaite's own poetic use of 'nam', 'nyam', 'nomminit' and of the whole Bantu concept of 'nommo'. We learn that '[t]he word (*nommo* or name) is held to contain secret, power . . .':

People feel a name is so important that a change in his name could transform a person's life. In traditional society, in fact, people often try to hide their names. That is why a Nigerian, for example, has so many names. Not only is it difficult to remember them, it is difficult to know which is the name that the man regards or identifies as his *nam*. If you call the wrong name you can't damage him. Rumpelstiltskin in the German fable and Shemo-limmo in the Jamaican tale are other examples of this.

(Brathwaite, *R* 236–237)

The importance of the highly poetic 'Nightwash' episode of *Mother Poem* can now be recognised. If the male coloniser of empire, personified in the figure of 'ogrady', to whom the piece is addressed, can be prevented from naming the poet by his own name, the 'maim what me/mudda me name' (*MP* 64), then he can be linguistically and culturally outwitted by the Bajan nation-language adoption of ancient African ritual. No matter how hard ogrady tries to beat the slave-poet into submission (notice the play on maim/name), his identity is veiled, hidden, secure. The note on the word 'nomminit', typical of Brathwaite's notes in its tone of bare understatement and partial decoding of the secrets of his text, runs as follows:

> p. 64, 1, 9. nomminit: nation-language sound/word for 'cultural domination', literally 'the gobbling up of the (other's) name'.
>
> (Brathwaite, *MP* 121)

Similarly, the note for 'nam' itself is quoted below, since it demonstrates the wordplay techniques which underlie and inform the whole trilogy and, again, is symptomatic of the kind of annotation which we must learn to read not just as explication and commentary, but as an integral part of the poetic text itself:

> p. 62, l. 8. nam: secret name, soul-source, connected with nyam (eat), yam (root food), nyame (name of god). Nam is the heart of our *nation-language* which comes into conflict with the cultural imperial authority of Prospero (O'Grady), pp. 58–64.
>
> (Brathwaite, *MP* 121)

Jumping forward, briefly, to the notes for *X/Self*, we should compare this definition with another explanation of 'nam' which again stresses the political implications of the word in relation to its colonial past, a whole new frame of reference being carried along in the same three letters:

> *Nam* (the title of the poem and word used throughout the work) means not only *soul*/atom but *indestructible self/sense of culture under crisis*. Its meaning involves root words from many cultures (meaning 'soul'; but also (for me) *man* in disguise (*man* spelled backwards)); and the *main* or *mane* of *name* after the weak *e* or tail has been eaten by the conquistador; leaving life (*a*/alpha) protected by the boulder

consonants *n* and *m*. In its future, *nam* is capable of atomic explosion: *nam . . . dynamo . . . dynamite* and apotheosis: *nam . . . nyam . . . onyame*

(Brathwaite, *XS* 127)

The neologising tendency which gives rise to words such as 'poopapadoo' and 'boobabaloo' (*MP* 64) is again dependent on our knowledge of the 'onomatopoeia and sound-symbols' of nommo in which 'a kind of conjuration . . . the same magical/miracle tradition as the conjurman' means that 'Vibrations awake at the centre of words' (*R* 238). The conjurman figure or 'word see-er' of African descent becomes the male poet of oral tradition and of performance poetry and in this respect Brathwaite reemphasises his Modernist hand. The belief that the poet could redeem or act as social prophet was a persistent theme of the European literary avant-garde throughout the twenties and thirties and in this way the second trilogy's linguistic gendering is seen to rewrite or reconfigure the history of empire not simply by replacing it with nation-language, but by infusing certain experimental principles of British Modernism with the environmental experience of the Barbadian mindset towards the word. The textscape of this long poem thus becomes a triage point for wounded British, Bajan and African masculinities.

The three long poem examples I have used above, then, have intrinsic merit when addressing questions about the representation of male identity – political, linguistic and ideological. But they also have extrinsic value for those interested in using such extended texts within a teaching context. Such value that links the life of the text to the lives of real readers may take several forms, and it is to these broadly educational concerns that I now turn in Part 2.

Pedagogy: Teaching the lifelong poem to male students

While the poems above only hint at the importance of masculinity in the contemporary long poem, and do need to be lived with and more carefully explored to appreciate the lifelong elements of their inscription, nevertheless they appear to trigger some interesting reactions in the seminar room. These range from classic 'male inexpressiveness' involving poor levels of self-disclosure (Balswick 1988), to masculinity being performed as the 'flight from the feminine' (Kimmel 2001), and link no doubt to wider historical interpretations beyond the institution regarding 'hegemonic masculinity' (Tosh 2004).[17] However, in the absence of firm data on the subject, let me begin by listing some empirically observed behaviours by male students while delivering this material:

1. An attempt to advise the tutor that the text was too difficult for other students on the course.
2. The taking the tutor aside at the end of the seminar to demonstrate that the student had superior cultural knowledge about the poem which he needed to prove in the others' absence.
3. A male student who gradually took on the role of 'expert' within the group to impress female students at the expense of the group's formerly supportive dynamic.
4. A male student who would say nothing at all and hide in his shell for weeks at a time, only to announce at the end of the module that it was all far too basic for him.
5. A male learner who exhibited laddish body language and lethargic poses in an attempt to impress other 'mates' in the class so as to form a peer clique instead of a small learning group.
6. A participant who increasingly saw himself in the role of the tutor's apprentice, using great care and self-awareness in complex processes of deference and counter-transference.
7. A mature student who used his life experience to way-lay and side-track critical discussion and the group's own objective development of ideas.
8. A football fan whose interpretation of each text always seemed to bear upon a heroic male in Tottenham Hotspur FC.
9. A student with specific learning needs who used aggressive and self-aggrandising outbursts about the so-called poor interpretations of his peers.
10. A male student of modest ability, who felt he had to rectify his intellectual shortcomings by dominating group sessions with his voice alongside the careful maintenance of a tiresome and emotionally costly 'cool' aura.
11. The strategic men, always to be found 'down the pub' after each class, dropping in and out of sessions in a piston arrangement to minimise contact time.
12. Mutually supportive but detrimentally inseparable male students, who worked so well together that they inevitably drew attention to themselves as Tweedle Dum and Tweedle Dee and whom none of us ever reached.

13. A male gay student who used his sexuality to elicit sympathy and humour from the rest of the group while actually being both lazy and indulgent.

It would be too much by far to claim that these examples were limited to the delivery of a long poem module – indeed I can think of certain more destructive examples from core survey modules – but I am suggesting here that pseudo-epic, narrative poems in which the construction and performance of fragmentary masculinities is highlighted, can and do cause exaggerated male learning behaviours to be exhibited in the seminar space. If resistant-defensive mechanisms are to be turned to the advantage of the group as a whole, an aim which is achievable if rarely accomplished, the tutor cannot afford to situate her/himself in a position which overlooks, disregards or is silenced by such interventions. Neither intentionally complicit nor unintentionally condoning the actions of such difficult participants, the tutor may have to allow certain short-term antagonisms to run their course if medium and longer-term learning goals are to be achieved by the whole group.

Nor is the male tutor in some way magically immunised against errors in behaviour and judgement. Experience only goes so far in gauging the harmful effects of certain individuals' ego displays. The male tutor can react aggressively himself; can get drawn into an unsavoury battle of wills; can weaken in the face of manipulation and misdirection; can, in short, be little better or far worse than the male student himself. In such cases where the power shifts uneasily between tutor and group and back again, little of lasting pedagogic value is achieved.

Having said that it is speculative to account for the high incidence of awkward male behaviour (which I take to be group transference indicators of one sort or another) in regard to one particular genre or sub-genre such as the long poem, it seems nevertheless likely that because men and women construct their preferences differently when entering the text, a generic cause may in the end be responsible for such effects in the space of the seminar room. According to reader research undertaken by David Bleich in the 1980s, male students consistently looked for a strong narrative voice, whereas female students tended to perceive a narrative 'world':

> After collecting five response statements from each of the four men and four women, we found a significant gender-related difference in response only with regard to literary genre. We did not see that response varied significantly with the gender of the author, and we

did not find any obvious differences in the respondents' sheer use of language. [...] Men and women both perceived a strong lyric voice in the poetry, usually seeing it as the author's voice, while in the narrative men perceived a strong narrative voice, but women experienced the narrative as a 'world', without a particularly strong sense that this world was narrated into existence.

(Bleich 1986: 239)[18]

Long poems in the Lucanian, subversive mode, such as the three discussed above, are in the deliberate business of disrupting any sense of sustained narrative voice, yet they easily build a story-world, a world that is accessed through an accumulation of associated but disparate chunks of information. It would then be possible to suggest a correlation between evidence of frustrated male behaviours and an absence of 'strong narrative voice'. Put another way, when a certain group of texts offer a weak narrative voice, there is little for the male reader to buy into, less material with which to build either an empathetic or cognitive link. When narrative voice begins to fragment, weaken or flex, it seems the text-world is more easily made significant by female readers who do not perceive such features as an obstacle to building a meaningful whole.

Where does this leave us and what conclusions can we usefully draw? In the English Studies seminar room we know that the male student is almost certain to be in the minority. We also know, in my own institution, that he is statistically twice as unlikely to make it through his degree at all. This speaks of a pressing need to research and acknowledge the obstacles to learning experienced by male participants in Higher Education. Generic research by Bleich and others is a good start, but if we are to move beyond general identification of the problem and unverified suppositions on the cause, what we need next is some serious consideration of male student perspectives, specifically those on UK English courses. The trope of the defeated reader is not one any educator wishes to encourage; the trope of the male defeated reader, a faltering minority, still less so.

Notes

1. Ezra Pound, *The Cantos of Ezra Pound* (New York: New Directions, 1991), 3.
2. Lisa Robertson, 'Debbie: An Epic', in *The New Long Poem Anthology*, ed. Sharon Thesen (Vancouver: Talonbooks, 2001), 365. Michael Ondaatje, *The Long Poem Anthology* (Toronto: Coach House Press, 1979).

3. Susie, comment on 'Experiencing Reading/Writing the Long Poem', Crop-circlers Blog, comment posted 15 May 2006, http://www.cropcirclers.blogspot.com (accessed 4 March 2006).
4. Carroll F. Terrell, *A Companion to The Cantos of Ezra Pound* (Berkeley: University of California, 1993), 1. For a full discussion of the traditional Virgilian versus the subversive Lucanian epic modes, see David Quint's persuasive argument in *Epic and Empire: Politics and Generic Form from Virgil to Milton* (Princeton, NJ: Princeton University Press, 1993).
5. See Frank Davey and Ann Munton, eds, 'The Proceedings of the Long-liners Conference on the Canadian Long Poem, York University, Toronto, 29 May – 1 June 1984'. *Open Letter* 6.2 (1985).
6. Poe makes this statement in his well-known 1850 essay, 'The Poetic Principle'. He goes on, 'If, at any time, any very long poem were popular in reality, which I doubt, it is at least clear that no very long poem will ever be popular again'.
7. See, for example, Richard Payne Knight, *The Landscape: A Didactic Poem in Three Books* (1795), reprinted as facsimile of 2nd edition (Farnborough: Gregg, 1972).
8. Ed Dorn, *Gunslinger* (Durham, NC: Duke University Press, 1989). Hereafter *G* in the text.
9. Erik Cohen, 'A Phenomenology of Tourist Experiences' *Sociology* 13 (1979), 179–201.
10. Robert Kroetsch, *Completed Field Notes: The Long Poems of Robert Kroetsch* (Toronto: McClelland and Stewart, 1989). Hereafter *CFN* in the text.
11. George Woodcock, *George Woodcock's Introduction to Canadian Poetry* (Toronto: ECW Press, 1993), 168.
12. Robert Kroetsch, *The Lovely Treachery of Words* (Toronto: Oxford University Press, 1989). Hereafter *LTW* in the text.
13. Woodcock, *George Woodcock's Introduction to Canadian Poetry* 166.
14. Ibid., 157.
15. Kamau Brathwaite, *Ancestors: A Reinvention of Mother Poem, Sun Poem, and X/Self* (New York: New Directions, 2001). Note, however, that references in the text are to *Mother Poem* (*MP*), *Sun Poem* (*SP*) and *X/Self* (*XS*) all originally published by Oxford University Press in 1977, 1982 and 1987.
16. Kamau Brathwaite, 'The African Presence in Caribbean Literature', in *Roots* (Michigan: Arbour, 1993). Hereafter *R* in the text.
17. Jack Balswick, *The Inexpressive Male* (Lexington, Mass: Lexington, 1988); Michael S. Kimmel, 'Masculinity as Homophobia: Fear, Shame and Silence in the Construction of Gender Identity', in Stephen M. Whitehead and Frank J. Barrett, eds, *The Masculinities Reader* (Cambridge: Polity, 2001), 266–287; and John Tosh, 'Hegemonic Masculinity and the History of Gender', in Stefan Dudink, Karen Hagemann and John Tosh, eds, *Masculinities in Politics and War: Gendering Modern History* (Manchester: MUP, 2004), 41–60.
18. David Bleich, 'Gender Interests in Reading and Language', in Elizabeth A. Flynn and Patrocinio P. Schweickart, eds, *Gender and Reading: Essays on Readers, Texts, and Contexts* (Baltimore and London: Johns Hopkins UP, 1986), 234–266.

10
Autobiographical Narratives in the Teaching of Masculinities

John Beynon

Introduction

This chapter is rooted in Cultural Studies, within which much valuable deconstructive work on gender (both femininities and masculinities) has taken place over the past two or so decades. Cultural Studies is the archetypal inter-disciplinary field, drawing upon, on the one hand, the Humanities (linguistics and literary studies, whether literary theory, text analysis, content analysis, narratology and stylistics) and, on the other, the Social Sciences (particularly ethnography, visual ethnography, life history, oral reminiscence and narrative analysis). Meanwhile, the recent 'narrative turn' in social research has witnessed a renewed interest in the autobiographical narrative, not only its form and content, but also its function and purpose (for example, Crossley 2000; Elliott 2005; Mishler 1999). Oral reminiscence is about documenting events and experiences ('the spoken'), as well as about the narrator ('the speaker'). Although this chapter privileges the former, the latter focus upon function is now being widely reflected in Cultural Studies: my own most recent published work, for instance, examines how inmates sought to recover, create and display masculinity through narrative in the midst of the emasculating environment of prison (Beynon 2006).

Masculinities are not easy to teach for a multitude of reasons. One pedagogical strategy that is likely to result in a fruitful learning experience for students is collaborative, lecturer-led research, starting with theory, moving to fieldwork, then ending with analysis (and presentation). Below I outline such a project, currently work-in-progress, focusing upon autobiographical narratives on the theme of Old Industrial Man. In what follows I start by saying something about students as researchers and the nature of autobiographical reminiscence

(Section A); then I outline a model for conceptualising masculinities in all their varieties (Section B); and, finally, I comment upon two autobiographical narratives (Section C) taken from the ongoing study of former working men's experiences of the industrial past in South Wales, centring on changes in work-related working class male identity since the 1930s. What factors, I ask, have shaped working class masculinities in South Wales in the recent past?

Section A: Researching men's lives

Old Industrial Man, along with the manual work-based masculinity he espoused, has been dismissed as limited and limiting by feminists, academics and journalists alike (Beynon 2002). With the advent of more plural masculinities from the 1970s onwards, he has increasingly been vilified as an oppressive patriarch trapped within an armour-plated machismo, a dinosaur as outmoded as the smokestack industries in which he laboured. Indeed, the glitzy, liberated New Man has been skilfully crafted to represent all that the Old Man is now held not to have been, namely emotionally literate and understanding; feminised and liberated; and all-too-willing to contribute to the full range of domestic and child-rearing duties. But before Old Industrial Man finally disappears should we not look more carefully at him and what shaped his masculinity and contest a reductionist view, widely current in some quarters, that caricatures him as little more than an ill-educated, Walter Morel-like domestic tyrant.

Students as researchers

In my teaching of masculinities I have long encouraged students as acolyte ethnographers to explore the minutiae of men's lives and how masculinities are lived, experienced and 'brought off' in everyday life. I have recently been using the South Wales project above as a stimulus to get students started on their own data gathering, something I have done successfully with other ethnographic projects in the past. Whilst I certainly do not present my own research as a template to be slavishly copied by students, I do insist that they start with theory prior to collecting data.

Students have ready access to a wealth of oral reminiscence within their own families and communities that can be insightful into changes in the nature of work; gender relations; the division of domestic labour; social and sexual mores; past class composition and attitudes; recreational pursuits; community life and so on. Gathered by both the lecturer and his/her students as a collaborative activity it can quickly accumulate into a valuable, comprehensive, topic-based archive, in the process throwing up a host of issues about both masculinities and the nature of oral reminiscence itself as the research passes through a number of stages:

- preparation, including reading, locating suitable respondents, making the necessary arrangements, establishing rapport and so on.
- data collection based on sensitive, open-ended interviewing.
- data transcription and data coding and ordering.
- data analysis and presentation, whether as an oral and/or written report.

The nature of autobiographical reminiscence

Autobiographical reminiscence is a particularly fruitful way of exploring how masculinity was shaped and experienced in the recent past. Clearly such data reveals something of the 'way it was', although its limitations should be readily acknowledged at the outset: the 'life-as-told' is not the same as the 'life-as-lived'. Narratives are often suffused with strong emotions, retrospective musings, memory condensations and contradictions of which the speaker may be unaware. Nevertheless, cross-triangulated with further accounts of working experiences (and supplemented by archival and documentary sources) it can be an admirable starting-point for students-as-embryonic-researchers. It uses the 'living memory' of a previous generation to explore their lives, working experiences and, in this case, masculinities. Such data, whilst it can never be a transparent mirror of past 'reality', can certainly reflect something of 'the way things were'. It is worth reminding ourselves, too, that a number of mediations take place between 'what happened' and 'the account of what happened', between how events were experienced then and how they are recalled and perceived now. The 'recollected past' always sees past events interpreted through the screen of the present. What was once experienced is recreated in an oral narrative framed by spoken conventions and may not only be subject to memory distortion, but also to the familiar human tendency to bathe aspects of the past in a nostalgic glow.

These oral recollections undergo a further mediation as the researcher renders them into text, drawing now on written and even literary conventions. S/he may (or may not) attempt to convey (as do sociolinguistic scholars) dialect, accent, register, tone, speed of delivery and associated paralinguistic features. S/he may even have to go to considerable lengths to render comprehensible to the reader what was said, as Lewis (1961) did, for example, in his classic 'The Children of Sanchez'. Furthermore, the interviewer has a considerable authorial role because it is s/he who frames the questions; establishes the interview agenda; and seeks clarification and, thereby, forces respondents to focus and elaborate. In this sense such 'auto/biographical' (Stanley 1993) data is 'dually authored'. Also significant is how respondents interpret the interview situation; view the interviewer and the topic under discussion; and decide what is expected of them. This version of the past, then, is not based on 'static' archival sources: indeed, the great majority of men I have interviewed to date in South Wales have relished the occasion as a rare opportunity to be listened to attentively as they momentarily 'hold the stage' and talk about long-past experiences that had, in retrospect, often been rendered into key incidents used to 'explain' aspects of their life story.

Whilst autobiographical narratives can tell us a great deal about men's lives and masculinities (as ways of seeing and being) were personally experienced in the recent past, it is important not to let the richness of such data conceal the influence of socio-economic and cultural forces beyond the individual. It is because of this that I insist that students start with theory and locate their data gathering within a theoretical framework. In my experience most students can, with the necessary prior training, become competent data-gatherers, but there is a tendency for the data gathering to develop into an end in itself. Some students are reluctant to select or edit it and insist that it is sufficient for 'the voices' to stand for themselves. Many find it difficult, even unnecessary, to move from this autobiographical level to a more analytical, theory-informed one. In what follows, therefore, I emphasise the centrality of theory as a starting point to inform both data gathering and data analysis. I contextualise two autobiographical narratives within a conceptual model of masculinities derived from the work of Mead (1934) and through which I seek to demonstrate that, whilst masculinities are experienced and expressed personally, they are largely shaped by external cultural, economic, geographical and historical forces.

Section B: Starting with theory: A Meadian model

Much gender theorising has failed to capture the interplay between society and individual agency, between the macro and the micro. Indeed, a dogmatic biological determinism has been superseded by an undue emphasis upon individual agency, so much so that masculinity is in danger of being reduced to little more than what are taken to be stereotypical 'masculine' or 'feminine' appearance and behaviour, as follows (Figure 10.1):

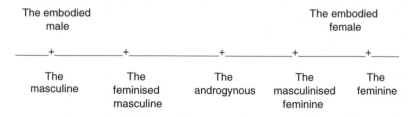

Figure 10.1   Gendered performative codes.

Indeed, no less a figure than Morgan (1992) writes that 'gender and masculinities may be understood as part of a Goffmanesque presentation of self, something which is negotiated (implicitly or explicitly) over a whole range of situations...we should think of doing masculinities rather than of being masculine' (1992: 47).

In an attempt to place the individual's personal 'bringing off' of masculinity more firmly into a wider social context I turn to Mead (1934) on identity and self, particularly his distinction between the 'Generalized Other', the 'I' and the 'Me'. I adapt this to propose a conceptual framework based on four 'life domains' to encapsulate the ongoing dynamic between the overarching social ('The Societal') and in which all our lives are embedded; the 'person inside' ('The Subjective'); the 'person-out-in-the-world' ('The Interactional'); and the unfolding 'Life Story' that chronicles, reflects upon and continuously seeks to make sense of the 'life-as-it-has-been-and-is-being-lived'. I believe such a model facilitates a better appreciation of the complexity of masculinities-in-the-plural (and also, of course, of femininities) and their socio-cultural formations. It is, of course, a diagrammatic representation of something that is far from static, with each of the life domains evolving as the life unfolds and the individual's sense of gendered identity gradually shifts under the influence of day-by-day experience, the ageing process and the ever-changing society in which the life is lived (Figure 10.2).

- *The Societal.* The equivalent of Mead's Generalized Other, the Societal operates on the level of discourse. It is analogous to the 'voice of society' as it 'speaks' to the individual through such agencies as family, culture and community; education; the state and legal

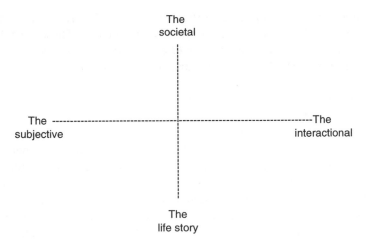

The
societal

The ---------------------------------------The
subjective   interactional

The
life story

Figure 10.2 A Meadian model of masculinities.

system; the mass media; and belief systems and so on. In other words, the Societal is about 'positioning' the 'male subject' by providing a regulatory framework, a template, for what is expected of the individual in order to 'be a man' and to demonstrate 'acceptable' masculinity. What is acceptable changes as social norms change and, furthermore, rarely does society speak in a single, unequivocal voice. What is more the individual can, of course, choose to accept, reject or modify these 'lifescript' prescriptions (what Harris 1995, aptly describes as the 'messages men hear'). The former relatively (but only relatively) fixed gendered behavioural codes relating to 'being a man' and 'being a woman' have today expanded and become both more various and more fluid. Indeed, the sheer proliferation of masculinities (that is, ways of 'being a man') in our time has led to the claim that there is 'a crisis' as essentialist views (which narrowly equate gender with biology) have been challenged, even overtaken, by those that define gender in more cultural terms.

- *The Subjective.* The equivalent of Mead's 'Me', this refers to the person's social construction of self and identity, more specifically of an interior sense of gendered identity and of how the individual determines himself (or herself) to be a masculine (or feminine) 'subject'. Whilst care has to be taken about mapping the accounts people give of themselves too closely onto interior subjectivities, autobiographical accounts are indicative both of how they view the world and of how they wish to be seen. These narratives are an essential part of the (direct and indirect) everyday presentation of self, which brings us neatly to the next domain, namely the Interactional.

- *The Interactional.* The equivalent of Mead's 'I', this draws specific attention to the outward and performative aspects of gender (e.g. Butler 1990). It refers to the 'actor' out in the world, 'enacting' masculinities in real life settings being informed by, but also informing, the 'Me'. From a dramaturgical standpoint (Goffman 1959) men and women today (in Western culture) have available to them an extended range of masculine and feminine presentational 'fronts', even moving between the two as the occasion demands. Indeed, the gendered link between the 'I' and the 'Me' is today is less direct, as illustrated in Figure 10.1, where the embodied male or female (the physical level) has access to a range of presentational and behavioural positions (the cultural level) across a continuum from, at its extremes, the overtly 'masculine' and the overtly 'feminine'. Gilmore (1990) and Cornwall and Lindisfarne (1994) are amongst the most insightful on 'doing masculinity' and it is certainly the case that more studies of 'masculinities-as-lived' are now appearing (e.g. Beynon 2006; Blackshaw 2003; Williamson 2004; Winlow 2001). However, many more ethnographies of how masculinities are 'brought off' in a variety of settings are badly needed.

- *The Life Story.* Our life story is the outcome of the ongoing interaction of the three previous life domains. We make sense of our life story by means of autobiographical narratives, especially the ones we tell ourselves, continuously updating it on the basis of new experiences. Our lives and the directions they take are never free of society, but are suffused by it, although the scope for considerable individual agency always exists. Morgan (1992) usefully refers to 'gendered life courses' in which 'characteristics – age, material status, class, ethnicity and so on – are not simply added to each other, but are seen in terms of a dynamic interaction over time and in relation to other life courses' (1992: 45). By scanning across the past, present and future (whether in thought or through autobiographical narrative) the individual attempts to render his/her still unfolding life story orderly and meaningful, a point I will return to later.

Section C: Two autobiographical narratives

Old Industrial Man in South Wales

It has to be remembered that South Wales was at the forefront of the Industrial Revolution and throughout the nineteenth century into the first half of the twentieth was a major centre of coal mining and heavy metal working. The gradual decline in the demand for coal finally culminated in the Miner's Strike of 1984–1985 against the closure of their industry by the Thatcher Government. Thereafter 'dirty jobs' were replaced by lower paid, light-industry-based and insecure 'clean ones'. What was left of Old Industrial Man in post-industrial, post-Devolution Wales has now finally disappeared, whether in mining, steel making or docking, along with the distinctive, class-based masculine culture associated with him, living on now only in the memories of elderly men.

Carrying out fieldwork in South Wales today, therefore, involves not only a research journey, but also a geographical one from a once heavily industrialised landscape (and the vibrant human activity therein) to a recently (and sharply) de-industrialised one. My respondents (the oldest to date is 97, the youngest 60) to date have either been formally approached to be interviewed or are people with whom I have just fallen into conversation. The formally arranged interviews have taken place in a variety of locales from an old peoples' residential home to pubs, clubs and a museum-based community memory project. Whilst I have occasionally tape-recorded I have mostly jotted down what was said, either at the time or as soon afterwards as possible. I have been greatly aided in this by using Pitman Shorthand, a useful skill acquired as a young journalist.

I want now to reproduce and comment upon two lengthy transcripts taken from the project in South Wales, the first by 'Handy Jack' and the second by 'Posh Dai'.

'Handy Jack'

I interviewed Jack (born Pontypridd, Rhondda, in 1916) in a Day Centre for the Elderly, where he 'helped out' by 'doing things around the place'. His delivery was interspersed with long pauses (indicated in the text) as he battled with an electrical plug he was changing on a hoover. He tells of his frantic search for work and itinerant lifestyle as a young man during the Depression and his subsequent willingness to 'have a go' at anything. At the age of nearly 90 he was still active, forever busy undertaking 'odd jobs' around his community. His narrative is a mixture of pride (at always having provided for his family) and envy (at what he sees as the 'cushy' lives of young men today).

I'm 'handy' – that is, I can turn my hand to virtually anything – plumbing, electrics, roofing, decorating, brick-laying, mechanics, car spraying, fitting windows, even digging ditches, if needs be! 'Handy Jack' is what everbody calls me, always have! (Laughs) I learned by watching, asking questions and doing. I served my apprenticeship 'on-the-job', so to speak. I'm no good at reading and writing, these (holds up his hands) are my brains! I still do odd jobs about the place. If it wasn't for me half the houses round here would have fallen down years ago! (Laughs) When I started in the 1930s there was bugger-all work in Ponty. So I packed my gear into a little canvas bag and went chasing after the work like you'd chase a rabbit! I was young and strong then. You'd go where it was! So I went everywhere – Berkshire, London, down to Devon, Bristol, Manchester, Liverpool – you name it, I've been there! I've been running, ducking and weaving ever since! I was a right little tough nut – still am! Put yourself first was what I learned 'cos no one else would! Mind you, I often think what my life might have been like if only my early circumstances had been different. But I always put bread on the table 'cos I was prepared to work eighteen hours a day if needs be, six days a week. I did it for years, but I always took Sundays off 'cos I'm a bit religious and I was brought up to regard Sabbath as a day of rest... Today? My grandson today sees far more of his kids in one day than I did in a month and does far more with them. I was always too busy scratching a living! I only ever saw them for an hour here and there and they grew up in next to no time! They were babies one moment, teenagers the next! My grandson isn't in that position. He had paternity leave when his kids were born! Just think of the answer I'd have got in my time if I'd asked for paternity leave! (Laughs) And he's as good as any woman about the place, cooks, cleans, does everything. His wife has a full-time job. The way things are going right now men will stay at home and women will be the breadwinners. Men and women could disappear – you'll not be able to tell the difference! My wife never had a job. I brought the bacon home, she raised the kids – that's the way it was then, that was the deal. Most working men wouldn't allow their wives to work, even if there'd been jobs around. It would have been a blow to their pride, their manhood. The man was the breadwinner, the woman the nest-maker, full stop!... Today is far better, no question about it! There's far more choices available. They're not pigeon-holed in the way my generation was. Then if you were a man, you were told to do this, this, then that! If you were a women, this, this and this! The path was laid out for you and you were pushed hard on your way and that was that!...I wasn't eased out of the nest at thirteen, I was bloody well hurled! (Laughs) It was start earning a crust or starve! Simple as that! The afternoon I left school my mother and father stood together and said, 'You've done with your schooling now, son, so get out and look for a job!'. (Laughs) Easier said than done, given thousands were unemployed at the time and everywhere you went there was a hundred waiting in front of you! So off I went and I've been scurrying around ever since!....Young men today don't know they're born compared to when I started. They've got it cushy!

'Posh Dai'

David, a distinguished diplomat and University Chancellor (born in the Gower 1943) relates the indelible impression a summer job on Swansea Docks prior to going to University more than 40 years ago made on him. Born into a well-off, professional family (his father had been a Western Circuit judge, his mother a general practitioner (GP)) and privately educated, he was an observer of the industrial working class. I interviewed him in his palatial London home and his narrative was delivered in a slow, deliberate tone. From the summit of all he has achieved in his successful career, he looks back nostalgically and concludes that some of his Swansea stevedores of the early 1960s were 'the finest kind of men imaginable'.

It was July, 1962, and I was 18 and had a place up at Oxford that Autumn. A pal of mine had landed a holiday job on the Docks and he asked me to join him. I didn't need the money and looked upon it as an adventure, really, a bit of a lark. We turned up early one lovely, sunny morning and were given the job of stacking sacks of flour from Weaver's Mill onto pallets ready for loading on board. They weighed a ton! At the end of each day my arms were dead! I'd cycle home covered in flour from head to foot, jump straight into a piping hot bath and then regularly fall fast asleep! Then, as the days passed, Johnny Walsh, my pal, and I began to come into contact with some of the dockers. And, of course, in those days there were hundreds of them. As 'College Boys' we were a prime target for their wicked humour. You soon learned to think before you spoke! From the moment I first opened my mouth I was nicknamed 'Posh Dai'! (Laughs) As we got to know them better some absolutely amazing characters began to emerge. There was a group of World War II squaddies who told wonderful stories and who'd clearly gone through God knows what and many of whom I now realise (forty years on!) were still deeply traumatised, but who had had to button it all up and get on as best they could and feed their kids. 'Press on regardless' was their motto and that's what they did – came home and just got on with it. But of all of them there was one character I'll never forget, a great shambling bear of a guy with the biggest shoulders I've ever seen on a man. His name was Edward Evans, but everyone knew him as Big Ed! He was a genuine working class intellectual who had left school at 14, gone to sea, then had worked on the docks for most of his life. Anyway, every fortnight or so he and a few of his chums used to take their flasks of tea and sandwiches during lunch hour (11.30 to 12.30) to this little brick storage shed on the King's Dock and there they would sit around and discuss a particular book they had all read since they last met! Today it would be called a book club. They invited Johnny and me along because, as students, I suppose they thought we would be able to contribute something. We weren't at all sure what to expect. I think we thought it would be a bit of a laugh! You know– Zane Grey, 'Titbits', 'The Reader's Digest', 'News of the World' – that sort of thing! We were right little snobs, but were we in for a big shock, boy were we in for a shock! As soon as they started we knew straightaway that we were way out of our depth, that we were high and dry! I remember the book under discussion was Anthony Sampson's 'Anatomy of Britain', which hadn't long been published. These ordinary working men- and there was about a dozen of them there! – had read Marx, Engels, Galbraith, Maynard Keynes, Weber, Durkheim, Freud, Tolstoy! I was never to come across a more intense, animated, informed seminar in any of the universities I subsequently attended including, after Oxford, Yale. They'd never had the remotest chance of an education – they'd done it for themselves, not for job advancement. But at the end of the day they were still stevedores. At 12.30 sharp they all stood up and went back to their loading and unloading! Looking back they were the finest kind of men imaginable and they deserved to go to Oxford far more than I did. All I'd done was pass a few exams! They'd been pushed around all their working life but had found dignity in books and ideas. There was no Open University then, just the WEA, Coleg Harlech and Ruskin, if you could get a place. I'd been brought up in a very closed world of private schooling, church and sport and I was very naive. From then on I had the deepest respect for self-educated and self-made people who climb a very steep hill with no help from anyone. For kids like me it was so much easier. We were born near the top of the hill, whereas they started off at the very bottom. Things would have been different if I'd been born in St. Thomas! I'll always think of them as heroic. In fact, those six weeks over forty years ago was an experience that, looking back, I can honestly say marked me for life. It changed the way I looked at the world. There are so many lessons in the past for future generations. It made me determined to ensure, as far as I could, that such terrible intellectual wastage was never repeated.

Different worlds: 'Handy Jack' and 'Posh Dai'

Jack and David provide vivid and insightful portraits of two very different worlds, namely Jack's impoverished Valleys' background in the 1930s and David's privileged Gower upbringing in the early 1960s. Both highlight the centrality of class to their subsequent life traject- ories (Stearns 1990) and both are portraits of 'respectability', given that the South Wales industrial working class has often being depicted as straddling a continuum between the hard-working 'respectable-and- aspiring' as opposed to the idle 'rough-and-feckless' (Croll 2000). If the former willingly availed themselves of whatever self-improving oppor- tunities were available (like education), the latter was more associated with riotous behaviour and immorality. Both are 'initiation-into-the- real-world' stories and each shifts between past, present and future, combining the retrospective and the prospective as they each relate a seminal event which each now imbues, in hindsight, with consider- able significance. There the similarities largely end, because whereas for Jack leaving school marked the onset of a lifetime of 'scratching a living', David's summer job was more akin to a participant observa- tion project. For Jack, it was being 'hurled out of the nest' at 13 into a life of labour (of 'running, ducking and weaving'), whereas David's encounter with the dockside 'book club' was, albeit in a different way, also a life-transforming experience. Both narratives recreate the past but, in the process, tell us much about the speakers' present outlooks and life styles. If one looks upon Old Industrial Man from the 'inside' (Jack- as-participant), the other does so from the 'outside' (David-as-observer). In both cases a fuller, more rounded and multi-dimensional, nuanced picture of Old Industrial Man emerges than in the empty stereotype which so often surfaces in both the academic and the popular press. Finally, both come to a definite conclusion namely, 'Young men today don't know they're born compared to when I started. They've got it cushy!'; and 'It made me determined to ensure, as far as I could, that such terrible intellectual wastage was never repeated'.

How typical the historical cameos portrayed are would obviously need to be substantiated by further data, but it can be confidently asserted that something of the 'way things were' comes through. Jack's narrative, in particular, tells us much about gender roles and domestic labour encapsulated in his Old Man masculinity in comparison to his grandson's more New Man masculinity. Moreover, the pursuit of work across the country was the common experience of many young Welsh working class men in the 1930s and there were undoubtedly scores of unfulfilled working class intellectuals like Big Ed scattered throughout South Wales industrial communities. More to the point, a number of masculinities are depicted: the young Jack's pursuit of work; the old 'tough nut's' continuing 'busyness' even today; Jack's 'new age' domesticated grandson; David's dogged World War II survivors who 'came home and just got on with it'; his group of unfulfilled working class intellectuals of nearly half a century ago, led by Big Ed; and David's own confident, upper middle class, high achiever masculinity.

Time in the autobiographical narrative

There are obviously many ways in which narratives might be analysed. Elliott (2005) comments that 'there is no standard approach or list of procedures that is generally recognised as representing the narrative method of analysis' (2005: 36). Indeed, Mishler (1995), a leading figure in narrative research, in reviewing the numerous competing approaches, talks of a 'state of near anarchy in the field' (1995: 88). I want to take, as an indicative example, an approach foreshadowed by the poet Seamus Heaney (2003) when he argues that, riding on the back of language, the ability to contemplate simultaneously the present, past and future is uniquely human. One way of investigating this is by means of 'time perspectives' and 'time tenses' (Schutz 1971), something Ricoeur (1981, 1984, 1985, 1988) takes further by distinguishing between 'the chronological' (the manner in which a narrative is composed of recalled events) and 'the non-chronological' (the manner in which the narrative construes meaning out of those events). Both are evident in Jack and David's narratival sense-making. More recently Roberts (2004a, 2004b) has argued that the understanding of our lives through narrative is accomplished by means of a combination of, firstly, 'tense' (for example, the past-in-the-present); and, secondly, 'orientation' (or mood). He notes how in his study of Blaina and Nantyglo respondents ranged over the past, present and future as they surveyed the changes to their own lives and to that of their communities as past, present and future were plotted. Indeed, for Roberts (2004b) the individual life is 'formed within memory' as we 'reflect, but also objectify, our existence in giving it a meaning' (2004b: 172). Such life history narratives are undertaken within the 'interpretation of time... past selves are re-lived, re-visualised and revised: future selves are "re-hearsed" ' (2004b: 176). Also, in examining the past from the vantage point of the present we invariably tend to review not only the actual ones but, also, the possible outcomes that might have, in different circumstances, taken place. This is evident in both Jack's and David's narrative when they comment respectively that 'I often think what my life might have been like if only my circumstances had been different' and 'Things would have been different if I'd been born in St. Thomas!' (the dockside area of Swansea). Roberts then goes on to identify nine 'narratival tenses' (Figure 10.3).

The life story

	Past	Present	Future
Past	Past-in-the-past.	Present-in-the-past.	Future-in-the-past.
Present	Past-in-the-present.	Present in the-present.	Future-in-the-present.
Future	Past-in-the-future.	Present-in-the-future.	Future-in-the-future.

Figure 10.3 Narratival tenses (after Roberts 2004b).

In the light of these I now return to 'Handy Jack's' and 'Posh Dai's' autobiographical narratives. Each of the nine tenses is evident in both, particularly in Jack's, who is particularly promiscuous in his time shifts.

- *Past-in-the-past.* 'I was young and strong then' (Jack).
- *Present-in-the-past.* 'Same as now – I never had a choice' (Jack).
- *Future-in-the past.* 'We must ensure that the terrible intellectual wastage that took place then is never repeated in the future' (David).
- *Past-in-the-present.* 'I was a right little tough nut- still am!' (Jack).
- *Present-in-the-present.* 'My grandson today sees more of his kids in a day than I did in a month' (Jack).
- *Future-in-the-present.* 'I'll always think of them as heroes' (David).

- *Past-in-the-future.* 'There are so many lessons in the past for future generations' (David).
- *Present-in-the-future.* 'The way things are going right now men will stay at home and the women will be the breadwinners' (Jack).
- *Future-in-the-future.* 'Men and women could disappear – you'll not be able to tell the difference!' (Jack).

So where does this lead us?

Conclusion: Matters arising

I want to conclude by restating my opening argument that there is much to recommend the theory-led collection and analysis of autobiographical narratives in 'teaching masculinities'. The pedagogical uses are twofold: the first relates to masculinities *per se*, the second to the nature of the text.

As far as masculinities are concerned, the charting of the minutiae of men's lived experience in the recent past can correct the bland assumptions currently being made concerning the Old Industrial Man. A lecturer-led, collaborative project with students can quickly establish a rich data bank. Referring back to Figure 10.2, autobiographical narratives can serve a number of functions.

- *The Societal.* Narratives can reveal much about the social forces bearing down upon the individual and helping to shape masculinities at a particular time in a particular place.
- *The Subjective.* Narratives can tell us much about how the narrator views the world, this subjectivity being closely allied to social, cultural and geographical positioning.
- *The Interactional.* Narratives can be indicative of how the narrator presents himself to the world and how he wishes to be seen, with how something is said being as revealing as what is said.
- *The Life Course* provides a picture of how a life has unfolded and how masculinity has been experienced and changed. The role of class in helping determine the ensuing life course is considerable, as is amply evident from both the narratives reproduced above.

Although text-related issues are less relevant to this book than the above, the autobiographical narrative also raises interesting issues about:

- the collection and transcription of texts, namely how the material was elicited, recorded and the authorial decisions taken during the process of 'textualisation'.
- the (selective) role of memory in recreating the past as viewed through the visor of the present with an eye on the future.
- narratives as retrospective meaning-making, identity-related projects.
- the 'emplotment' (Ricoeur 1984, 1985, 1988) of the narrative and the speaker's skills as a raconteur and so on.

And, of course, many more...

References

Beynon, J. (2002), *Masculinities and Culture*, Buckingham: Open University Press.

Beynon, J. (2006), 'Lies' or 'identity projects'?: Inmate narratives in HMP. Cityton, *Subject Matters*, Summer, 2(2): 1–32.

Blackshaw, T. (2003), *Leisure Life: Myth, Masculinity and Modernity*, London: Routledge.

Butler, J. (1990), *Gender Trouble, Feminism and the Subversion of Identity*, London: Routledge.

Cornwall, A. and Lindisfarne, N. (1994, eds), *Dislocating Masculinity: Comparative Ethnographies*, London: Routledge.

Croll, A.J. (2000), *Civilizing the Urban: Popular Culture and Public Space in Merthyr, 1870–1914*, Cardiff: University of Wales Press.

Crossley, M. (2000), *Introducing Narrative Psychology: Self, Trauma and the Construction of Meaning*, Buckingham: Open University Press.

Elliott, J. (2005), *Using Narrative in Social Research*, London: Sage Publications.

Gilmore, D. (1990), *Manhood in the Making: Cultural Concepts of Masculinity*, New Haven: Yale University Press.

Goffman, E. (1959), *The Presentation of Self in Everyday Life*, Harmondsworth: Penguin.

Harris, I.M. (1995), *Messages Men Hear: Constructing Masculinities*, London: Taylor & Francis.

Heaney, S. (2003), *Room to Rhyme*, Dundee: University of Dundee.

Lewis, O. (1961), *The Children of Sanchez: The Autobiography of a Mexican Family*, New York: Random House.

Mead, G.H. (1934), *Mind, Self and Society*, Chicago: University of Chicago Press.

Mishler, E.G. (1995), Models of narrative analysis: A typology, *Journal of Narrative and Life History*, 5(2): 87–123.

Mishler, E.G. (1999), *Storylines*, Cambridge, MA: Harvard University Press.

Morgan, D.H.G. (1992), *Discovering Men*, London: Routledge.

Ricoeur, P. (1981), Narrative time, in Mitchell, W.J.T. (ed.), *On Narrative*, Chicago: Chicago University Press.

Ricoeur, P. (1984, 1985, 1988), *Time and Narrative*, 3 volumes, Chicago: Chicago University Press.

Roberts, B. (1999), Welsh identity in a former mining village: Social images and imagined communities, in Fevre, R. and Thompson, A. (eds), *Nation, Identity and Social Theory: Perspectives from Wales*, Cardiff: University of Wales Press.

Roberts, B. (2004a), Biography, time and local history-making, *Rethinking History*, March, 8(1): 89–102.

Roberts, B. (2004b), Health narratives, time perspectives and self-images, *Social Theory & Health*, 2, 170–183.

Schutz, A. (1971), On time, in Natanson, M. (ed.), *Collected Papers, 1: The Problem of Social Reality*, The Hague: Martinus Nijhoff.

Smith, B. and Sparkes, A. (2004), Men, sport and spinal injury, *Disability and Society*, 19(6): 509–612.

Stanley, L. (1993), On auto/biography, in *Sociology*, February, 27(1), 41–52.

Stearns, P.N. (1990), *Be a Man! Males in Modern Society*, New York: Holmes and Meier.

Winlow, S. (2001), *Badfellas: Crime, Tradition and New Masculinities*, Oxford: Berg.

Williamson, H. (2004), *The Milltown Boys Revisited*, Oxford: Berg.

11
Atrocity and Transitivity

Cris Yelland

This discussion is based on the idea of using linguistic analysis as a 'point of entry'[1] into a series of debates. In the first instance, I shall look at some specifics of historiography; later, I shall use the same linguistic features as a point of entry into a much broader debate, about masculinity. In each case, the use of linguistic analysis is not at all a substitute for knowledge of the debate itself, but the focus on linguistic detail provides a heuristic tool for arranging and understanding material.

Teaching transitivity

Any course concerned with linguistic approaches to texts is likely to include some attention to transitivity: transitivity is one of the most powerful analytic tools which linguistic approaches have. As is often the case in linguistics, there are differing and competing models of transitivity, each with slightly different terminology. The most usual is that of Berry[2] as used by Burton,[3] but Hodge and Kress offer a model of their own in *Language as Ideology*, and Fowler's later study of newspaper language works with a more developed model still.[4] In the present, basically pedagogic, context, the theoretical differences between these different models are of little importance – I shall work with a small number of concepts which are common to all the different models of transitivity available.

Most of the time, linguistic approaches are taught in a structural way (to borrow the term from language teaching). The tutor outlines the theory and concepts, then there are lots of examples, and then the students work through analyses of their own. Working this way is also working with a model of pedagogic power in which understanding flows from tutor to students, especially as the technical terminology of linguistics is, and sounds, difficult for the uninitiated. One of the attractions of linguistic approaches is their hard-edged 'scientific' promise, and the question of how 'scientific' they are is a very long-standing area of debate.[5] In the present discussion I want to adopt a different approach, one which more resembles a situational approach (in language teaching terms) or in more general educational terms is about problem-based learning. I am going to begin with a question in historiography, about the accounts given of a particular episode in the Vietnam War, the massacre at My Lai on 16 March 1968, and use only a small part of the terminology available under the heading of 'transit-ivity' to describe differences between the accounts. Then I will extend the analysis, but by discussing the texts in different contexts, not by introducing more terminology. Finally, I shall offer a follow-up exercise and questions. Follow-ups of this kind are a familiar part of linguistics-based discussions and pedagogy.

Writing about the Vietnam War

Before starting the discussion, I want to apologise in advance for the harrowing nature of the material I shall be looking at. It can seem trivial or impertinent to do linguistic analysis of an event like the massacre at My Lai. Nevertheless, I believe that this kind of analysis is worthwhile and necessary. Representations of past wars and proposals for future wars are continuing features of the world, and that fact makes historiography, and the analysis of historiography, important.

The first account I shall discuss is from a history of the Vietnam War by an American journalist and Pulitzer Prize winner, Neil Sheehan. Sheehan's *A Bright Shining Lie* is deeply concerned with questions of masculinity, and it understands and presents the Vietnam War partly in terms of masculine rites of passage. Sheehan was one of a small group of journalists in Vietnam in the early 1960s who were nicknamed the 'Young Turks'.[6] They had bad relationships with their official 'fathers', the US Generals who wanted them to 'get on the team' and use their journalism to support whatever the military line on the progress of the War might be. Instead, Sheehan found a father figure in a more independent-minded Army officer, Colonel John Vann. When he wrote his history of the War, he structured it around Vann, using him as a metaphor for US involvement in Vietnam. A selection of quotations from Sheehan in an interview in 1988 shows how deeply he admired Vann as an embodiment of traditional masculinity:

> Vann helped us to understand the war in a way that other advisors couldn't, because he was fearless...we were trying to come to grips

with this ourselves, and this man helped us come to grips with it in
a way we wouldn't have been able to do without him...

He was in Vietnam to fight other men, not to kill somebody's
mother or sister or kid...

First of all he was a marvelous soldier, a natural leader of men in
war, he was fearless and he had an indomitable will to win...[7]

As well as this very positive model of a tough but nurturing
masculinity, *A Bright Shining Lie* engages with a range of crises and problems about fathering and masculinity more generally. The book opens
with a dramatic demonstration of values in crisis, at Vann's funeral in
1972. The range of mourners was unusually varied. President Nixon
was there, and so was Daniel Ellsberg. Vann's widow was there, but
the couple had divorced only months earlier. Vann's son Jesse, a draft
resistor, was there, and had placed half his torn-up draft card in his
father's coffin. He was only dissuaded at the last minute from handing
the other half to the President in person. Sheehan used the funeral as
the opening of *A Bright Shining Lie* to dramatise the conflicting legacy
which Vann had left: in Sheehan's sympathetic account of Jesse Vann,
the father's military virtues of courage and independence issue most
clearly in the draft resistor son.

There are other crises of masculinity which are crucial to *A Bright
Shining Lie*. One theme of the book is the familiar one of a son's recognition of his father's sexuality. Vann was a compulsive philanderer, who
had been accused of unlawful carnal knowledge of a teenage girl (Vann
was cleared, but confessed his guilt to his wife, and to Sheehan). Vann
was married, but had two mistresses in Vietnam. In interview, Sheehan
described his sense of growing involvement with Vann, not as simple
admiration, but as a more mysterious fascination:

And he had this dark personal side...He was a lot more complicated
than I had realised...Turned out that no one knew John Vann.[8]

One of the most memorable[9] parts of *A Bright Shining Lie* is its account
of My Lai:

The American soldiers and junior officers shot old men, women, boys,
girls,and babies. One soldier missed a baby lying on the ground twice
with a .45 pistol as his comrades laughed at his marksmanship. He
stood over the child and fired a third time. The soldiers beat women
with rifle butts and raped some and sodomized others before shooting
them. They shot the water buffaloes, the pigs and the chickens. They

threw the dead animals into the wells to poison the water. They tossed satchel charges into the bomb shelters under the houses. A lot of the inhabitants had fled into the shelters. Those who leaped out to escape the explosives were gunned down. All of the houses were put to the torch.[10]

This passage is harrowingly hard to read. The effect derives from a number of things. There is the nature of the acts described, and the appalling detail; there is the syntax – a sequence of brutally short sentences. There is also the lexis, which is curt and concrete. I want to look in more detail now at a different aspect of the passage – its transitivity.

Transitive material action processes

A process is a 'material' process when it describes something happening in or on the material world. Most of the processes in the above passage are brutally material: 'shot ... beat ... raped ... sodomised ... threw ... tossed'. The relentless violence of the passage is increased by the fact that there is hardly any variation in it; almost all the processes are material, and there is no indication of either thought or feeling on the soldiers' part or anyone else's, other than the 'laughed'.

A material process is said to be an 'action' process when it has, usually, a human being performing it, or at least something animate. There is a difference between 'John burst the balloon', which is a material action process, and 'The river burst its banks', which is a material 'event' process. The difference relates to an important assumption which we normally make – that people act purposefully, whereas inanimate things do not. Almost all the processes in the passage are material action processes.

Finally, the processes are all transitive. A process is 'transitive' when it affects someone or something other than the performer of it. 'Mary moved the book' is transitive, whereas 'Mary moved' is not. Mary seems more powerful in the transitive process; she is capable of acting on the world around her. In the passage above, the US soldiers are agents in a sequence of transitive material action processes. They seem irresistibly powerful, especially as their actions are listed in a strikingly repetitive form: 'They did a. They did b. They did c and d and e etc'. The change comes at the end of the passage, where the soldiers' last actions, gunning down villagers and putting houses to the torch, are given in a different form, the agentless passive. This is a formation which I shall discuss in detail later. Here, it serves to reduce the intensity of the description at the paragraph's end, ready for a return to more orthodox history-writing.

To sum up, the Sheehan passage is shocking; it is a marked departure from the norm of history-writing, and its lexis, syntax and transitivity all reinforce each other in producing its very powerful effect.

The second account I shall consider is very different. It comes from a later collection of essays on the Vietnam War:

> On 16 March 1968, a company of US soldiers had landed by helicopter near My Lai, a hamlet in the 'Free Fire Zone' established near the provincial capital of Quang Ngai. The Americans, mostly young and inexperienced, had taken casualties from snipers and booby-traps, and were thoroughly upset and demoralised. Expecting to trap Viet Cong at My Lai, they instead found only women, children and old men. During the hours that followed, these civilians were murdered and their homes razed. There was no justification for an act that, according to the final US investigation, took the lives of 347 innocent non-combatants.[11]

Several things differentiate this account from Sheehan's. The list includes:

Mental processes. Here, the mental condition of the US soldiers gets quite a lot of attention; they had taken casualties;[12] they were 'thoroughly upset and demoralised', and they were 'expecting' to encounter Viet Cong. The effect, coupled with the earlier statement that they were 'mostly young and inexperienced', is to invite the reader to empathise with the US soldiers. In Sheehan's account, by contrast, there are no mental processes given.

Agentless passives. This is the biggest single difference between this account and Sheehan's. The events at My Lai are reduced to two processes, civilians being murdered and their homes razed, and in both cases these are acts without agents. The transformation involved is a common, and ideologically crucial, one. The active-voice clause, 'US soldiers murdered civilians' becomes 'Civilians were murdered by US soldiers' and then the agent is deleted to produce 'Civilians were murdered.' The effect is to occlude agency and responsibility for the massacre. Other acts, the torture and sexual abuse, are occluded in a different way: they are not mentioned at all.

Nominalised non-human agent. In this account, it was not US soldiers who killed civilians – it was 'an act' that took their lives. Like the agentless passive, this is a device of agent-deletion, or at least agent-concealment.

It is appropriate here to set out the processes in which the US soldiers are participants. They:

Material processes	Mental processes
had landed	were thoroughly upset
had taken casualties	[were] expecting to trap Viet Cong
found instead only women etc.	

At which point, half way through the account, the US soldiers disappear from view, and the massacre is carried out by persons unknown, or by an impersonal 'act'.

I have described the agentless passive as the crucial construction in the second passage, and I shall go on to argue that it is ideologically very significant. Before I do that, it is only fair to point out that the construction has a number of effects, and there are a number of possible reasons for a writer to use it. One of them is 'fronting' or 'thematisation'. The passive transformation reverses the order of front and back in a clause, so that 'the soldiers killed the villagers' becomes 'the villagers were killed by the soldiers'. Another reason for using the agentless passive is that it may well not be possible to know with certainty who did what in a situation as complicated and intense as the massacre at My Lai. Witnesses often feared punishment themselves, or were reluctant to incriminate others, or were just confused.[13] Finally, a powerful motive for using agentless passives is simply that they are common in history-writing, impersonal, and thus appropriate for a relatively formal discourse.

Nevertheless, there is a correlation between ideology and the agentless passive in descriptions of My Lai. The book from which the second passage comes is a collection of essays on the Vietnam War which argue that the war was justified, and that it was won militarily but lost politically. The book has a foreword by the General Westmoreland who was US Commander in Chief in Vietnam until 1968. It is easy enough to see a connection between the defence of US military involvement in Vietnam and the evasive transitivity of the passage quoted. In the next two sections I shall argue that this correlation holds good more widely than simply being true of these two texts.

Historiography – The revisionist position and the neo-conservative challenge

American historiography of the Vietnam War has been strongly influenced by issues and arguments outside that war – arguments about the nature of the Soviet Union, and about political developments in Central America. Melanson draws a contrast between an immediately post-1975 consensus about the Vietnam War, which he calls a 'revisionist' position,[14] and a later 'neo-conservative revisionist' position. Sheehan's *A Bright Shining Lie* belongs to the earlier, revisionist, school of thought, even though it was not published until much later. Sheehan has described how he began work on the book in the mid-1970s, and planned to spend 'three or four years' on it. Circumstances dictated that he would take 15 years.[15]

The revisionist position was strongly associated with the Carter administration, and with Carter's criticisms of the Vietnam War. As President, Carter described America's involvement in Vietnam as indicative of 'moral bankruptcy'[16] (although as Governor of Georgia in 1971 he had called for support for Lt Calley).[17] Carter's foreign policy was widely seen by its domestic critics as a neurotic response to defeat in Vietnam. It was swiftly 'rebuked' by three events which seemed to challenge the United States' status as the world's leading superpower. These were the Soviet invasion of Afghanistan, the hostage crisis in Iran and the Sandinista challenge in Nicaragua. Carter's defeat by Reagan in 1980 involved a return to a more traditionally confrontational foreign policy; part of the justification for this would be a change in the historiography of the Vietnam War:

> To reiterate, the neo-conservative revisionists had correctly claimed that the orthodox understanding of Vietnam had to be overturned before a revitalised strategy of anti-Communist containment could be effectively justified. A revised memory of Vietnam was a first step along the road to a truly resurgent American foreign policy.[18]

This is the position taken by, for example, Moore's collection of essays on the War.[19] Two things emerge very consistently from the work by the political commentators, journalists and ex-servicemen who are the book's contributors. These are: firstly, the Vietnam War was fought bravely and effectively, and was won militarily but let down by weak politicians (the 'stab-in-the-back' argument); secondly, Central America is the new Vietnam. In this debate between revisionists and neo-conservatives, the My Lai massacre had particular status. For critics of the Vietnam War, and of potential future wars, it was a strong argument in their favour; for neo-conservatives, what happened at My Lai needed to be minimised or occluded. Apart from one dismissive reference, Moore's book does not mention My Lai at all.

War is hell – Atrocity and crocodile tears

Another neo-conservative apologist, Michael Lind, adopts a slightly different strategy, what Bilton and Sim describe as the 'war is hell' argument. In this argument, atrocity is commonplace and inevitable, and so there is no point in complaining about it. In his one paragraph mentioning My Lai, Lind claims that atrocity is ubiquitous in American military history: 'Individual acts of murder, rape and looting have been committed by US troops in every American war'.[20]

The 'war is hell' argument is important because it pretends to be much more critical of the atrocity at My Lai than it actually is. Because of this, I shall spend a little more time on it, looking at a paper by Stephen Ambrose, one of the contributors to the conference on My Lai at Tulane University, Louisiana, in 1993. Professor Ambrose was a military historian and, like Lind, he begins by asserting that atrocity is ubiquitous, and thus unavoidable, and also like Lind, ends with reasserting the *status quo ante*. Ambrose's paper opens and continues on a folksy note: 'We have a painful task – to examine a side of war that is awfully hard to face up to but is always there'.[21]

Like Lind, Ambrose is perfectly explicit about agency when he is describing atrocities in the nineteenth century, or even in World War II. His purpose in doing so, however, is to minimise the effect of My Lai as much as he can. He begins his paper with a very curious argument, that combat is a uniquely stressful experience, which is surely true, and moves from there to the conclusion that nobody who has not been in combat has any right to judge what happens there, which is dangerously false.[22]

When he comes to discuss My Lai, Ambrose has various arguments to offer to explain the massacre. Lieutenant Calley lost control. The system of rotation of individual tours of duty was a bad one because it increased the stress and disorientation felt by individual soldiers. Finally, Ambrose ends his discussion with a reassertion of his pride in the US Army, which, he claims, was the only army in the world, which would have publicly investigated the events at My Lai. All of which is strongly argued, but Ambrose was strongly criticised by a member of the audience who pointed out the multiple falsehoods in his account. The US Army did not investigate My Lai until forced to; before then, they had lied about it and covered it up. Calley did not lose control, either of himself or of his men; every account of him at My Lai, including his own, describes him as being in control. The system of rotating individuals may well have been a bad one in general[23] but as it happened C Company had all arrived in Vietnam as a unit, and this argument does not work in their case.[24]

So far, the analysis of transitivity has had a heuristic effect, leading out into a consideration of the historiography of the Vietnam War and its relationship with subsequent political debates. Within that context, different formations of transitivity correlate with and function in positions in debates, so that the question of agency, especially, is one which features in attempts to minimise the significance of My Lai, or, more rarely, to stress it. There is widespread agreement about the facts of what happened at My Lai; nevertheless, different formations of transitivity offer different versions of what happened, and of how important it is. At this point, I want to use the analysis of transitivity to broaden the argument further; once again, however, I shall use transitivity as the point of entry into the discussion.

Ordinary men: Transitivity and masculinity

The Vietnam War was the most problematic war in American history. It was the longest war, the most expensive, the only war the United States lost, the war with most opposition to it and so on. The contrast which many people, from serving soldiers to historians, drew most often was between the complexities of the Vietnam War and the moral clarities of World War II. In particular, Herzog and Faludi both describe a powerful contrast between entanglement in Vietnam and the heroic achievements of D-Day in 1944.[25] One of the heroic aspects of World War II, in the West at least, was that it was relatively free of atrocity against civilians by Allied infantry.[26] Atrocity against civilians in the Normandy campaign was perceived as something characteristic of the enemy. Here is a description by an American historian of a German atrocity against civilians in the Normandy campaign:

> An exception was the 2nd SS Panzer Division (*Das Reich*) which had been in Army Group G reserve at Toulouse, and was bombed, strafed and harassed throughout its move by the Resistance and Allied air. This division had earned notoriety for one of the most shameful acts of brutality committed during the Second World War: the annihilation of the village of Ouradour-sur-Glane, near Limoges, in reprisal for suspected concealment of explosives. The entire population of the village had been rounded up, the men locked in barns and the women and children in the church. Six hundred and forty-two people were then machine-gunned or burned to death and the village burned to

the ground. Only remnants of this once elite division arrived intact in Normandy.[27]

The striking thing about this description is how closely it resembles the second passage about My Lai discussed earlier. It has the same 'shape' in terms of transitivity as the earlier passage. It begins from the point of view of the soldiers, not the civilians, and sees the soldiers as suffering from the actions of others. They were 'bombed, strafed and harassed' on their journey north to Normandy. Then there is a very odd shift to the past perfect tense, 'had earned notoriety', which seems to imply that the Division had committed its atrocity before the Normandy campaign began. This is quite false – they murdered the population of Oradour on 10 June 1944. The acts themselves are described in six agentless passive clauses, 'had been rounded up... locked in barns... [locked] in the church... people were then machine-gunned... [were] burned to death... the village [was] burned to the ground'. At the end, the description returns to explicit agency when it constructs the SS as victim; 'Only remnants of this once elite division arrived intact in Normandy'. That last sentence is downright odd – it implies that it is not clear whether the soldiers of the division were the victims of Allied attack, or of their own criminality.

In discussing the transitivity of passages about the Vietnam War, it was possible to link devices like agentless passives to a neo-conservative defence of the US Army in Vietnam. That connection is not available here, in the sense that Professor d'Este is obviously not defending either the atrocity at Oradour, or the SS in general. Yet the Oradour passage minimises the impact of the atrocity, just as the neo-conservative descriptions of My Lai do, and, like them, sees it in large part from the point of view of the perpetrators, not the victims. Interestingly, this does not mean that the language resembles actual participant testimony. When people who have committed atrocities talk about it, they characteristically do so in a direct, explicit way which does not obscure agency. One brief example to illustrate this is the description by one of the soldiers in C Company, who corrects himself to make agency explicit:

And the mothers were hugging their children, but they kept on firing. Well, we kept on firing.[28]

Of all the descriptions we have looked at, the passage from Sheehan is in fact much the closest to the way that participants describe what they have done. There are no doubt differences between writing and speech at issue here – we probably expect greater explicitness in speech than in writing; the agentless passive style is a distinctively written form which sounds very evasive indeed if spoken.[29] If the agentless passive style is written in some sense in exculpation of participants, or from their point of view, but it does not resemble the language of participants, then what is it? As the similarity between the descriptions of My Lai and the description of the Oradour massacre shows, the question goes beyond the historiography of the Vietnam War.

The agentless passive style and the direct style with agency not obscured correlate with different constructions of masculinity. In particular, they relate to different ways of dealing with the implications of masculine atrocity. It is true that atrocity against civilians had particular prominence in writing about the Vietnam War: for Fertel, atrocity is the 'primal scene' of Vietnam fiction;[30] for Jeffords, it is 'the figure' of Vietnam writing.[31] Testimony to the Dellums Committee described atrocity as routine in Vietnam.[32] Beyond the question of atrocity in Vietnam, however, is the broader question of what ordinary men are capable of.

Browning's *Ordinary Men*[33] is a study of atrocities committed between 1942 and 1944 by an armed police unit in German-occupied Poland. Using this as a starting-point, Browning discusses how it is that ordinary men can commit appalling acts. Using a combination of historical research and social psychology, for instance the Stanford 'prison' experiment of 1971[34] and Milgram's famous 'obedience to authority' experiment,[35] Browning concludes that the acts of Reserve Police Battalion 101 in butchering several hundred civilians are within the range of normal, or at least very possible, masculine behaviour. He finds that atrocity is not determined or inevitable: there is always the possibility of resistance. However, given the 'right' circumstances, men will commit atrocities. The factors which Browning lists as the 'right' circumstances are, apart from war, all ominously ordinary: racism; war; deference to authority; career advancement; bureaucratisation; peer-group pressure.[36] The list ends with the question,

> If the men of Reserve Police Battalion 101 could become killers under such circumstances, what group of men cannot?[37]

The same disturbing ordinariness is clear in the soldiers of C Company. Their leader, Lieutenant Calley, was described as 'horribly typical'[38] by Mary McCarthy, and his conduct at My Lai was based on very ordinary motives – deference to authority and desire to impress his superior officer, Captain Medina. The expert psychiatrist witness at Calley's court martial was certain that Calley was sane, and was not suffering from any form of psychosis or neurosis,[39] other than a 'compulsion' to obey orders. The soldiers of C Company were not unusual for US soldiers in Vietnam; their only deviation from the statistical norm was that their educational level was slightly higher than average.[40]

The stylistic choice of whether to be explicit about agency or to occlude it by agentless passives, nominalisations and other means, is significant in this broader context, of examining and questioning masculinity. Two recent works of historical research are especially relevant here: one is Bourke's *An Intimate History of Killing*[41] and the other Faludi's *Stiffed*. Both of these make extensive and explicit use of participant testimony; both are thus more direct and explicit about agency than is usual in historiography; both are concerned to explore aspects of masculine behaviour which have been de-emphasised or hidden because they are highly problematic. In Bourke's case (to drastically simplify a long and complex argument) the received opinion is that men in combat are primarily concerned to avoid danger and to survive, but this received view omits a primary motive for many soldiers, which is pleasure in killing. Using letters and other forms of participant testimony from World War I, World War II and Vietnam, Bourke reaches the conclusion that some aspects of military life which are considered most horrible in civilian society, notably pleasure in killing, in fact appeal to very powerful desires in many men.

Faludi's argument is more narrowly focussed historically, on the 'baby boom' generation of men born between 1940 and 1960. In a series of case studies, one of which is about My Lai, she argues that this generation of men has been so damaged by economic change that it has proved unable to achieve an adequate masculinity which would compare with the historic victories of its fathers, or to pass on adequate masculinity to its sons. My Lai she sees as a consequence of inadequate fathering, and her discussion of the atrocity understands C Company as a kind of dysfunctional family. She describes the Vietnam War in general as 'a defining event of American masculinity',[42] an event which C Company failed to negotiate successfully. Faludi describes the relationship between officers in an army, especially non-commissioned officers, and ordinary soldiers, as traditionally based on a kind of fathering; older men support younger ones through a process of initiation into achieved masculinity. In the US Army in Vietnam, she argues, this traditional military culture was replaced by a managerialist culture which had lost touch with authentic masculine values: the result was that C Company did not behave like a family, but like a different masculine organisation, a street gang. Street gangs, Faludi says, are well known to fill 'a void created by the absence of fathers'.[43]

Conclusion

Sheehan's description of the massacre at My Lai is unforgettably vivid. It is also part of his angry critique of the 'false fathers', the Generals Westmoreland and Harkins, and their masters, who fought the Vietnam War in a way that made atrocity 'inevitable'.[44] Foregrounding My Lai is one of the aspects of *A Bright Shining Lie* which make it work as metaphorical exploration of masculinity as well as political history. The technical means which achieve this include using the explicit transitivity which is characteristic of participant testimony, not the transitivity with agent deleted or obscured of conservative historiography. Many accounts of My Lai seek to keep it within the bounds of the acceptable, the in-need-of-minor-reform, or the inevitable. They seek, in other words, not to be worried about it. Sheehan is one writer (Bourke and Faludi are others) for whom My Lai and events like it bring about a profound questioning of what it means to be American, or military, or male. Not using agentless passives in the orthodox fashion is one defamiliarisation which enables the questioning to start.

Follow-up exercise

Lieutenant Calley

In these extracts from Lieutenant Calley's court-martial, how does his transitivity indicate a confused or inconsistent sense of his own responsibility for his actions at My Lai? Does he see himself as powerful or powerless? (Calley's words are in response to the defence lawyer's questions.)

Q: Now, did you see some live Vietnamese while you were going through the village?
A: I saw two, sir.
Q: All right. Now, tell us, was there an incident concerning those two?
A: Yes sir. I shot and killed both of them.
Q: Under what circumstances?
A: There was a large concrete house and I kind of stepped up on the porch and looked in the window. There was about six to eight individuals laying on the floor, apparently dead. And one man was going for the window. I shot him. There was another man standing

in a fireplace. He looked like he had just come out of the fireplace, or out of the chimney. And I shot him, sir.

[Calley is asked a question about whether he was right to kill women and children]

A: Well, I was ordered to go in there and destroy the enemy. That was my job on that day. That was the mission I was given. I did not sit down and think in terms of men, women and children. They were all classified the same, and that was the classification that we dealt with.

Q: Who gave you that classification the last time you got it?

A: Captain Medina, sir.

Q: Now, I will ask you this, Lieutenant Calley: Whatever you did at My Lai on that occasion, I will ask you whether in your opinion you were acting rightly and according to your understanding of your directions and orders?

A: I felt then and I still do that I acted as I was directed, and I carried out the orders that I was given, and I do not feel wrong in doing so, sir.

Notes

1. Roger Fowler, *Literature as Social Discourse* (London: Batsford 1981) 27.
2. Margaret Berry, *Introduction to Systemic Linguistics* (London: Batsford 1975).
3. Deirdre Burton, 'Through Glass Darkly: Through Dark Glasses', in Ronald Carter (ed.) *Language and Literature* (London: Allen & Unwin 1982) 194–214.
4. Roger Fowler, *Language in the News: Discourse and Ideology in the Press* (London: Routledge 1991).
5. The debate goes back to Frank W. Bateson, 'Literature and Linguistics: A Reply', in *Essays in Criticism* 17: 3 (1967) 335–347, and 'Language and Literature: A Reply' in *Essays in Criticism* 18: 2 (1968) 176–182. It continued with Peter Barry, 'The Limitations of Stylistics', in *Essays in Criticism* 38: 3 (1988) 175–189, and with a series of debates in the 1990s: Peter Mackay, 'Mything the point', in *Language and Communication* 16: 1 (1996) 81–93. Mick Short responded in Short *et al.* 'Stylistics, Criticism and Mythrepresentation Again' in *Language and Literature* 7: 1 (1998) 39–50. Mackay replied in 'There Goes the Other Foot' in *Language and Literature* 8: 1 (1999) 59–65, and Short and Willie van Peer responded in 'A reply to Mackay', in *Language and Literature* 8: 3 (1999) 269–275. See also Henry Widdowson, 'Discourse Analysis: A Critical View', in *Language and Literature* 4: 3 (1995); Norman Fairclough, 'A Reply to Henry Widdowson's 'Discourse analysis', in *Language and Literature* 5: 1 (1996) 49–55, and Widdowson's 'Reply to Fairclough', in *Language and Literature* 57–69.
6. William Prochnau, *Once Upon A Distant War: David Halberstam, Neil Sheehan, Peter Arnett – Young War Correspondents and Their Early Vietnam Battles* (New York: Random House 1995).

7. Neil Sheehan, in conversation with Harry Kreisler in the 'Conversations with History' series at Berkeley Institute of International Studies: http://globetrotter/berkeley.edu/conversations/Sheehan.html (29 May 2006). See also http://www.refstar.com/vietnam/sheehan_interview.html (29 May 2006).

8. Ibid.

9. One demonstration of the unforgettable quality of Sheehan's description is that whole phrases from it appear in a later travel book about South-East Asia, Lucretia Stewart's *Tiger Balm* (London: Chatto & Windus 1992) 118–121, and also in Mark Kurlansky's *1968* (London: Vintage 2005) 106. I am not suggesting that Stewart's or Kurlansky's accounts of My Lai, which are very fully researched, and in Kurlansky's case fully referenced, are plagiarised; but Sheehan's account has clearly stuck in both their minds.

10. Neil Sheehan, *A Bright Shining Lie* (London: Picador 1990) 689.

11. Bernard C. Nalty (ed.) *The Vietnam War* (London: Salamander 1998) 233.

12. On the issue of casualties, it should be pointed out that C Company had suffered rather fewer casualties than comparable units, that their most recent casualty had been two days before the massacre, and that they had already expressed their unhappiness at the death of Sgt Cox on 14 March by beating up some children and shooting and beating to death an unarmed woman they found in a rice paddy. See Michael Bilton and Kevin Sim, *Four Hours in My Lai* (London: Penguin 1992) 92–93.

13. See Mary McCarthy, *Medina* (New York: Harcourt Brace Jovanovich 1972) 19–20, 39–42, 56–57, and Richard Hammer, *One Morning in the War* (London: Rupert Hart-Davis 1970) 142–143, 182–183.

14. Richard Melanson, *Writing History and Making Policy: The Cold War, Vietnam and Revisionism* (Lanham, MD: University Press of America 1983)

15. Sheehan at Berkeley.

16. Melanson, *Writing History and Making Policy* 142.

17. Bilton and Sim, *Four Hours in My Lai* 340.

18. Melanson, 206.

19. John. N. Moore (ed.) *The Vietnam Debate: A Fresh Look at the Arguments* (Lanham, MD: University Press of America 1990).

20. Michael Lind, *Vietnam: The Necessary War* (New York: Simon & Schuster 1999).

21. Stephen Ambrose, 'Atrocities in Historical Perspective', in David Anderson (ed.) *Facing My Lai* (Lawrence, KS: University of Kansas Press 1998) 107–120.

22. At this point, it is appropriate to cite the novelist Tim O'Brien, who was on combat duty in Quang Ngai at about the same time as the men who committed atrocities at My Lai. He is insistent that the men of C Company who committed atrocities are self-confessed murderers and should be severely punished. See Tim O'Brien, 'The Mystery of My Lai', in Anderson, *Facing My Lai* 171–178.

23. The fact that American soldiers arrived at the war and left it as individuals is cited by Herzog as one of the features of the Vietnam War which made it especially disorienting. See Tobey Herzog, *Vietnam War Stories: Innocence Lost* (London: Routledge 1992) 47–48 and Herzog's response to John Leland, 'Writing About Vietnam' in *College English* 43: 7 (November 1981) 739–745.

24. Ambrose, 'Atrocities in Historical Perspective' 118.

25. See Herzog, and also Susan Faludi, *Stiffed: The Betrayal of Modern Man* (London: Chatto & Windus 1999), Part 1: 'The Promise of Postwar Manhood'.
26. Only relatively. See, for example, Stanley Whitehouse and George Bennett, *Fear is the Foe* (London: Robert Hale 1995) 132–134.
27. Carlo d'Este, *Decision in Normandy* (London: Collins 1983) footnote to 233.
28. Quoted in Bilton and Sim, 262. For participant testimony about My Lai, see *The Listener*, 8 April 1971, and about the Vietnam War in general, Richard Stacewitz, *Winter Soldiers: An Oral History of the Vietnam Veterans Against the War* (New York: Twayne 1997).
29. As it does in passages from Lt Calley's testimony at his court martial. See http://www.law.umkc.edu/faculty/projects/ftrials/mylai/MYL_calt.HTM (29 May 2006).
30. Robert J. Fertel, in Anderson (ed.) 199.
31. Susan Jeffords, *The Remasculinization of America* (Bloomington: Indiana UP 1989) 73.
32. Hearings of the Dellums Committee on War Crimes in Vietnam: http://members.aol.com/warlibrary/vwch1.htm (29 May 2006).
33. Christopher Browning, *Ordinary Men: Reserve Police Battalion 101 and the Final Solution in Poland* (London: Penguin 2001).
34. http://www.prisonexp.org/index.html (29 May 2006).
35. Stanley Milgram, *Obedience to Authority: An Experimental View* (New York: Simon & Schuster, 1974). Milgram studied transcripts from My Lai in writing the book: http://cla.calpoly.edu/~cslem/Temp/Obey/history.html (29 May 2006).
36. Browning's list of circumstances which tend to atrocity is very similar to Robert Jay Lifton's definition of an 'atrocity-creating situation'. See Robert Jay Lifton, *Home From the War* (New York: Simon & Schuster 1973) and 'Conditions of Atrocity', in *The Nation*, 31 May 2004.
37. Browning, *Ordinary Men* 189.
38. Mary McCarthy, *Medina* 14.
39. http://www.law.umkc.edu/faculty/projects/ftrials/mylai/Myl_tALVER.htm (29 May 2006).
40. Hays Parks, in Anderson (ed.) 138.
41. J. Bourke, *An Intimate History of Killing* (London: Granta 2000).
42. Faludi, *Stiffed* 298.
43. Ibid., 328.
44. Sheehan, *A Bright Shining Lie* 690.

Works cited

Ambrose, S. 'Atrocities in Historical Perspective', in Anderson, D. (ed.) *Facing My Lai*, Lawrence, KS: University of Kansas Press 1998 107–120.
Barry, P. 'The Limitations of Stylistics', in *Essays in Criticism* 38: 3 (1988) 175–189.
Bateson, F.W. 'Literature and Linguistics: A Reply', in *Essays in Criticism* 17: 3 (1967) 335–347.
Bateson, F.W. 'Language and Literature: A Reply', in *Essays in Criticism* 18: 2 (1968) 176–182.
Berry, Margaret, *Introduction to Systemic Linguistics*, London: Batsford 1975.

Bilton, M. and Sim, K. *Four Hours in My Lai*, London: Penguin 1992.

Bourke, J. *An Intimate History of Killing*, London: Granta 2000.

Browning, C. *Ordinary Men: Reserve Police Battalion 101 and the Final Solution in Poland*, London: Penguin 2001.

Burton, D. 'Through Glass Darkly: Through Dark Glasses', in Carter, R. (ed.) *Language and Literature*, London: Allen & Unwin 1982.

D'Este, C. *Decision in Normandy*, London: Collins 1983.

Fairclough, N. 'A reply to Henry Widdowson's "Discourse Analysis" ', in *Language and Literature* 5: 1 (1996) 49–55.

Faludi, S. *Stiffed: The Betrayal of Modern Man*, London: Chatto & Windus 1999.

Fowler, R. *Literature as Social Discourse*, London: Batsford 1981.

Fowler, R. *Language in the News: Discourse and Ideology in the Press*, London: Routledge 1991.

Hammer, R. *One Morning in the War*, London: Rupert Hart-Davies 1970.

Herzog, T. *Vietnam War Stories: Innocence Lost*, London: Routledge 1992.

Herzog, T. 'Writing About Vietnam', in *College English* 43: 7 (November 1981) 739–745.

Jeffords, S. *The Remasculinization of America*, Bloomington, IN: Indiana University Press 1989.

Kurlansky, M. *1968*, London: Vintage 2005.

Lifton, R.J. *Home From the War*, New York: Simon & Schuster 1973.

Lifton, R.J. 'Conditions of Atrocity', in *The Nation* 31 May 2004.

Lind, M. *Vietnam: The Necessary War*, New York: Simon & Schuster 1999.

Mackay, P. 'Mything the Point', in *Language and Communication* 16: 1 (1996) 81–93.

Mackay, P. 'There Goes the Other Foot', in *Language and Literature* 8: 1 (1999) 59–65.

McCarthy, M. *Medina*, New York: Harcourt Brace Jovanovich 1972.

Melanson, R. *Writing History and Making Policy: The Cold War, Vietnam and Revisionism*, Lanham, MD: University Press of America 1983.

Milgram, S. *Obedience to Authority: An Experimental View*, New York: Simon & Schuster 1974.

Moore, J.N. (ed.) *The Vietnam Debate: A Fresh Look at the Arguments*, Lanham, MD: University Press of America 1990.

Nalty, B.C. (ed.) *The Vietnam War*, London: Salamander 1998.

O'Brien, T. 'The Mystery of My Lai', in Anderson, D. (ed.) *Facing My Lai*, Lawrence, KS: University of Kansas Press 1998 171–178.

Prochnau, W. *Once Upon A Distant War: David Halberstam, Neil Sheehan, Peter Arnett – Young War Correspondents and Their Early Vietnam Battles*, New York: Random House 1995.

Sheehan, N. *A Bright Shining Lie*, London: Picador 1990.

Short, M. *et al.* 'Stylistics, Criticism and Mythrepresentation Again', in *Language and Literature* 7: 1 (1998) 39–50.

Short, M. and van Peer, W. 'A Reply to Mackay', in *Language and Literature* 8: 3 (1999) 269–275.

Stacewitz, R. *Winter Soldiers: An Oral History of the Vietnam Veterans Against the War*, New York: Twayne 1997.

Stewart, L. *Tiger Balm*, London: Chatto & Windus 1992.

Whitehouse, S. and Bennett, G. *Fear is the Foe*, London: Robert Hale 1995.

Widdowson, H. 'Reply to Fairclough', in *Language and Literature* 5: 1 (1996) 57–69.

Online sources

Conversations with Neil Sheehan

http://globetrotter/berkeley.edu/conversations/Sheehan.html (29 May 2006)
http://www.refstar.com/vietnam/sheehan_interview.html (29 May 2006)

Court martial of Lt Calley

http://www.law.umkc.edu/faculty/projects/ftrials/mylai/MYL_calt.HTM (29 May 2006)
http://www.law.umkc.edu/faculty/projects/ftrials/mylai/Myl_tALVER.htm (29 May 2006)

Dellums Committee on War Crimes in Vietnam

http://members.aol.com/warlibrary/vwch1.htm (29 May 2006)

Obedience to authority and the Stanford prison experiment

http://cla.calpoly.edu/~cslem/Temp/Obey/history.html (29 May 2006)
http://www.prisonexp.org.index.html (29 May 2006)

12
Taking Possession of Knowledge: The Masculine Academic in Don DeLillo's *White Noise*

Ruth Helyer

Don DeLillo's 1986 novel *White Noise* provides a narrative which critiques the educational reproduction of masculinities.[1] The lecturers in his 'School of American Environments' are portrayed as shallow and insecure, desperate to outdo each other in feats of masculinity which resemble rites of passage rather than pedagogic experiences. In the Western world manliness has come to be closely aligned with reasonable behaviour. Victor Seidler reiterates the way in which reason is put forward as, the 'legislator of reality', thus gaining authority for men to form, and educate, a world according to their notion.[2] This construction prioritises rationality and requires that men should live a careful and controlled life – ignoring instincts and any uncivilised urges to instead mimic what has been taught to them. DeLillo's academics noticeably struggle to align their urges with their society's expectations.

Jack Gladney, the text's central protagonist, strives to fulfil the idea of 'authentic' masculine identity. Despite his chaotic postmodern setting, his conventional principles prompt him to insist that, 'people need to be reassured by someone in a position of authority that a certain way to do something is the right way or the wrong way' (*W.N.* p. 172). His fellow teachers are obsessed by the most banal things, including bodily functions; toilet and hygiene habits; handling consumables and their packaging; de-coding celebrity and nostalgia. They use their work as part of their striving to make connections which validate some viable masculine framework; their chair, Alfonse Stompanato, giving them the blueprint for the manly academic, 'large, sardonic, dark-staring, with scarred brows and a furious beard fringed in grey' (*W.N.* p. 65). Jack lives in the hope that his academic status is capable of elevating and protecting:

> I'm not just a college professor. I'm the head of a department. I don't see myself fleeing an airborne toxic event. That's for people who live in mobile homes out in the scrubby parts of the county.
>
> (*W.N.* p. 117)

He teaches 'Hitler Studies' yet the transfer of knowledge and the encouragement of analytical debate are not his priorities. He sees his career, rather, as an opportunity to create an impenetrable front for himself. He tries to appropriate Hitler's larger than life image as his own in a recycling aimed at absorbing his overwhelming fear of death. His colleague Murray J. Siskind compliments him:

> You've established a wonderful thing here with Hitler. You created it, you nurtured it, you made it your own. Nobody on the faculty of any college or university in this part of the country can as much as utter the word Hitler without a nod in your direction, literally or metaphorically. This is the center, the unquestioned source. He is now your Hitler, Gladney's Hitler.
>
> (*W.N.* p. 11)

Murray is eager to imitate Hitler Studies by substituting Elvis, convinced that the representation of any male icon will suffice in the act of myth creation. Jack's contribution to the sustenance of such myths leaves him living in constant fear of being exposed as a fraud. He comments on Murray's conscious creation of 'the male academic':

> There was something touching about the fact that Murray was dressed almost totally in corduroy. I had the feeling that since the age of eleven in his crowded plot of concrete he'd associated this sturdy fabric with higher learning in some impossibly distant and tree shaded place.
>
> (*W.N.* p. 11)

Not only does Murray construct this image for himself, he constructs academic courses he feels will court success, based upon Jack's experience. Jack makes a guest appearance at Murray's initial Elvis lecture to give it his official seal of approval (*W.N.* pp. 71–72) and comments afterwards that, 'I had been generous with the power and madness at my disposal' (*W.N.* p. 73). There is a certain ambiguity surrounding whose madness this is, Jack's, Hitler's or both. He comments further on the fragility of the created image, 'We all had an aura to maintain and by sharing mine with a friend I was risking the very things that made me untouchable' (*W.N.* p. 74). Jack's identity is completely bound up in ideas of academic self-aggrandisement. He foregrounds personal object-ives; sharing insight and support are not cited in his list of priorities.

By choosing to create and teach a course about Hitler, Jack illustrates the inherent irony of attempting to 'teach' in a society deemed post-modern. Rather than dismissing grand narratives, teaching potentially perpetuates them. He does not take the opportunity to re-visit and re-assess the myths surrounding Hitler but rather validates fascist beliefs by adhering to an 'approved version'. Again there is no room for student discussion: their role is rapt attentiveness. Lecturers presenting an undis-puted version of an event or identity become inextricably implicated in what they are discussing. As N. Katherine Hayles summarises it, 'We are involved in what we would describe'.[3] Insider knowledge, like self-knowledge, illustrates a certain level of self-consciousness. Tradi-tionally college novels present professors as objects of ridicule, either intellectuals who cannot cope with life, or power-hungry individuals, eager to dominate others. Both of these unflattering descriptions fit Jack to a certain extent. The students do not simply study a narrative history, rather they are encouraged to respond adoringly to Professor Gladney, endowing him with the same hypnotic power his subject matter commands. Jack claims to be teaching 'Advanced Nazism' due to Hitler's alignment with television. He feels that both have the same dictatorial power over the enthralled masses, absorbing and destroying any conflicting opinions. Like the Nazi faithful, Jack's students give up their minds to him and the education system; they give up their individual powers of determination to become part of a crowd, a mass consciousness.[4]

What Georges Bataille terms, the, 'isolation of individual separate-ness' undoubtedly makes crowds more attractive.[5] However, as well as offering a certain homogenous comfort they are also, paradoxically, frightening and threatening, with their potential to crush and obliterate. Ironically, Jack's charade with Hitler Studies only serves to make him more vulnerable as he creates a front of invincible power impossible to live up to, 'Hitler...I spoke the name often, hoping it would overpower my insecure sentence structure' (*W.N.* p. 274). He lives in fear of his fellow professors and the 'actual Germans' at his forthcoming confer-ence discovering that his grasp of the German language is inadequate, or that the innocuous name 'Jack' is loitering behind the grandiose initials J.A.K., describing his situation as, 'living...on the edge of a landscape of vast shame' (*W.N.* p. 31). He scrabbles around for origins, hiding his ageing eyes and body behind dark glasses and academic robes. He has compromised himself by taking the academic gown and the relative security that goes with it in exchange for the unfettered vibrancy of new and disturbing ideas. His methods of 'teaching' Hitler are dogmatically predetermined. He has begun to nervously admit that 'Hitler Studies' puts him further away from his potential to have a 'real' self, if such an autonomous state can ever be achieved:

> The chancellor had advised me, back in 1968, to do something about my name and appearance if I wanted to be taken seriously as a Hitler innovator. Jack Gladney would not do, he said, and asked me what other names I might have at my disposal. We finally agreed that I should invent an extra initial and call myself J.A.K. Gladney, a tag I wore like a borrowed suit. The chancellor warned against what he called my tendency to make a feeble presentation of self. He strongly suggested I gain weight. He wanted me to 'grow out' into Hitler. He himself was tall, paunchy, ruddy, jowly, big-footed and dull. A formidable combination. I had the advantages of substantial height, big hands, big feet, but badly needed bulk, or so he believed – an air of unhealthy excess, of padding and exaggeration, hulking massiveness. If I could become more ugly, he seemed to be suggesting, it would help my career enormously. So Hitler gave me something to grow into and develop toward... The glasses with thick black heavy frames and dark lenses were my own idea... Babette said [the disguise] intimated dignity and prestige. I am the false character that follows the name around.
>
> (*W.N.* pp. 16–17)

He demonstrates Jean Baudrillard's allegation that representation has replaced reality in a surface-focused, 'hyper-real' society. Jack's creation of an academic persona supersedes the real, in that it dares to suggest that there is nothing below the surface. The constructed stereotypical 'College Professor' he strives to be is an effort to reflect a certain aspirational 'perfection' beyond what can exist.[6] Baudrillard focuses on the false and created nature of much of contemporary life, where, amongst the abundance of copies and representations, fixed narratives of instruction become an anathema.

New and different personae can be invented, and gradually authentic-
ated. The Chancellor does not admit to re-inventing Jack; he insinuates
that he is filling out his 'true self'. The term 're-invent' suggests that
what is being replaced was already an invention, part of a circularity
of creation amply illustrated by his fellow university lecturers who are
former journalists, sportsmen and celebrity bodyguards, merely rein-
vented as 'teachers'. The J.A.K. Gladney that develops is simply another
disguise; Jack is no nearer to any tangible reality. Instead of security,
gleaned from the comfort of the elusive 'authentic', Jack is caught up in
his own hype, cocooned in self-myth, like Hitler, his hero and academic
inspiration. Both men are masquerading behind a show of power, which
is merely a façade waiting to be discovered. Indeed when one of his ex-
wives asks Jack how his academic job is going the conversation breathes
life into the long-dead aggressor. The question, 'How is Hitler?', brings
the reply: 'Fine, solid, dependable' (*W.N.* p. 89). Jack is referring to what
Hitler's image is doing for his career.

Hitler asked Albert Speer to design buildings to represent the
Nazi party, which would decay magnificently, and astonish posterity
(*W.N.* pp. 257–258). These architectural decisions encouraged him to
believe that he could control the future. He thought that by ensuring
definite and predictable happenings he would create his own grand
narrative. Ironically, by trying to predict the future and dictate
nostalgia, he suspends chronology and emphasises the difficulty in ever
assessing modernity and postmodernity as separate entities. Traditionally the present is lived in, whilst looking to the future, with the past
firmly behind. However, Lyotard suggests that viewing the future as
experienced before the past is a way of coming to terms with postmodern times: '*Post modern* would have to be understood according to
the paradox of the future (*post*) anterior (*modo*)'.[7] Jack, like his hero, tries
to control his future, but his impersonation of power cannot save him
from dying anymore than Hitler could keep himself from ruin.

Universities, and other educational institutions, where popular culture
vies with more traditional subjects, further illustrate this complex relationship between grand narratives and postmodernity. The courses
of learning do not exist chronologically, or historically, but instead
compete with each other for validity and superiority, within an uncom-
fortably incestuous, yet at the same time competitive, environment. The
traditional academic study of literature could be viewed as an archetypal
grand narrative with its veneration of the 'Canon', an approved version
with verifiable origins. What is taught centres upon 'authentic' literature; that which has already met with official approval. Contemporary

courses which offer the study of films and television adverts (in Jack's university there are 'full professors ... who read nothing but cereal boxes' *W.N.* p. 10), present alternatives. However, if these alternatives are simply destined to become the grand narratives of the future, with accepted readings reproduced in multiple text books, then individual interpretation becomes part of a new normative, rather than part of a multiplicity capable of overturning one official version.

Amongst the multiple strands forming society there are inevitably sections that, for whatever reason, cannot adequately represent themselves. Jean François Lyotard names these unpresentable sections the 'differend', claiming them to be incommensurable with the dominant societal 'norms', yet no less valid.[8] The danger is that these small sections will be ignored or abused. Lyotard suggests that this can be avoided by celebrating the 'differend', 'Let us wage war on totality; let us be witnesses to the unpresentable; let us activate the differences and save the honor of the name'.[9] He acknowledges that it is easier to accept the majority opinion but wants to at least make the effort to question and analyse, to refuse the, 'consolation of correct forms ... consensus of taste and common ... nostalgia'.[10] Such common accord can be seen directly illustrated in *White Noise* by 'The Most Photographed Barn', especially when scrutinised in the light of John Frow's writing on tourism, returned to later in the chapter. As Frow states, nostalgia makes no allowance for 'difference'.

Jack's wife Babette's son, Wilder, is an example of difference with his protracted crying, lasting over seven hours (*W.N.* p. 79), and his inability (or refusal) to speak. He is 'wilder' than the rest of the family, actively, and seemingly instinctively, resisting the civilising potential of 'teaching'. He demonstrates his lack of cohesion with the modern world by looking behind the television set for his mother after her brief appearance on the screen and pedalling his tricycle across the motorway (*W.N.* p. 322). Murray claims, 'You cherish this simpleton blessing of his' (*W.N.* p. 289). Learning and the amassing of knowledge only increases fear. Rather than thinking of Wilder as retarded Jack sees him as, 'the spirit of genius at work' (*W.N.* p. 209) and the family treat him as special and revered:

> His great round head, set as it was on a small-limbed and squattish body, gave him the look of a primitive clay figurine, some household idol of obscure and cultic derivation.
>
> (*W.N.* p. 242)

The value they place on Wilder is reminiscent of what Michel Foucault suggests in *Madness & Civilisation*. He claims that before the inception of lunatic asylums those failing to comply with limited societal categories as deviant or pathological would have been viewed as having something special to offer, a certain insight or wisdom setting them apart from ordinary mortals.[11] When the asylum burns down (*W.N.* p. 239), watched by Jack and Heinrich, it is a postmodern symbol for the overturning of such set categories, or at least some re-assessment of who decides what constitutes 'normal'.

Jack's safe and contained version of what can be classed as 'normal' is challenged repeatedly by the events and characters of the narrative. His German teacher (portrayed as threatening and uncivilised) communicates in American-English, the German language he teaches in his rented room (secretly, in the case of Jack) is associated with primitive regression; unformed, undisciplined and untutored. Jack comments on the transformation Mr Dunlop undergoes when he reverts to German:

> When he switched from English to German, it was as though a cord had been twisted in his larynx. An abrupt emotion entered his voice, a scrape and gargle that sounded like the stirring of some beast's ambition. He gaped at me and gestured, he croaked, he verged on strangulation. Sounds came spewing from the base of his tongue, harsh noises damp with passion. He was only demonstrating certain basic pronunciation patterns but the transformation in his face and voice made me think he was making a passage between levels of being.
>
> (*W.N.* p. 32)

The teacher's unbounded return to his preferred language is not his only breaching of boundaries, Jack finds it disturbingly inappropriate when Dunlop puts his fingers into his mouth, 'Once he reached in with his right hand to adjust my tongue. It was a strange and terrible moment, an act of haunting intimacy. No one had ever handled my tongue before' (*W.N.* p. 173). Jack begins his relationship with this man by doubting his masculinity due to the softness of his skin, an opinion which is shallow, but relatively harmless, 'Soft hands in a man give me pause. Soft skin in general. Baby skin. I don't think he shaves' (*W.N.* p. 32). His doubts connect to Mr Dunlop's seeming inability to face teaching within the public domain; all of his transference of knowledge goes on behind closed doors in a barricaded room (*W.N.* p. 238). Jack's perseverance with the tuition, despite grave doubts, demonstrates his desperation to master the German language. This centrality (and ambiguity) of language is underpinned by Jack's addiction to erotic literature, and Babette's objection to some of the phrases used, translating them, as she does, in ways far beyond Jack's thought patterns:

> I don't want you to choose anything that has men inside women, quote-quote, or men entering women. 'I entered her.' 'He entered me.' We're not lobbies or elevators. 'I wanted him inside me,' as if he could crawl completely in, sign the register, sleep, eat, so forth. Can we agree on that? I don't care what these people do as long as they don't enter or get entered.
>
> (W.N. p. 29)

Babette and Mr Dunlop are aligned with one another as 'feminine'; they are united by difference and categorised as inferior. Jack, by contrast, is the archetypal hero, a college professor: knowledgeable; North American; white; middle-class and male. His possession of knowledge is tied to control and, therefore, masculinity, but as the doctor tells Jack, ever eager for facts, 'knowledge changes every day' (*W.N.* p. 280). These changes are reflected in the endless lists of fashionable commodities his children compulsively recite, and the frequent mis-translations arising from the changing and overlapping meanings of words. The result is conversations doomed to remain forever misunderstood. Such changes make Jack uneasy, as his manly image and his pedagogic superiority must be constantly re-assessed and his claims to dominance justified. It is impossible to conceive masculinity as unitary and coherent amongst such fluidity. The vastness of what seems 'unknowable' is overwhelming and aligns living with uncertainty and chance. Man must gamble if he wants to find out more than he already knows, or experience more than he is already experiencing. Bataille links this risk-taking with constructed identities and posits that these should be cast aside. 'Communication' cannot take place from one full and intact being to another: it requires beings who have put the being within themselves *at stake*, have placed it at the limit of death, of nothingness.[12]

Jack's fear of death, and his subsequent fear of sex's potential to similarly overwhelm completely, are irrevocably tied to a fear of literally 'letting go' of identity and the comfort of constructs. Jack is happier sifting through, selecting and blending what has always already been done, this circularity carries inferences of continuation rather than ending. When a colleague suggests that awareness of death makes humans cherish life he begins to question the value of knowledge, 'Does knowledge of impending death make life precious? What good is a preciousness based on fear and anxiety? It's an anxious quivering thing' (*W.N.* p. 284). Jack's insistence that it is more comfortable and pleasant not to 'know' could easily negate his own employment, which, after all, hinges on the need to pass on what you 'know'. Jack's extreme response in his bid to become a little more intimate with death, is the attempted murder of Babette's lover, spurred on by a philosophising Murray, 'He dies, you live' (*W.N.* p. 291). If you are not an acting body then by default you become a body being acted upon. Jack is furthering the intimacy with death already fostered via his close connections to the mass murderer he has chosen as his pedagogical focus.

Jack is a voracious consumer; desperately clinging to the belief that, 'Here we don't die, we shop' (*W.N.* p. 38). He is convinced that the amount he buys is directly linked to his validity as a 'male', 'provider', 'academic' and, most crucially, 'living entity'. 'The sheer plenitude those crowded bags suggested, [...] the sense of replenishment [...] the sense of well-being, the security and contentment these products brought' (*W.N.* p. 20). He believes that his acquisitiveness and his eagerness to enter into the exchange system will ensure that he remains alive. Baudrillard's comments on America's commodified culture likewise align it with death:

> The proliferation of technical gadgetry inside the house, beneath it, around it, like drips in an intensive care ward, the TV, stereo, and video which provide communication with the beyond, the car (or cars) that connect one up to that great shopper's funeral parlour, the supermarket, and lastly, the wife and children, as glowing symptoms of success... everything here testifies to death having found its ideal home.[13]

Jack relies on his surface appearance to deflect death. When one of his colleagues sees him away from the campus, denuded of his academic uniform and trademark sunglasses, and comments that, 'You look so harmless Jack. A big, harmless, ageing, indistinct sort of guy' (*W.N.* p. 83), he is horrified and afraid at the suggestion of his lack of substance. He takes his family on a spending-spree in the Mid-Village Mall to counteract his feelings of unease. This provides material goods to support his construction of an identity, and also offers him therapy and affirmation. He claims that what he spends comes back to him in the form of 'existential credit' (*W.N.* p. 84). He lavishes gifts on both his family and himself and consequently feels rewarded, underlining the affirmative aspects of purchasing and consuming; the business of exchange, 'I began to grow in value and self-regard. I filled myself out, found new aspects of myself, located a person I'd forgotten existed' (*W.N.* p. 84). Jack's behaviour recalls the ancient tribal ritual of gift-giving, 'Potlatch', a ruinous act of outdoing and undoing, which Bataille suggests always more acutely answers something in the giver.[14]

The crowds shown in supermarkets and malls trying their utmost to sustain an identity, hence a life, are the same crowds who attend Jack's lectures. Jack's son Heinrich comments on how becoming part of a crowd can be likened to becoming part of a machine, impersonal and technological, doing as you are told to make the larger machine run efficiently. Baudrillard also confirms the way in which modern life is increasingly experienced as part of a mechanical crowd. He terms them, 'the masses', huge ungainly and inert. However, when confronted by multiplicity and choice they ironically still huddle together to carry out the same acts and buy the same products and services, accepting the lecturer's version, totally in the thrall of what Baudrillard terms, 'The networks of influence',[15] powerfully mass-mediated images. The students use their studies as part of this consuming lifestyle. Jack craves the purported safety his lofty academic position offers. His students long to ape his confidence and knowledge, eager to create clones. Their unquestioning approach to Jack's knowledge perpetuates, rather than breaks down, grand narratives. Day-to-day life is not homogenous, and the same for everybody in every place, it is instead disorderly, frag-mented, heterogeneous. The fact that the human sciences are known as 'disciplines' speaks of Academia's efforts to tame this unruly mess. Jack believes that his students are attracted to the concept of the crowd for its potential to offer a safety in numbers. As a personal and obsessive fear of death dominates his life he presumes that his students share this terror, claiming that they come together to form, 'a shield against their own dying. To become a crowd is to keep out death. To break off from the crowd is to risk death as an individual' (*W.N.* p. 73). Ironically such mute obedience also brings death closer. As the narrative progresses Jack realises this and tries to stop conforming, to 'escape the pull of the earth, the gravitational leaf-flutter that brings us hourly closer to dying. Simply stop obeying' (*W.N.* p. 303).

Academic colleagues Jack and Murray become part of the crowd when they visit the site of, 'The Most Photographed Barn in America' and discuss the collective perception of this famous tourist site, 'No one sees the barn...We're not here to capture an image, we're here to maintain one' (*W.N.* p. 12). Frow suggests that humans' acceptance of constructed representations as lived reality results in them being linked to their surroundings by a constant mediation of words and texts, for example, an adherence to the instructions on maps and billboards. Jack and Murray illustrate this by responding to the textual commentary on what is purported to be a site of interest in much the same way that Jack's students respond to his 'teaching'; both sets of behaviour helping to perpetuate mythical narratives. Frow describes this reification as a process of acknowledging a definitive 'type', 'suffused with ideality, giving on to the type of the beautiful, or the extraordinary, or the culturally authentic'.[16] Reality is therefore not palpable, but rather revealed emblematically, through signs and symbols. Murray and Jack follow posters advertising the barn, and imitate the other tourists, who are also doing what those who came before them did. Again, like Jack's students they are driven by a hunger both to belong, and to place other people and events within this belonging, what Frow describes as 'nostalgia for a lost authenticity'.[17] The authenticity is not 'mislaid' but lost because it never existed and so can never be reclaimed. Such mythologising of 'types' results in an attraction to typicality, and consequently to societal constructions, like normative masculinity, being lived as reality. Within the education system adhering to the particulars of type fosters a culture of sameness, inevitably leading to feelings of non-validity for non-conformers. Postmodern theory encourages variety and multiplicity; the empowerment of thinking and feeling for yourself. However, Jack, rather than welcoming this liberty, as both university professor and man, is afraid and suspicious of it.

Frow discusses perpetual imitation in the light of the Platonic simulacrum; a copy of a copy. The act of copying endows the copied with a certain validity, even reality, much in the manner that man can be seen to be endlessly copying himself via the education system. This is Baudrillardian hyper-reality, more real than real. It is a world consisting of closed, self-referring systems where 'ideas' of what constitutes reality are indefinitely reproducible and the consumption of these reproduced images dominates to the point of replacing experience, with future definitions made against that which is already a reproduction within a thoroughly commodified society.[18] Supposed originals, often offered as part of an accepted canon of knowledge, are actually copies: 'tradition'; 'heritage'; 'the past', are all part, like the famous barn, of the nostalgia for a lost authenticity that never was. Foucault suggests that, '[Man] constitutes representations by means of which he lives'.[19] In other words these surface representations are what come to be known as 'reality'.

Jack's questioning of this reality leads him to take a highly techno-logical health check. He is unnerved to see his existence translated as a series of 'pulsing stars' and 'flashing numbers' on a computer screen. His reduction to, 'the sum total of (his) data' (*W.N.* p. 141) seems strangely appropriate for a teacher who relies on, and believes in, what is in his data banks. Just as his teaching encourages, rather than ostra-cises, fascism, so too does the technology to which he is drawn, for its purported power to save or extend his life, paradoxically offer the opportunity for others to alienate him from his own body and his own death. As he summarises, 'It makes you feel like a stranger in your own dying' (*W.N.* p. 142). He longs for the supposed security of his invented identity, 'I wanted my academic gown and dark glasses' (*W.N.* p. 142) and is clinical, even patronising, about the deaths of others, 'An emer-gency ward ... where people come in gun-shot, slashed, sleepy-eyed with opium compounds, broken needles in their arms. These things have nothing to do with my own eventual death, non-violent, small-town, thoughtful' (*W.N.* p. 76).

His nonchalant stereotyping of deathly circumstances, with his own death 'booked in' to be peaceful and thoughtful merely because he is an academic, is now being rudely questioned by the probing, and apparently sinister, technology. Like the Mylex suits worn by the rescue workers, whose composition compromises the precision of the vital computer readouts, the cure is worse than the disease. Jack feels afraid and distant from his own flesh and concludes that a healthy person would become ill after the tests, with their insinuations that the body is rendered superfluous in cyberspace. Modern citizens are conditioned not to question the knowledge of 'The Doctor', 'The Scientist' or 'The Teacher', even if this requires the feigning of ignorance about 'The Self'. Accepted knowledge overrules anything a person thinks he knows, even to the extent that instilled attitudes are accepted as gut reactions, in an illustration of Marx's 'false consciousness' or, as Victor Seidler terms it, 'We can be so used to constructing our experience according to how we think that things ought to be, that it can be difficult to acknowledge any emotions and feelings that go against these images'.[20]

Lyotard claims that this determination to prove, to label and to tie down is impossible to satisfy due to the evolving and circular status of life.[21] There is always room to question, to discuss and explore further. He also predicts that if knowledge is accepted as finite and passed on as unquestionable it will come to be accrued instantly with the implantation of microchips in the brain, without any studying or analysis. Recalling Jack's description of the experimental drug Dylar this, literally, presents 'technology with a human face' (*W.N.* p. 211). If knowledge is intrinsically bonded to the creation of masculinity because of the control it offers, then technology, via such developments as microchips in the brain, can be viewed as a direct threat to masculinity, as presently perceived. The rapid progression of computer technology includes the enormous resources of the internet, comparable to a microchip in the brain, where learning is superfluous because someone, or rather something, will do the knowing on your behalf. But as Jack's eldest son, Heinrich comments, 'What good is knowledge if it just floats in the air? It goes from computer to computer. It changes and grows every second of every day. But nobody actually knows anything (*W.N.* p. 149). The idea that technology will not just help humans but will in fact replace them is once again apparent.

The value of knowledge and what can be learned is intrinsic to the father–son relationship. Jack does not know what to teach Heinrich, a failure which only adds to his anxiety. He tries to establish a 'normal' relationship with him by taking him to watch the local mental asylum burning down, believing that there is something primal about such raging destruction and the virile physicality of firefighters that cannot help but unite a father and son. Despite his pride in his scholarly lifestyle, and his arrogant belief that academia will shield him Jack remains uneasy about his lack of physical skills, feeling that this makes him less of a 'man'. He comments, 'What could be more useless than a man who couldn't fix a dripping faucet – fundamentally useless, dead to history, to the messages in his genes?' (*W.N.* p. 245). The action of the narrative suggests that perhaps there are no such messages and that men are emulating what they believe their society requires of them. Jack is torn between his modernist principles and his chaotic postmodern situation, ensuring that his psyche remains undecided about whether to emulate a philosopher or a firefighter. His lectures have become dramatic productions – rehearsed and copied; his carefully honed identity as male academic makes him the central protagonist of his own play, spectacular and revered yet ultimately unfulfilling.

Notes

1. Don DeLillo, *White Noise* (London: Picador, 1986). Further references to this text are made in parentheses within the body of the chapter.
2. Victor J. Seidler, *Unreasonable Men: Masculinity & Social Theory* (London: Routledge, 1994), p. 65.
3. N. Katherine Hayles, *The Cosmic Web: Scientific Field Models & Literary Strategies in the Twentieth Century* (Ithaca: Cornell University Press, 1984), p. 20.

4. Don DeLillo's *Mao II* (London: Jonathan Cape, 1991), also illustrates this crowd mentality with the combination of photographic images and narrative.
5. Georges Bataille, *Eroticism*, Trans. Mary Dalwood (London: M. Boyars, 1987), p. 20.
6. Jean Baudrillard, *Simulations*, Trans. P. Foss and P. Patton (New York: Semiotext(e) 1983), pp. 1–4.
7. Jean-Francois Lyotard, *The Postmodern Condition: A Report on Knowledge*, Trans. Geoff Bennington and Brian Massumi (Minneapolis: University of Minnesota Press, 1984), p. 81.
8. Lyotard, *The Differend: Phrases in Dispute* (Minneapolis: University of Minnesota Press, 1988).
9. Jean-Francois Lyotard, *The Postmodern Condition*, p. 82.
10. Jean-Francois Lyotard, *The Postmodern Explained to Children* (London: Turnaround, 1992), p. 24.
11. Michel Foucault, *Madness & Civilisation: A History of Insanity in the Age of Reason*, Trans. Richard Howard (London: Routledge, 1993).
12. Georges Bataille writing about Nietzsche, quoted by Derrida in *Writing & Difference* (London: Routledge & Kegan Paul, 1978), p. 263. Italics in original.
13. Ibid.
14. Georges Bataille, *The Accursed Share*, Trans. Robert Hurley (London: Zone Books, 1988), pp. 68–69. Marcel Mauss discusses 'potlatch' in *The Gift: The Form & Reason for Exchange in Archaic Societies*, Trans. W.D. Halls (London: Routledge, 1990).
15. Jean Baudrillard, 'The Ecstasy of Communication', *Postmodern Culture*, Ed. Hal Foster (London: Pluto, 1985), p. 133. The 'masses' are also discussed in, *In the Shadow of the Silent Majorities* (New York: Semiotext(e), 1983).
16. John Frow, *Time & Commodity Culture: Essays in Cultural Theory & Postmodernity* (Oxford: Clarendon Press, 1997), p. 67.
17. Ibid.
18. Baudrillard, *In the Shadow of the Silent Majorities*.
19. Michel Foucault, *The Order of Things: An Archaelogy of the Human Sciences* (London: Routledge, 2000), p. 352.
20. Seidler, *Unreasonable Men*, p. 138.
21. Lyotard, *The Postmodern Condition*, p. 79.

Bibliography

Bataille, Georges. *Eroticism*, Trans. Mary Dalwood (London: M. Boyars, 1987).
——. *The Accursed Share*, Trans. Robert Hurley (London: Zone Books, 1988).
Baudrillard, Jean. *Simulations*, Trans. P. Foss and P. Patton (New York: Semiotext(e),1983).
——. *In the Shadow of the Silent Majorities* (New York: Semiotext(e), 1983).
——. 'The Ecstasy of Communication', *Postmodern Culture*, Ed. Hal Foster (London: Pluto, 1985).
——. *America* (London: Verso, 1999).
Connell, R.W. *Masculinities* (Cambridge: Polity, 2005).
DeLillo, Don. *White Noise* (London: Picador, 1986).
——. *Mao II* (London: Jonathan Cape, 1991).

Derrida, Jacques. *Writing & Difference* (London: Routledge & Kegan Paul, 1978).

Edwards, Tim. *Cultures of Masculinity* (London: Routledge, 2006).

Foucault, Michel. *Madness & Civilisation: A History of Insanity in the Age of Reason,* Trans. Richard Howard (London: Routledge, 1993).

——. *The Order of Things: An Archaelogy of the Human Sciences* (London: Routledge, 2000).

Frow, John. *Time & Commodity Culture: Essays in Cultural Theory & Postmodernity* (Oxford: Clarendon Press, 1997).

Hayles N. Katherine. *The Cosmic Web: Scientific Field Models & Literary Strategies in the Twentieth Century* (Ithaca: Cornell University Press, 1984).

Lyotard, Jean-Francois. *The Postmodern Condition: A Report on Knowledge,* Trans. Geoff Bennington & Brian Massumi (Minneapolis: University of Minnesota Press, 1984).

——. *The Differend: Phrases in Dispute* (Minneapolis: University of Minnesota Press, 1988).

——. *The Postmodern Explained to Children* (London: Turnaround, 1992).

Mauss, Marcel. *The Gift: The Form & Reason for Exchange in Archaic Societies,* Trans. W.D. Halls (London: Routledge, 1990).

Seidler, Victor J. *Unreasonable Men: Masculinity & Social Theory* (London: Routledge, 1994).

——. *Man Enough: Embodying Masculinities* (London: Sage, 1997).

Simon, William. *Postmodern Sexualities* (London: Routledge, 1996).

13
High Visibility: Teaching Ladlit

Alice Ferrebe

Contemporary study of literary masculinities is under pinned by a founding assumption: that the specificity of male gender constructions and experience is initially, and tactically, hidden beneath the textual surface. Antony Easthope began the influential *What A Man's Gotta Do* with a claim that, 'despite all that has been written over the past twenty years on femininity and feminism, masculinity has stayed pretty well concealed. This has always been its ruse to hold on to its power' (Easthope 1990: 1). At Liverpool John Moores University, an important part of our work on the gender-based English modules is engaged with uncovering the (male) gendered particularity of purportedly 'universal' themes, in the man-making experiments of Victor Frankenstein, for example, and the contemporary parables of Ian McEwan. In the 1997 article 'Integrating Men Into the Curriculum', Michael Kimmel, himself a founding father of the contemporary paradigm of masculinity studies, has traced a similar blind-spot in teaching as well as textual processes, remarking of the 'educational endeavour' that 'at every moment in the process, men are invisible'. They are invisible, he claims, 'as men' (Kimmel 1996: 181): that is, as men involved in a complex negotiation and performance of gender. It is, of course, precisely this failure to see the dynamics of masculinity at work in teaching and its designated texts that this volume seeks to redress.

When teaching Ladlit, the most prominent genre of British male fictional self-expression of the 1990s, this trope of invisibility, and its attendant pedagogical practices, are disrupted. 'A man would never set out to write a book on the peculiar situation of the human male', Simone de Beauvoir claimed with understandable conviction in *The Second Sex* in 1949 (De Beauvoir 1988: 15), yet much of the work of, for example, Mike Gayle, Nick Hornby and Tony Parsons, is driven by precisely this purpose. In a 2002 piece entitled 'Ladlit', Elaine Showalter traces an English continuum in the genre beginning in the 1950s, from Amis *père* through *fils* to Hornby, reaching its demise with the century 'as traditional distinctions of maturity and coming-of-age collapsed' (Showalter 2002: 76). She characterises the style of the deceased genre as 'comic in the traditional sense that it had a happy ending. It was romantic in the modern sense that it confronted men's fear and final embrace of marriage, and adult responsibilities. It was confessional in the post-modern sense that the male protagonists and unreliable first-person narrators betrayed beneath their bravado the story of their insecurities' (2002: 60). Showalter nominates Martin Amis's 1984 novel *Money* as the apotheosis of Ladlit. This honour she bestows with reference to the initial invisibility of the novel's covert gendered dynamics, in particular its 'subtextual worries about marriage and paternity' (2002: 69) and the 'suppressed identification with fairy-tale romance' (2002: 70) gradually unveiled by John Self's creeping obsession with the Royal Wedding.

Crossing the categories of the comic, romantic and post-modern, as well as incorporating the *Bildungsroman*, Showalter's taxonomy prompts an awareness of 'Ladlit' as a highly contestable genre category. The term's contemporary commercial origins ensure a semantic multi-tasking that allows it to designate on demand the sanctioned literary fiction of Martin Amis, John King's violent reworkings of the hoolie book in his football trilogy, or Tony Parsons' carefully populist and eminently popular novels, with the gender composition of readership altering in each case. Such contestation, however, does not concern us in this chapter, which uses as Ladlit case studies selected novels by Nick Hornby and Tony Parsons. These texts' narratives – their confessional modes, registers of address, themes and characterisation – merit their discussion as at least partially representative of this shifty genre. Importantly too, for the purposes of my discussion, they are the texts that I have most recently taught. The following consideration of classroom gender dynamics is prompted by the way in which these Ladlit novels disrupt the normative practice of masculinity studies by making the male gender, its performances and structural contradictions, highly visible.

Three years of teaching these novels to undergraduates has yielded (perhaps only) one reliable maxim – male students don't write about Ladlit. Their work in the analysis of literary gender (like that of many of their female peers) gravitates towards the project I have already outlined as common practice in masculinity studies, a practice owing much debt and deference to feminist literary criticism. Choosing instead to write about texts by, for example, William Golding, D.H. Lawrence or John Fowles, they prefer to unearth masculinity, the deeper anxieties and contradictions that lie beneath a textual surface fostering that illusion of existential equality, the 'human condition'. In a discipline ('English') that tends towards concerns most conventionally designated feminine, this task, for practitioners of either gender, may be seen as satisfyingly dynamic, a kind of 'muscular archaeology' akin to that enacted by Indiana Jones and his post-feminist successor, Lara Croft. Paradoxically, the 'deep truths' to be mined here are not organic, but rather the post-structuralist ultimatum of gender's artificiality. Relishing the performance of machismo while exposing the insubstantiality of its foundations: naturally, this sense of conflict between the aim of a theoretical paradigm and its attendant gender assumptions and dramaturgical pleasures is not new. Robert Scholes was worrying at the clash between feminism and Derridean aspirations of rationality and intellectual dominance in the 1987 piece 'Reading as a Man' (though pleasure does not figure in his account of deconstruction). Complicating these gender dynamics still further, however, we can also think of this kind of critical work as contributing to the characterisation of English as feminine, concerned as it is with the revelation and validation of deep emotional realities. In other words, our pedagogic practices are performances too, and they are fraught with conflicting gender implications.

In 'Performing Gender Identity: Young Men's Talk and the Construction of Heterosexual Masculinity', Deborah Cameron remarks upon the way in which the vignettes of 'typical' masculine and feminine behaviour in popular self-help manuals could reverse genders without compromising plausibility. The notorious male reluctance to ask directions while driving, for example, can be understood as motivated by anxiety at appearing ignorant. However, citing instead a predominant female reluctance easily prompts explanations of a desire to avoid imposing upon others and/or placing oneself in a position of physical vulnerability. This Cameron uses as a means of stressing such scenarios to be part not of a presiding empirical, or essential, experience, but rather scenes in various dominant, performative, cultural narratives. She concludes that:

> The behaviour of men and women, whatever its substance may happen to be in any specific instance, is invariably read through a more general discourse on gender difference itself. That discourse is subsequently invoked to *explain* the pattern of gender differentiation

in people's behaviour; whereas it might be more enlightening to say the discourse *constructs* the differentiation, makes it visible *as* differentiation

(Cameron 2002: 443)

This chapter, then, aims to trace some of these constitutive discourses and the gender differentiation they make visible within the masculinity studies classroom, in the dynamics of its theoretical models, its teacher-talk, and student responses. It is not a detailed ethnographic study of classroom conversations, but instead an often speculative product of recent experience of teaching gender-focused modules and working on contemporary British male-authored fiction, intended to illicit further debate and welcome suggestions. It finds in Ladlit, with its insistent confessional register and characteristic political and thematic concerns, a useful engine for generating these gendered discourses in both texts and their teaching, as well as an informative site of epistemological conflict between conceptions of masculinity as both essentialist and performative.

Performing Ladlit

Ladlit's register characteristically cultivates a sense of unmediated, interpersonal communication between a first-person narrator and his reader. The title of Nick Hornby's 1995 *High Fidelity* puns, of course, on the novel's themes of long-playing records and potentially long-lasting relationships, but it is fitting too for its aspirations authentically to reproduce a narrative voice, that of Rob Fleming, without aural distortion. In *The Bonds of Love*, psychoanalyst Jessica Benjamin refers to what she calls 'the exchange of recognition' amidst friendly social interaction, during which each participant gains 'that response from the other which makes meaningful the feelings, intentions and actions of the self' (Benjamin 1990: 12). This process of inter-recognition is crucial, of course, to laddishness – as Martin Amis put it in an interview with Alan Rushbridger: 'A lad is not a lad by himself, he's only a lad when he's with the lads. You can't walk around in your own house being a lad, can you? It's a communal activity' (Amis 2000: 2). In *High Fidelity*, Rob's confession makes regular appeals for this exchange of homosocial validation with an ideal laddish reader: 'I never remember their birthdays – you don't do you, unless you are of the female persuasion?' (Hornby 1995: 170). Though couched as an inevitable, and biological characteristic, recognition of this forgetful trait is generated in a reader, whatever their gender and propensity with calendars, by their supplying the necessary cultural script to make the trait meaningful, that is that laddish masculinity involves a reflex carelessness of social niceties.

Yet a Habermasian ideal speech situation, that consensual, rational, total act of social communication, is far from assured, either in Hornby's novel or the genre more widely. The referent of Rob's insistent 'you' register frequently shifts, appealing often to this unlikely figure of the bookish lad (reading being a most unladdish activity), but also to Laura, his ex-partner. Rob is partially engaged in trying to hurt Laura, as, for example, with the news of her failure to appear in the top-five of his 'memorable split-ups', because 'those places are reserved for the kind of humiliations and heartbreaks that you're just not capable of delivering' (1995: 9). Yet he often, and ostentatiously, addresses her as representative of a female moral authority. His deference to this female superego figure is symbolic of his identity not as a New Lad, but as that older, Eighties stereotype, the New Man: 'You'd say that this was childish, Laura. You'd say that it is stupid of me to compare Rob and Jackie with Rob and Laura who are in their mid-thirties, established, living together' (1995: 20). Indeed, Rob appeals to so many differing cultural scripts, so many competing gender discourses and stereotypes, for validation or condemnation; the hapless lad, the pitiful wimp (in the cinema queue, 1995: 117–118), the wise female, the unfair feminist (1995: 156); that the ideal interpretive community for his confession becomes hopelessly fragmented and confused.

This confusion surrounding audience is reflected in the patterns, and volume, of the genre's sales. A 2004 article in the US publication *Publishers Weekly* quotes Leah Rex, fiction buyer for Borders bookshop, claiming that 'the only place lad lit exists as a viable genre is in the imaginations of publishers'.[1] Some American companies have attempted to address sales flagging further after an initial failure to match their media hype by including novels by, for example, Mike Gayle, within established chick-lit imprints. This demonstrates the Ladlit market's tacit anomaly: that this alleged indicator and communicator of a new masculinity is only purchased and read with any avidity by women. Showalter's recognition of the romance element of Ladlit might invite further investigation of the processes of identification between female readers and the voice and sexual politics of the genre. In *Reading the Romance*, Janice A. Radway observes the way in which 'in ideal romances the hero is constructed androgynously. Although the women were clearly taken with his spectacularly masculine phallic power, in their voluntary comments and in their revealed preferences they emphasized equally that his capacity for tenderness and attentive concern was essential as well' (Radway 1994: 13). These gender identifications Radway characterises as central to the (female) reading of romance, and their conflicts and androgynously constructed heroes coincide suggestively with those of Ladlit, not least in the simultaneous nostalgia for and dissatisfaction with traditional gendered stereotypes that they demonstrate. Certainly the notable reluctance of my male students to engage with Ladlit texts in their written work seems worthy of more consideration than space permits here.

More arresting still is the wider confusion apparent in student discussion of, for example, *High Fidelity*, over precisely which of the conflicting gender discourses present in the text it might be most satisfactory, or, in the context of looming assessment, 'most correct', to espouse. In relation to traditional masculine traits of rationality and taciturnity, the novel's confessional tone is easily cast as feminised – domesticated gossip rather than sanctified proclamation. Such lowly associations, of course, interfere still further with Ladlit's claims to be an authentically male form of communication, as well as its much-hyped claims to be authentically new. Yet both claims, authentically masculine or feminised, are constituted by the same antithesis between maleness and confession. In the article 'The narrative construction of reality', Jerome Bruner invokes the idea of 'tellability' in social conversation, of having a point, which he identifies in contemporary Western culture as usually involving deviance from the expected norm: a breach of what he calls the 'canonical script' (Bruner 1991: 11). The tellability of Ladlit confessions relies upon exactly such a breach, that of a canonical script inscribing men as 'naturally' unable to communicate their emotions. The contemporary canonical gender script of English as a discipline in higher education, of course, seeks to estrange such assumptions in favour of a post-structuralist discourse of performativity and deconstruction of the 'natural' and inevitable, with an attendant promise of political and social liberation. Nick Hornby's earlier, autobiographical *Fever Pitch* explicitly seeks to reclaim masculinity from fashionable cultural discourses perceived as pejoratively artificial rather than dynamically constitutive:

Masculinity has somehow acquired a more specific, less abstract meaning than femininity. Many people seem to regard femininity as a quality; but according to a large number of both men and women, masculinity is a shared set of assumptions and values that men can either accept or reject. You like football? Then you also like soul

music, beer, thumping people, grabbing ladies' breasts, and money.
You're a rugby or cricket man? You like Dire Straits or Mozart, wine,
pinching ladies' bottoms and money. You don't fit into either camp?
Macho, nein danke? In which case it must follow that you're a pacifist
vegetarian, studiously oblivious to the charms of Michelle Pfeiffer.

(Hornby 1993: 79–80)

In defence, his football fanaticism Hornby genders genetically, and occasionally pathologically, male, and roots it firmly in a series of childhood traumas, predominantly his parents' divorce: 'I would have to be
extraordinarily literal to believe that the Arsenal fever about to grip me
had nothing to do with all this mess. (And I wonder how many other
fans, if they were to examine the circumstances that led up to their obsession, could find some sort of equivalent Freudian drama?)' (1993: 17).

Tony Parsons is similarly intent upon delineating 'natural' male traits
and linking them, if not to childhood *per se*, then to an 'inner child'
within his protagonist Harry Silver. Parsons's 1999 novel *Man and Boy*
draws attention to the possibility of the titular 'boy' role being filled
not just by Harry's son Pat but by Harry himself, a boy still innocent enough to be granted forgiveness for his inadequacies – infidelity
and inarticulacy among them (a similar pun and project is apparent in
Hornby's 1998 novel *About a Boy*). In the sequel *Man and Wife* (2002)
this is made still more explicit by an amplified role for Harry's mother
and the narrative's investment in the organic wisdom of her frequent,
home-spun truisms: 'My Mum was right. Pat was in a right old pickle.
Her boy was in a right old pickle. It took me quite a while longer to
realise that my mother was talking about me' (Parsons 2002: 74). His
mother's adages are set in opposition to the phony macho banter he
encounters daily in his job as a television producer, where his colleagues
tend to speak 'as though working in television was a lot like running an
undercover SAS unit in South Armagh' (1999: 59). This crucial binary
of social performance (compromising, debilitating) and essential identity (organic, nurtured in the domestic sphere) coincides instructively
within the central theme of Parsons's novel sequence – fatherhood.
The figure of the father forms a similar nexus of competing discourses of
the 'natural' and the 'social', the biological and the epistemological. The
high visibility of the negotiation in *Man and Boy* of laddish (or childlike)
masculinity, together with the simplicity of its narrative construction
and expression relative to the more explicitly literary fiction on the
course, freed the better part of the seminar devoted to it for the consideration of recent understandings of fatherhood. Though initially careful

to acknowledge the need for an increased cultural recognition and protection of fathers' rights, discussion soon focused upon a prolonged condemnation of the hero during his crucial period of education in Parsons' *Bildungsroman*: Harry Silver's (3 months) crash course in single parenthood. Students' suspicions were especially aggravated by overt textual attempts to garner a recognition of heroism by implication for Harry: 'I did our shopping at the local supermarket. It was only a 5-minute driveaway, but I was gone for quite a while because I was secretly watching all the women I took to be single mothers. I had never even thought about them before, but now I saw that these women were heroes. Real heroes' (1999: 80). The narrator seeks an own-brand heroism to match that of his warrior father, whose medals are invoked insistently in nostalgia for war-won, state-sanctioned masculine self-assertion. One student read similarly pathetic aspirations in the media images of representatives of the (now disbanded) 'Fathers for Justice' group, balanced precariously on the edifices of public structures in the tattered costumes of out-dated comic book heroes.

My students are acutely aware of the inadequacies of contemporary discourses surrounding fatherhood, specifically the recurring trope of male childcare as admirable but part-time, hierarchically arranged below a full-time mother/line-manager and centred upon more frivolous duties such as entertainment and sports coaching. It is often difficult to discern, however, whether their condemnation stems from the rejection of this particular, culturally prescribed performance of fatherhood, or from an inherent bias against performativity *per se*, as it is judged against an indistinct but abiding concept of essentialism. The model of masculinity provided by *Man and Boy*, and Ladlit more generally, was similarly judged as 'artificial', a judgement that would strike at the core of Harry's insecurities: 'In my heart,' he tells us, 'I believed that Gina was only pretending to be a housewife, while I pretended to be my father' (1999: 21). This sense of inauthenticity is both provoked and amplified by the overt appeals for sympathy by its narrator, and the overt publicity surrounding the genre that brands it purveyor of a 'new' British masculinity. Such scepticism towards 'alternative' (and commercialised) masculinities is apparent in R.W. Connell's charge of 'complicity' in *Masculinities* (1995), which he levels against men who present themselves as personally reformed whilst continuing to accept the persistent privileges of a patriarchy dressed in more fashionable discourses. Students display a distinct lack of patience with Harry Silver's confession of his anxieties and the 'exchange of recognition' his narrative voice repeatedly entreats. We debated this relationship – Harry's special pleading and our most common response, the reflex retort of the need for a stiffer upper lip – as a possible British (or specifically English) and more subdued version of the explicit US discourse of 'white male as victim' circulating in some of our other set texts (Chuck Palahniuk's 1996 *Fight Club*, for example). This discourse has been met with some equally explicit reactions, such as that in *Epistemology of the Closet* as Eve Kosofsky Sedgwick, with characteristic verve and venom, diagnoses a high level of self-pity in non-gay men in contemporary American society:

> The sacred tears of the heterosexual man: rare and precious liquor whose properties, we are led to believe, are rivalled only by the *lacrimae Christi* whose secretion is such a speciality of religious kitsch. What charm, compared to this chrism of the gratuitous, can reside in the all too predictable tears of women, of gay men, of people with something to cry about?
>
> (Sedgwick 1990: 145–146)

Performing pedagogy

Another important dynamic within this discussion is, of course, the influence of my own talk around and about the text. Though pale in comparison to Sedgwick's rhetoric, my own frustration with the failure of Tony Parsons' text to yield insight into anything other than the superficiality of its own narrative constructions (and an attendant uncertainty about how, and whether, to include such popular fictions on the 'Representing Masculinities' module in the future) was undoubtedly communicated in my lecture on Ladlit that preceded the seminar.

Indeed, a previous experience might suggest that my own gender alone is enough to elicit certain calculated student responses. An assessment on the same module the year before involved a critical written response to a piece of writing about masculinity presented 'blind' (that is, with date but no source). This, I had conjectured, would serve a number of purposes. On a basic level, it would initiate analytical engagement with contemporary gender debates. It should also encourage awareness of the kind of assumptions made in response to the figure (and gender) of an author-figure; of the textual work done to position readers; and of theoretical, or non-fictional, texts to be as open to insights through the close reading of their style and narrative as the literary. The selected extract, from Rosalind Coward's *Sacred Cows: Is Feminism Relevant to the New Millennium?* (1999), focused on precisely the idea of the 'invisibility' of men that began this piece. In it, Coward notes the way in which men were 'often absent from discourses' (Coward 2000: 96–97), and traces the accelerating deconstruction of what she calls 'ungendered man' (2000: 97) from the early 1980s onwards. Her central anecdote; the proposal 'a few years ago' (2000: 97) of a session to discuss the (now ubiquitous) idea of a 'crisis of masculinity' on a Women's Studies course, and its rejection by the course leader as irrelevant and imperialistic; together with Coward's assessment of 'feminism's hostility to any male self-consciousness' (2000: 98), led all but one student (in a cohort of 50) to assume a male author. The critique of feminism was automatically judged to equate to maleness. By such logic, of course, female = feminist: my very presence in the classroom, I can thus assume, invokes a pro-feminist discourse that students need to negotiate (not that such a skill is not a crucial one). This awareness, no doubt, is amplified by my determined deconstruction of a favoured (and disheartening) opening conversational gambit in class, especially for female first-year students: 'I'm not a feminist but . . .'. The wise (or at least well-informed) woman and the unfair feminist: the roles projected upon me as a female tutor of masculinity studies can be as contradictory and stereotypified as the female figures in *High Fidelity* noted above.

Jane Sunderland has noticed the circulation in contemporary culture of what she calls the 'Boys will be Boys' discourse, which seeks to excuse boys from particular kinds of effort. In wider social debate, Sunderland notes, this is usually academic effort, and we have seen how, within Ladlit, its remit is expanded to prompt exoneration, say, for forgetting birthdays (*High Fidelity*) or even, in Silver's case, infidelity: 'The reason that most men stray is opportunity, and the joy of meaningless sex should never be underestimated. It had been a meaningless, opportunistic coupling. That's what I had liked most about it' (Sunderland 2004: 43). Sunderland identifies too a 'Poor Boys' discourse, usually related to the received wisdom that boys are unable to communicate effectively. As already discussed, Ladlit's characteristic register is predicated precisely upon this discourse, its Poor Boy/Man narrators dependent for the tellability of their tales and their (precarious) contemporary constructions of heroism on the idea of a daring male breach of emotional self-repression. In a seminar dedicated to an overview and analysis of theoretical writing about masculinity, we considered David Morgan's innovative 'critical autobiography' *Discovering Men* (1992), in particular his account of his own experience of fatherhood. Morgan says of his son that 'I have tried many times to talk about what's going on between us but he sees this as my usual 'ear-grinding' and doesn't seem to want to notice that I'm in the process of changing' (Morgan 1990: 107). Initial condemnation of the text's perceived 'special pleading' was swift and as ironic as Sedgwick's comments above. This has regularly been my experience: that students react the same way to the register characteristic of (male) theoretical writing about masculinity as they do to that of Ladlit, and that this reaction is motivated for the most part by a judgement of stylistic similarity. Students' critical responses to Michael Kimmel's 1994 essay 'Masculinity as Homophobia: Fear, Shame and Silence in the Construction of Gender Identity' indicated a suspicion of the textual manipulation inherent in the 'we' register of the piece comparable to reaction against, for example, Hornby's insistent appeal to shared, homosocial experience through the repetition of 'you'. Such a response, of course, is also prompted by the assignment's context in a module that self-declaredly aims to critique masculine, universalising modes of address. The fact that Kimmel's use of 'we' functions to undermine such universalisation by its explicitly gender-specific address (its solidarity demanding the male reader's negotiation of personal complicity) was almost exclusively overlooked. This points to the crucial need for teachers of gender studies to place emphasis upon the context of theoretical writing, prompting the understanding of, say, Morgan's autobiographical work as an interventionary gambit in a longer process of political change. Yet it also indicates an interesting ambivalence: well-steeped now in popular discourses of male confession and male performances of emotional honesty, my students demonstrate a wariness of both the occlusion and the amplification of male particularity.

A similar ambivalence, I would suggest, is present within contemporary masculinity studies more widely. The confessionalist strand within men's studies claims the lingering Enlightenment paradigm of the opposition between reason and emotion as a source of male repression at the same time as a feminist approach denounces it as a patriarchal political instrument. There remains an abiding and endemic confusion between the competing demands of the masculine denial of emotion as both male power gambit and as a male curse. We are left anxious about our inability to distinguish the 'Poor Boys' from the Good Men. Such anxiety has been partially eclipsed by the academic move into more fluid and Foucaultian critiques of power and discourse, yet such critiques too are rife with gendered dynamics. The vacillating allegiance between explanations of biology and performance observed in Nick Hornby's *Fever Pitch*, for example, is not absent from the masculinity studies classroom. There too, discourses of liberation, complicity and blame are regularly mobilised to various ends. An enduring, unexamined link between masculinity and maleness allows, depending on our agenda, either punishment for men for their legacy of privilege, or the promise of solidarity and progress for a group long-debilitated by the demands of the society in which it exists. Binary oppositions, gender amongst them, I am suggesting, are reinscribed as well as renounced.

Last year a taciturn (male) student submitted an essay which struggled to construct a biological explanation for gendered characteristics (the only such agenda apparent amongst a group of 50). After my initial response to the unsatisfactory and insubstantial nature of an old argument, I was struck with a strong sense that I had failed to provide him with any materials with the potential to progress his argument (this, surely, being one of my key professional roles). When steeped in post-structuralist practice, essentialism seems easy to dismiss, and I realised I had done this somewhat perfunctorily on the module, with a look at Robert Bly's *Iron John: A Book about Men* – his metaphor of the 'hairy man' (Bly 1999: 6) provoking much amusement – and the more serious condemnation of an essay by Abby L. Ferber drawing parallels between the discourses of the mythopoetic movement and the white supremacist movement. Ladlit texts might be similarly easily discarded, with the ready visibility of their underlying essentialism robbing critical readers of the potential pleasure of muscular archaeological practice. In upholding the ways in which it is discourse that constitutes 'the natural', it is possible to forget the way in which these discourses *about* discourses construct the paradigms, or 'truths', by which we teach: one being that essentialism is essentially fallacious. It is possible, too, to forget the way in which such discourses are gendered. I mentioned above the need for teachers to contextualise political moves such as the adoption of the personal register by men's movement writing in order to temper quick student condemnation of the outdated. My own response in this situation has most often been to draw comparison with Second Wave Feminist tactics – in this case with attempts to dismantle the possibility of the (inherently patriarchal) objective stance in theoretical writing. This impulse – of justifying the trajectory of masculinity studies by reference to the implicitly more advanced but parallel progress of feminism – seems on reflection suggestive of a more fundamental paradigm underlying contemporary gender studies: the reflex feminisation of good practice.

In *The Aristos*, the seductively adolescent conviction of which hints at its position as John Fowles's first written book, the ninety-third aphorism provides a useful indication of the mythic and dualistic nature of its author's proto-feminism:

> Adam is stasis or conservatism; Eve is kinesis, or progress. Adam societies are ones in which the man and the father, male gods, exact strict obedience to established institutions and norms of behaviour, as during a majority of the periods of history in our era. The Victorian is a typical such period. Eve Societies are those in which the woman and the mother, female gods, encourage innovation and experiment, and fresh definitions, aims, modes of feeling. The Renaissance and our own are typical such ages.
>
> (1980: 165–166)

This seems quaint now, yet I want to posit the idea that our own current canonical script within the gender studies classroom is constituted by and constitutive of just this sense of an 'Eve society'. Sunderland identifies a discourse she brands that of 'Bounded masculinity/Unbounded femininity', noting that it is 'highly situated' (Sunderland 2004: 89), for in many cultural contexts normative feminine practices remains as hidebound and resistant to transgression as their masculine counterparts. However just such a discourse, I am suggesting, is situated, and often highly venerated, in contemporary Western academia. Within it, the liberational potential of difference and differance is preached, whilst leaving unexamined an enduring binary which privileges performativity and post-structuralism above essentialism precisely by a process of gendering. In *Sacred Cows* Coward coins the neologism 'womanism', defined as 'feminism's vulgate' and 'a sort of popularized version of feminism which acclaims everything women do and disparages men' (Coward 2000: 11). 'Womanism', then, connotes a potent confusion of the terms and associations of feminism with those of both the female and the traditional feminine. In the discourse of 'Bounded masculinity/Unbounded femininity', practices recognised as having more potential to achieve progress, to admit transgression and allow play are gendered in this womanist way – they are, purportedly, 'more' post-structuralist and thus superior. Like Rob to Laura in *High Fidelity*, the appeal is to a type of knowledge validated by the gender placed upon it. As in Ladlit more generally, the epistemological structure of gender categories, though still binary, is fraught with both essentialist and anti-essentialist assumptions and implications. In a striking reversal from traditionalist gender configurations, such a discourse uses a coalescent (and perceivedly transcendent) masculinity/maleness to signify an out-dated and logocentric reliance upon biological and bodily explanation, a narrative easily read in the primal solutions of set-texts like *Fight Club*, or the investment in the power of biological fatherhood in *Man and Boy*.

The presiding sense of antagonism here is, of course, disappointing: the Battle of the Sexes updated to that of the Genders. Yet I am seeking here not so much to condemn this contemporary discourse as to admit some complicity with it, in the hope of prompting a shared recognition of its relative robustness within masculinity studies, and of the role that essentialist and transcendent ideals still play in the classroom, and in analytical work. At the crest of the Second Wave in 1979, Angela Carter wrote in *The Sadeian Woman* of the silliness of the notion of matriarchal goddesses. 'If a revival of the myths of these cults gives [us] emotional satisfaction,' she warned, 'it does so at the price of obscuring the real conditions of life' (Carter 1993: 5); and those of our teaching and critical paradigms too. A great portion of our work on gender-focused modules must still remain the expunging of the invisibility of masculinity, and the exposing of the naturalising discourses that are mobilised to conceal it. Yet despite the high visibility and narrative simplicity of masculinity that characterises the genre, Ladlit has hopefully emerged from this discussion as an interestingly conflicted site generative of wider and vital questions about gender, textual address and classroom practice.

Note

1. Natalie Danford, 'Lad Lit Hits the Skids', *Publishers Weekly*, 29 March 2004.

Works cited

Amis, Martin. Interview. 'All About My Father'. By Alan Rusbridger. *The Guardian*, 8 May 2000. 2.
——. *Money: A Suicide Note*. 1984. Harmondsworth: Penguin, 1985.
De Beauvoir, Simone. *The Second Sex*. 1949. London: Picador, 1988.
Benjamin, Jessica. *The Bonds of Love*. London: Virago, 1990.
Bly, Robert. *Iron John: A Book About Men*. 1990. Shaftesbury, Dorset: Element Books Ltd, 1999.
Bruner, Jerome. 'The Narrative Construction of Reality'. *Critical Inquiry* 18 (1) 1991. 1–21.
Cameron, Deborah. 'Performing Gender Identity: Young Men's Talk and the Construction of Heterosexual Masculinity' In *The Discourse Reader*. Eds Adam Jaworski and Nikolas Coupland. London: Routledge, 2002. pp. 442–458.
Carter, Angela. *The Sadeian Woman*. 1979. London: Virago, 1993.

Connell, R.W. *Masculinities*. Cambridge: Polity, 1995.

Coward, Rosalind. *Sacred Cows: Is Feminism Relevant to the New Millennium?* London: Harper Collins, 2000.

Danford, Natalie. 'Lad Lit Hits the Skids', *Publishers Weekly*, 29 March 2004.

Easthope, Antony. *What a Man's Gotta Do: The Masculine Myth in Popular Culture*. Boston: Unwin Hyman, 1990.

Ferber, Abby L., 'Racial Warriors and Weekend Warriors: The Construction of Masculinity in Mythopoetic and White Supremacist Discourse', In *Feminism and Masculinities*. Ed. Peter F. Murphy. Oxford: Oxford University Press, 2004. pp. 228–243.

Fowles, John. *The Aristos*. 1964. London: Triad/Granada, 1980.

Hornby, Nick. *About A Boy*. London: Victor Gollancz Ltd., 1998.

——. *Fever Pitch*. 1992. London: Victor Gollancz Ltd., 1993.

——. *High Fidelity*. 1995. London: Indigo, 1996.

Kimmel, Michael. 'Integrating Men Into the Curriculum'. *Duke Journal of Gender Law and Policy* 4 1996. 181–195.

——. 'Masculinity as Homophobia: Fear, Shame and Silence in the Construction of Gender Identity', In *Theorizing Masculinities*. Eds Harry Brod and Michael Kaufman. Thousand Oaks, CA: Sage, 1994. pp. 119–141.

Morgan, David H.J. *Discovering Men*. London: Hyman, 1990.

Palahniuk, Chuck. *Fight Club*. London: Vintage, 1997.

Parsons, Tony. *Man and Boy*. 1999. London: Harper Collins, 2000.

——. *Man and Wife*. 2002. London: Harper Collins, 2003.

Radway, Janice A. *Reading The Romance: Women, Patriarchy and Popular Literature*. London: Verso, 1994.

Scholes, Robert. 'Reading as a Man', In *Men in Feminism*. Eds Alice Jardine and Paul Smith. London: Methuen, 1987. pp. 204–218.

Sedgwick, Eve Kosofsky. *Epistemology of the Closet*. Berkeley: University of California Press, 1990.

Showalter, Elaine. 'Ladlit', In *On Modern British Fiction*. Ed. Zachary Leader. Oxford: Oxford University Press, 2002. pp. 60–76.

Sunderland, Jane. *Gendered Discourses*. Basingstoke: Palgrave Macmillan, 2004.

Afterword

From the editor

This book represents one step on a long journey, and one which might perhaps be personally exemplified. It was as an adult education tutor in the early 1980s that I first realised how problematic was masculinity in English Studies. Men represented a small minority in classes (indeed there were classes in which I was the *only* man). Yet – with some exceptions – the men who *were* present plainly felt they had a special relationship both to me as male tutor and to the subject matter. On average, men took disproportionately more airtime, and worked harder to demonstrate their superior grasp of the topic. Many of them both enjoyed the attention of women and simultaneously needed to establish that they had a special, even if often rivalrous, relationship with me as tutor. 'We', I was sometimes made to feel, shared an intellectual authority which created for us what might now be called a homosocial bond (the word was not yet available to us) in our superiority to women students. As both Mark Dooley and Chris Thurgar-Dawson note in their chapters, it is difficult for the male tutor not to respond to – or even to be drawn into – the behaviours they describe. At the same time, we should not see the masculine performance of the subject as solely one more ruse for the assertion of male power. Tutors both male and female need to be sensitive to the legitimate subjective needs of those men drawn to the subject – reading, among other things, being the secret domain of shy and perhaps bullied boys.

There were a number of historical reasons for a growing self-awareness of myself as a male teacher. In the Workers Education Association and in university adult continuing education, feminism fuelled a rapid growth in women's education. Courses under titles like 'New Opportunities for Women' (and an early generation of creative writing courses) supplied much of the surviving political energy of British adult education. And the larger environment contributed strongly to the growth of a feminist politics of education. For these were years of crisis in the cold war, the era of the deployment in Britain of US cruise missiles as part of the North Atlantic Treaty Organisation (NATO) 'twin track' policy; of 'protest and survive', of the Greenham peace camp, and the resurgence of the Campaign for Nuclear Disarmament (CND). The indictment of patriarchy and of men as witting or unwitting agents of terminal devastation was intellectually and politically convincing. These were the circumstances in which scattered 'men's groups' set about trying to re-think their own complicity in oppression and violence. In these circumstances, the drive to dominate symbolic meanings and access to ideas – even at the microlevel of the literature group – started to seem more significant. Was the compulsion to establish or maintain control over the generation of privileged meanings simply one mutation of a much larger history, a history where (as the new Theory was simultaneously arguing) it no longer made sense to separate out material and symbolic power?

While the environment has changed, those or related questions have not gone away. The dominant apocalyptic narrative has shifted from thermo-nuclear exchange to environmental catastrophe. Few people would now uncomplicatedly attribute to one gender alone responsibility for pillaging the earth. Yet this does not mean that men and masculinity are no longer problems. Very real gender inequalities persist. Internationally, patriarchy is on the warpath, enlisting dispossessed (and not so dispossessed) young men in a macabre body politics of the Word. Commitment to a transformative gender politics requires attention not only to the symbolic forms in which inequalities are reproduced. It demands a radical critique of nostalgia for subservience to the Father God.

We are not in this book calling for an obsessive re-routing of Literary and Textual Studies. We do not seek to revive a cultural politics of guilt or accusation. Yet, while we have no clear-cut policy recommendations to make, we write out of a shared belief that highly wrought symbolic forms provide a terrain for the examination and gradual extension of human agency. In the disciplines which are the subject of this book, we need to estrange the taken-for-grantedness of hegemonic masculinity and its perspectives. The biological basis of masculinity, we have argued, leaves what Ross Chambers has referred to as 'room for manoeuvre'.[1] But if teachers and their students are serious about change, then they have to look beyond the establishment of magisterial commentary on text to a conscious intervention in the gendered situations in which that discussion takes place.

Note

1. Chambers, Ross. *Room for Maneuver: Reading the Oppositional in Narrative.* Chicago: University of Chicago Press. 1991.

Index